THE CLASSICS OF **WESTERN SPIRITUALITY**

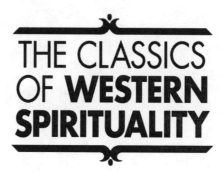

THE CLASSICS OF WESTERN SPIRITUALITY
A Library of the Great Spiritual Masters

Bishop Kallistos of Diokleia—Fellow of Pembroke College, Oxford, Spalding Lecturer in Eastern Orthodox Studies, Oxford University, England

Azim Nanji—Director, The Institute of Ismaili Studies, London, England

Seyyed Hossein Nasr—Professor of Islamic Studies, George Washington University, Washington, DC

Raimon Panikkar—Professor Emeritus, Department of Religious Studies, University of California at Santa Barbara, CA

Sandra M. Schneiders—Professor of New Testament Studies and Spirituality, Jesuit School of Theology, Berkeley, CA

Michael A. Sells—John Henry Barrows Professor of Islamic History and Literature, University of Chicago Divinity School

Huston Smith—Thomas J. Watson Professor of Religion Emeritus, Syracuse University, Syracuse, NY

John R. Sommerfeldt—Professor of History, University of Dallas, Irving, TX

David Steindl-Rast—Spiritual Author, Benedictine Grange, West Redding, CT

David Tracy—Greeley Professor of Roman Catholic Studies, Divinity School, University of Chicago, Chicago, IL

The Most Rev. and Rt. Hon. Rowan D. Williams—Archbishop of Canterbury.

Abū al-Ḥasan al-Shushtarī

SONGS OF LOVE AND DEVOTION

TRANSLATED AND INTRODUCED BY
LOURDES MARÍA ALVAREZ

FORWORD BY
MICHAEL A. SELLS

PAULIST PRESS
NEW YORK • MAHWAH

Cover Art: iStockphoto. Used with permission.

Cover and caseside design by Cynthia Dunne, www.bluefarmdesign.com
Book design by Lynn Else

Library of Congress Cataloging-in-Publication Data

Shushtari, ʻAli ibn ʻAbd Allah, 1213 or 14-1269.
[Selections. English 2009]
Abū al-Ḥasan al-Shushtarī : songs of love and devotion / [translated by] Lourdes María Alvarez ; foreword by Michael A. Sells.
p. cm.—(The classics of western spirituality)
Includes bibliographical references and index.
ISBN 978-0-8091-4594-2 (alk. paper) — ISBN 978-0-8091-0582-3 (alk. paper)
I. Alvarez, Lourdes María. II. Title.
PJ7755.S45A2 2009
892.7′134—dc22

2009000309

Published by Paulist Press
997 Macarthur Boulevard
Mahwah, New Jersey 07430

www.paulistpress.com

Printed and bound in the
United States of America

Contents

CONTENTS

CONTENTS

Contributors to This Volume

Translator of This Volume

LOURDES MARÍA ALVAREZ is associate professor of modern languages at the Catholic University of America in Washington, DC. She was a Fulbright Senior Scholar in Morocco in 2000–2001 and has studied Arabic language and literature in Morocco, Egypt, and several American universities. Her research interests include Hispano-Arabic poetry, medieval Islamic mysticism, and literary translation across linguistic and cultural boundaries. She has her PhD from Yale University.

Author of the Foreword

MICHAEL A. SELLS is a noted scholar of Qur'anic studies, Sufism, Arabic and Islamic love poetry, and mysticism. Among his many publications is *Early Islamic Mysticism* in the Classics of Western Spirituality (Paulist Press). He received his PhD from the University of Chicago, where he is now John Henry Barrows Professor of Islamic History and Literature in the Divinity School.

Foreword

It is a pleasure and privilege to welcome this latest contribution to the Classics of Western Civilization series: Abū al-Ḥasan al-Shushtarī's *Songs of Love and Devotion*, selected and translated by Lourdes María Alvarez. Within these passages there sounds forth—across an array of linguistic, theological, and artistic registers—an intensity of expression and vision that is likely to enrich the English-reading world for years to come.

As becomes clear in Lourdes Alvarez's textured introduction, the seventh Islamic (thirteenth Christian) century witnessed a tidal wave of poetic and spiritual energy flowing across the Arabic- and Persian-speaking worlds of Islam, despite geopolitical disasters epitomized by the fall of Cordoba to Castile in 1236 and the fall of Baghdad to the Mongols in 1258. Living and composing at the same time, intersecting with one another's travels, and keeping a discreet silence on any encounters with one another were Ibn al-'Arabī, Ibn al-Fāriḍ, Shushtarī, and al-Būṣīrī'—all towering figures in Arabic poetry and Sufi thought—and the Persian Sufi master poet Jalāluddīn Rūmī.[1]

Alvarez offers us a selection of major works that reveal Shushtarī at the axis of the major cultural and spiritual developments of his century. In the brilliantly translated verses that follow, we find a play of the vernacular—in theme and in genre—sounding alongside high metaphysics. We encounter neoclassical Bedouin love quests: neoclassical in the sense that these desert wanderings in search of the lost beloved are composed by the great urbanite poets, who place the poetic persona and the implied audience within those ancient abodes and twisting sounds of Arabia. We hear a poetic voice that ranges from hymns of cosmic dance to vulnerable personal confessions, from celebrations of doctrinal openness and the unlimited mystery behind all life to rousing polemics against moral, literary, theological, and legal critics.

In this foreword I will limit myself to some observations on two sets of poems in the volume. I begin with the following two verses from "I'm a sight to see":

You are the mirror of the glance,
the axis of time

Encompassed in you is what is dispersed
throughout time.

I am struck by the compact nature of these verses. The *you* that is the mirror of the glance (the glance being, by definition, a momentary act) is also called the axis of time, holding within itself all that time has dispersed. Similarly, these verses that form a momentary poetic glance within the expression of Shushtarī condense within themselves the developments in Arabic love poetry, *ghazal*, and Sufi understandings of mystical states of consciousness that had been unfolding over several centuries. It would be inappropriate to proceed further without a word on the poetic and scholarly skills that have come together to make such a couplet sound forth with a lyrical and idiomatic ease in English. For example, I note in the above verses the liquid ease with which the words flow into one another, the balanced and effective use of assonance, with one color provided by the conjoining of *s* and *x* sounds and another by the linkage of *r*'s and *l*'s. I note as well the manner in which hard and soft stress and stress inversion provide just the right measure of emphasis to key words and "language acts" within verses. The same qualities of pitch and measure can be found throughout the volume; take, for example, the translation of the poem "My art," a translation that seems to gain in its mesmerizing power on each rereading.

One of the final poems in the selection, the long *Nūniyya*, contains a clue, perhaps, to what we may hear in "I'm a sight to see" and even more directly to the poem in the same section entitled "Hidden in plain sight." In one movement of the *Nūniyya*, Shushtarī traces the power of reason from Hermes, Socrates, and Dhū al-Qarnayn (a Qur'anic figure associated by tradition with Alexander the Great) down to the Sufis of his own time, such as Ibn Sab`īn and Ibn al-`Arabī.[2] As Alvarez points out, this poem does far more than simply state a spiritual lineage. In his treatment of one enigmatic figure, Niffarī (d. 867),

Shushtarī writes that the power of reason "enraptured the essence of Niffarī" to the point that the affirmation of God's oneness "became his companion," and that "he was a speaker between two essences."

What might the poet have meant by saying that Niffarī affirmed the oneness of God until "it became his companion"? Or that he became a speaker between two essences? Or that he (singular) who is poor can see the essence into which we (plural) have plunged?

Let us return from the *Nūniyya* to verses from the lyrically condensed "Hidden in plain sight":

It is you who speak
  and you who listen.

Just when do you think what is absent will appear?
  God is the One with no other.

There is nothing like me,
  I am one.

And the very notion of place, in truth,
  is trouble.

I cannot help but hear in these verses a poetic play on some of the most famous of the "standings" of Niffarī. Like several poems in this selection, the poem in question speaks of oneness as a riddle but also promises to break open the riddle. In the work of Niffarī, absolute oneness, through which the Sufi seeker becomes one with God as his own separate self passes away in contemplation, results in a ghost dialogue: a speaker and hearer, a *you* and an *I*, continue their intimate discourses, but there is only one being remaining. In "Hidden in plain sight," the phrases *God is the One with no other* and *There is nothing like me* (an allusion to the Qur'anic verse 42:11) fit into the poetic flow in a natural fashion and participate in the performance of sudden shifts in voices and persons.[3]

In this poem, the affirmations of oneness—*God is the One with no other, There is nothing like me,* and *I am one*—show forth not merely as statements but as personae, characters, and agents. Who is speaking and who is listening? The poetic voice seems to exist between two essences indeed. Through her introductory treatment of the major

Sufi poetics of Shushtarī's time and the resurgence of interest in Niffarī, through her translation and explanation of the *Nūniyya*, and through her translation of poems like "Hidden in plain sight," Alvarez offers a tantalizing possibility: Could it be that in his *Nūniyya*, Shushtarī was not only setting for a poetic movement of history and consciousness across the ages, but was also signaling his own accomplishments as a poet, as well as the manner in which his verses perform poetically what each of the figures he mentions achieved historically?

In her introduction, Dr. Alvarez has explicated the strophic *zajal* and *muwashshaḥa* forms and the various levels of vernacular diction that help season such poetry. She also explains the lack of a common denominator between the Arabic vernacular of Shushtarī and any contemporary English vernacular, due to the potentially distracting ethnic registers of most strong English vernaculars today. What Alvarez has chosen to do is to use a soft touch with the vernacular, adding it in places where it will be particularly effective in English, as with the phrase *is trouble*. That colloquial expression then contrasts within the metaphysical deconstruction of the word *whereness* in the following verse. The result is that the statement opened by *I am one* ends with an embedded, double paradox. The goal, *I am one*, is to be found in the where-beyond whereness, a no-place beyond place. There, the one *I* is discovered—as *us*. In attempting to appreciate this verse in prose, I, of course, have lost its poetry. It is through the balances of aural and sonic features of the verse—elegantly reconstructed through translation—and through the shifts among first person, second person, and third person, and between the singular and the plural, that the poetic persona speaks from "between two essences." Below, I cite the moment where this *I am one* is linked to the seemingly contradictory affirmation *you will find us*. Between these two affirmations—of oneness and of community—there springs into expression the statement that the notion of place *is trouble*—a colloquial touch, subtly accomplished in translation, that announces that the oneness can and does embrace an implied *ḥaḍra*: an encounter, a meeting, an "audience," or a coming together.

It is you who speak
    and you who listen.

Just when do you think what is absent will appear?
    God is the One with no other.

There is nothing like me,
  I am one.

And the very notion of place, in truth,
  is trouble.
When you let go of "whereness,"
  you will find us.

When viewed as an abstraction, the mystical visions of Ibn al-Farīḍ, Ibn al-`Arabī, and Shushtarī, named by later writers as *waḥdat al-wujūd*, or "unity of existence," can appear cold or solipsistic when paraphrased or selectively quoted to claim a reality revealing itself to itself through the mirror of its own creative act. It is in the performative nature of their language that such static essentialisms are overcome in favor of a constant shift in perspectives between the ultimate unity beyond language and a sense of relational intimacy or homecoming that is brought into life around that ineffable oneness. I can find few more compelling responses to such abstracted representations of Sufi affirmation of oneness than these verses from Shushtarī's poem, which verses may themselves be a commentary on Niffarī (who, himself, as Alvarez points out, was brought to life and attention in the seventh Islamic century largely through the efforts of Ibn al-`Arabī). In absolute oneness, the *you* implied by the poem discovers the one, and in so doing experiences a homecoming, finding *us*.

My second observation begins with the following verses from "The lover's visit":

My heart's desire visited me, darkness fell away,
  in that union, he was generous.
He attended my *ḥaḍra*, the wine glass went round,
  and my hopes attained.

...

My beloved is my intimate confidant and my lamp,
  present, so close.

What drink! What wine! What a vintner!

What music! What song!
In a garden blooming with flowers
that fill us with light.
From their pulpits in the trees
the birds speak among us.

The first two verses quoted above speak of a *ḥaḍra*, a "session" or "soiree," that can refer to a gathering of devotees around a master, a one-on-one encounter of master and devotee, an encounter between God and a human, or even a group of poets, singers, and/or drinkers.[4] The third verse then brings us a moment of intimacy, with the lover and beloved close to one another. The poem evokes the Qur'anic "light" verse, in which the light of God is likened to that of a lamp, in a niche fueled by oil from a blessed olive tree, which needs no external spark to blaze forth, accenting the notion that the encounter occurs at night, away from others. The last set of verses quoted above offers a sense of the ecstatic sensibility—the flowers illumining the garden as if lit from within and the birds singing in the pulpits of trees—that bursts forth in the Arabic poetry of Shushtarī and his contemporaries.

At other times, the wine-séance can take on a ghostly sense. The extreme affirmation of life seems to meld into a performative acknowledgment of both human mortality and something beyond—as in these verses from "Wine from no wine press":

You who are unversed in this,
admit what you see:
The wine is passed round
and every one of us is drunk.
See the men here
with hearts abrim?

See them all dancing?
The secret is manifest in them,
for this they gave their lives
and their night has become day.

Within the wine-song, the timeless and cosmic vision can suddenly shift to the most humble, common, gently comic vision of the drunkard slumped in the corner of the bar, a shift cultivated by the Arabic and Persian poets. Take the following selected verses from "Many a cup," another poem that rings across linguistic registers into a natural and compelling English:

> My night has turned to day.
> The sun is mine and the stars.
> My dominion encompasses the depths.
>   My heart is the Atlas mountains.
>
> Your love has served me many a cup.
>
> When I looked away from myself,
> I saw myself, the writing of my being visible to me.
> What had been hidden
> appears to me,
>   its meaning beyond ordinary wealth.
>
> ...
>
> Look for me in the tavern.
> You will see me
> slumped among the wine jugs.
> I love—without restraint—the one
>   who revives the spirits of those who join with him.

"When I looked away from myself, / I saw myself, the writing of my being visible to me." In those verses, the transformation of perspective—from the self as "separate entity" to the self as "one with the one who has no other"—seems to take place before the eyes of the reader, as the self recedes into the universe-like vastness of the new persona. Then, with another sudden shift in perspective, the reader is invited to look for the poet-lover in the tavern, slumped among the wine jugs.

The poetic and spiritual refrain that sounds through this volume raises a number of questions. What is this wine? *Ah...* Is it the earthly wine or the heavenly? It is an ancient vintage, older than time, yet it seems to represent something as ephemeral as will, as elusive as a glance.[5] It is quaffed in order to forget the beloved but brings the beloved back to the mind. In it, the drinker, the lover, the devotee perish, yet it brings the dead to life. It seems to function at times like the remembrance of the beloved, as a wellspring of thought, emotion, and spiritual or moral acceleration. It is passed round among the members of the *ḥaḍra*, in a continual circling motion—like the motions of the heavenly spheres, the circumambulations of the pilgrim, the whirling of the dervishes, or the rounds of the choir that pass by and return as the refrain of the *zajal* or *muwashshaḥa*. The intoxication it brings seems to be aligned in theological terms with oneness itself, yet it is also the agent of that oneness, the elixir that allows those who drink it to become the one that they are.

In cultural terms, the wine-song represented by Shushtarī can be said to become the wine itself. The act of composing, transmitting, and performing it brings an intoxication no less than drinking the beverage. With each revival of the tradition, a new round forms. In that sense, Lourdes María Alvarez has just helped pass the cup, and I suspect she will be bringing others into the *ḥaḍra* taking place in the Arabic world during that remarkable century.

Michael Sells

NOTES

Dates of both the births and deaths of the five in Islamic and Christian years:

1. Ibn al-`Arabī	560/1165	638/1240
Ibn al-Fāriḍ	562/1181	632/1235
Rūmī	604/1207	672/1273
Būṣīrī	607/1211	c. 695/1295
Shushtarī	608/1212	663/1265

For Būṣīrī, see Suzanne Stetkevych, "From Text to Talisman: Al-Būṣīrī's Qaṣīdat al-Burdah (Mantle Ode) and the Supplicatory Ode," *Journal of Arabic Literature* 37, no. 2 (2006): 145–89.

2. For another example of a long Sufi poem offering a cosmic perspective of world history through the lens of reason or the melting of reason, see Ibn al-Fāriḍ's poetic summa, the *Tā'iyya*. In this regard, I would point out in particular the shadow-play section from the *Tā'iyya* (verses 269–706) in the powerful translation of Emil Homerin. See Emil Homerin, *`Umar Ibn al-Fāriḍ: Sufi Verse, Saintly Life*, Classics of Western Spirituality (Mahwah, NJ: Paulist Press, 2001), 269–75.

3. *The Mawáqif and Mukháṭabāt of Muḥammad Ibn `Abdi l-Jabbár al-Niffarí*, trans. A. J. Arberry (London: J. W. Gibb memorial, 1935), numbers 5, 6, 43, and 44, pp. 30–31, 79–80. Michael Sells, *Early Islamic Mysticism: Sufi, Qur'an, Mi`raj, Poetic, and Theological Writings*, Classics of Western Spirituality (Mahwah, NJ: Paulist Press, 2001), 284–91.

4. For a classic example of such a notion of poetic and bacchic conviviality, see the *muwashshaḥ* "Pass the cup around" attributed, according to the source, either to al-A`mā of Tudela (d. 1126) or to Ibn Baqī of Cordoba (d. 1150). The text can be found in Benjamin Liu and James Monroe, *Ten Hispano-Arabic Strophic Songs in the Modern Oral Tradition* (Berkeley: University of California Press, 1989), 54.

5. For the paradoxes and associations of wine in early Arabic poetry, see Philip F. Kennedy, *The Wine Song in Classical Arabic Poetry: Abū Nuwās and the Literary Tradition* (Oxford: Oxford University Press, 1997).

PART ONE

Praising God in the Language of Everyday Life

Praising God in the Language of Everyday Life

Introduction

> If your servant...has shown boldness in the formulation of his prayer, his water still belongs forever to your sea...If he spoke a hundred languages, in each tongue he would praise you; if he falls silent like those forsaken, you comprehend the language of him who has no words.
>
> —Nizami, *Leila and Majnun*

Late in the twelfth century, Niẓāmī (d.1217?), a poet from the region now known as Azerbaijan, wrote a lengthy poem in Persian, retelling the story of the tragic young lovers Qays and Layla, long a popular trope for Arab poets. Qays, who "was drowned in an ocean of love before he knew that there was such a thing," goes mad when he is separated from his beloved by her disapproving father.[1] Wandering the desert in rags, wholly consumed by his love, he is known to all as Majnūn Layla, "the one mad for Layla." Niẓāmī's poem is widely interpreted as a mystical allegory of man's passionate and uncontainable love for God, yet as Chelkowski observes, "it is virtually impossible to draw a clear line in Niẓāmī's poetry between the mystical and the erotic, between the sacred and the profane."[2] His provocative blurring of boundaries is noteworthy, especially as it signals an increasing willingness to read poetry as religious when it is not explicitly marked as such, an important milestone in the growing Islamic acceptance of the use of imaginative literature to explore the emotional and experiential side of the spiritual quest.

Equally significant however, is Niẓāmī's contribution to a growing body of Islamic literature in Persian—rather than Arabic—asserting the value of local language and its cultural specificities to speak of religious matters, even while accepting Arabic as the language of revelation. For centuries heated battles had raged about the place of languages other than Arabic in Islam: was Arabic a tool of cultural and religious integration, essential to proper exegesis, or the instrument of exclusion and marginalization of all that was not Arab? By Niẓāmī's time, Islamic mystics had begun to record poetry and song not just in Arabic and Persian, but in myriad local languages, dialects, and vernaculars. Several of these local languages had little or no written tradition, and it might be argued that, at least in the case of Turkish, the desire to record and transmit a mystical message provided a significant impetus to the development of a literary language. Indeed, much to the chagrin of the defenders of rigid orthodoxy, political centralization, and linguistic purity, by late in the twelfth century it seemed that Sufis from East to West were suddenly praising God in a hundred languages.

Islamic Spain was no exception. In the thirteenth century, a new mystical poetry emerged, appropriating not only the metrical patterns, rhyme schemes, and colloquial diction of popular Andalusian song, but also much of its iconoclastic spirit. Without a doubt, the most accomplished composer of these Andalusian songs, called *muwashshaḥāt* and *zajals*, was Abū al-Ḥasan al-Shushtarī (1212–69).[3] Shushtarī, however, was not the first to use these popular poetic forms for mystical expression. Instead another Andalusian, the prolific and multi-talented Sufi theorist, Muḥyī al-Dīn ibn al-ʿArabī (1165–1240), is credited with the first mystical *muwashshaḥāt*.[4] Yet Ibn al-ʿArabī, al-Shaykh al-Akbār (the Greatest Master), who wrote hundreds of dense treatises, a substantial corpus of difficult theosophical poetry and a slender volume of odes in the traditional Arabian style, *Tarjumān al-Ashwāq [The Interpreter of Desires]*, was uncomfortable with these casual Andalusian forms. Setting aside the matter of their mystical content and the challenges inherent in interpreting them, as artistic and poetic compositions, Ibn al-ʿArabī's *muwashshaḥāt* feel stiff and uneasy, not unlike what one might expect if a theologian with only passing knowledge of hip-hop culture began writing religious raps. By contrast, it was Shushtarī's special talent to use popular song and informal diction to talk about the divine. His were songs that could be enjoyed and interpreted at many levels, songs that not only rejected rank and privilege and championed voluntary poverty, but that themselves spoke in the simple and unexalted language of daily life, the vernacular language spoken by all—rather than the erudite language that separated the educated classes from the illiterate.

Shushtarī's popular songs won him wide recognition, recognition that went far beyond the hundreds of disciples who formed the Sufi brotherhood known as the Shushtariyya, an order eventually absorbed into the Shādhiliyya.[5] The poet also composed poems in the classical monorhyme style, several of which were commented by later Sufi writers.[6] His fame is highlighted by attacks against him by the outspoken critic of theosophical Sufism, Ibn Taymiyya (1263–1328), who called him "that composer of zajals."[7] As for Shushtarī's admirers, these included the one-time vizier of Granada and noted polymath Lisān al-Dīn Ibn al-Khaṭīb (1313–75), who, after his political fall it seems, wrote mystical *muwashshaḥāt* in what he himself called "Shushtarī-style."[8] Ibn ʿAbbād of Ronda (1333–90), an Andalusian who became an enormously influential figure in Moroccan Sufism, enthusiastically recommended Shushtarī's colloquial versse, noting that they elicited strong emotions for him, "especially if they are accompanied by music and beautiful voices." He further recommends that these songs be committed to writing "whenever possible."[9] In his writings on Sufism, the great historian of al-Andalus, Ibn Khaldūn (1332–82),[10] praises Shushtarī's verse despite his deep misgivings about the radical monism he perceived in the poet's master, Ibn Sabʿīn (c.1217–c.1269).[11] The historian and literary anthologist al-Maqqarī (1577–1632) calls him "the leader of those who strip bare and a blessing to those who wear the robes of the Sufis" (*amir al-mutajarradīn wā baraka lābisī al-khirqa*).[12] Shushtarī's earliest biographer, Aḥmad al-Ghubrīnī (d.1304), writes: "His poetry (*shiʿr*) was extraordinarily impressive and elegant (*ghāyat al-inṭibāʿ wa-l-malāḥa*), and he composed *muwashshaḥāt*, plays on words, and amusing zajals of the utmost beauty."[13] Shushtarī's influence even extended into Christian Europe, for the Catalan mystic Ramon Llull (1232–1315)—who read and wrote Arabic fluently—echoes one of Shushtarī's most famous refrains, "What care have I for others?/What care have they for me?" in *Blanquerna*, in which a character wanders the marketplace calling out: "'Little-care-I' or 'what-will-men-say'" (*diria hom,' o 'poc m'o preu*).[14]

The enduring appeal of Shushtarī's mystical songs is indicated not only by the dozens of extant manuscript copies of his *dīwān* (collected poems), now scattered in academic libraries, private collections and the libraries of Sufi brotherhoods around the world, but by the fact that his songs are also recorded in many songbooks, with information about their musical modes *(maqām)* and rhythms. The songbooks, such as the eighteenth-century *Kunnāsh al-Hā'ik*, are particularly interesting because they demonstrate the vitality of these songs as part of a popular repertoire that transcends secular or religious labels.[15] And to be sure, Shushtarī remains a towering figure in North African Sufism. From Morocco to Syria, his verses are well loved and oft recited; they are prominently featured in the mystical sessions of virtually every brotherhood, sung at funerals, and recorded by prominent artists.[16] Indeed, Aḥmad al-Khaligh, the host of a prestigious and widely broadcast Sufi radio show, features his poetry and songs on a regular basis and has called him the "greatest mystic poet of Islamic Spain and North Africa."[17] His songs are arguably the most vibrant—and the liveliest—element of Islamic Spain's cultural legacy. It would be hard to overstate his importance. Shushtarī, then, might be understood as the Rūmī of Western Islam.

In recent years the verse of Persian mystics like Niẓāmī and Ḥāfiẓ, and especially that of Rumi, has become familiar to international audiences and the subject of many translations and studies, but Sufi poetry in other languages—perhaps most surprisingly, in Arabic—has not enjoyed the same attention. This neglect is even more pronounced for popular poetry and song in the various vernacular dialects of Arabic. Doubtless, the principal reason for this inattention is the stigma attached to the spoken language—seen as a corruption of the pure Arabic of the Qur'ān and of high culture—even as it is used by all segments of the population in the course of daily life. (These dialects, it must be noted, are so different from one another and from standard Arabic that they can be mutually unintelligible. Standard Arabic, the language of books, political and religious addresses, and news broadcasts, is acquired through schooling; the language of private life, the language that roots one in a particular place, is the vernacular.) The tendency to exclude and marginalize the rare texts that do attempt to record the spoken register is not purely due to linguistic discrimination but is also a product of the daunting obstacles to their establishment and interpretation. Scribal error and emendation introduce some uncertainties, which are especially notable when the scribe is unfamiliar with the dialect being copied. Error and uncertainty are further compounded by code-switching between formal and informal registers and the use of nonstandard meter, for meter is oftentimes an important tool in deciphering or establishing a text. Further imprecision comes from the Arabic writing system itself, which generally relies on the reader's knowledge of the correct vocalization of words and in many cases allows the same graphic representation for a word in its standard and dialectal pronunciation.

In the instance of Shushtarī, we still lack a reliable Arabic edition of his *dīwān* or collected poems. The obstacles are many. There is no autograph copy of his *dīwān*, that is, a copy authenticated by the poet himself. This is unsurprising, as many *dīwāns* are collected posthumously; however, the imposing gap of nearly three centuries separating the composition (or presumed composition) and the dates of the earliest extant manuscript copies leaves many unanswered questions about when, where, and by whom his poems were gathered. Yet Shushtarī's popularity means that rather than the lacunae and uncertainties that attend a paucity of manuscripts, the reader faces the difficulties associated with a superabundance of manuscripts: variants, spurious interpolations, and false attributions. Manuscripts are scattered in American and European libraries and throughout the Islamic world: North Africa, the Levant, Turkey, and even Indonesia. Many more copies are thought to be in private collections or in small libraries attached to Sufi circles. ʿAlī Sāmī al-Nashshār's 1960 edition of the *dīwān* based on seventeen manuscripts from three separate manuscript traditions is a considerable achievement, despite being plagued by typographical errors, inconsistencies, and poor documentation of variants.[18] Federico Corriente's 1988 *Poesía estrófica: céjeles y/o muwaššaḥāt*, which he himself called a *pre-edición*, corrects quite a few problems found in Nashshār's edition, yet his transcription of text into Latin characters fixes the reading in a way that is inimical to the customary flexibility of the Arabic script.[19] Corriente is only interested in Shushtarī's popular strophic verse; his book excludes the thirty-seven monorhyme compositions collected by Nashshār. Furthermore, Corriente has relied on only one early yet incomplete manuscript to supplement his reading of

Nashshār's edition; he thus is unable to address a fair number of errors.[20]

In preparing this volume, I have meticulously checked Nashshār's edition against nine manuscripts. Of these, two stand out as the earliest and most reliable: Escorial 278, copied in 956/1549, and another, more complete manuscript apparently unknown to Nashshār (or Massignon), Yale Arabic Manuscript 21, copied in 1000/1591.[21] In the notes for each poem, I list page numbers for Nashshār's edition of the *Dīwān* followed by the number he assigned each poem; the same numbers serve for Corriente's transliterated edition and translation.[22] I also list the folios for the Yale and Escorial manuscripts. The changes seen in certain poems in later manuscripts provide evidence of Shushtarī's evolving legacy and the role of his compositions—and those ascribed to him—in Sufi devotional practice. Popular poems are sometimes shortened for singing, retaining the most dramatic or memorable lines; at other times new strophes are inserted; in still other cases controversial or obscure language is replaced. These changes are discussed in the notes when they present a special interest. However, to avoid overburdening the reader, in the majority of cases they pass unremarked, as variations that are common and expected in a living oral tradition.

The aim in the present volume is to make available a representative sample of Shushtarī's work; the criteria for any selection of this kind are, by necessity, subjective. There is, unfortunately, room for doubt about the authenticity of a substantial number of the poems attributed to Shushtarī, especially in later manuscripts. Although Nashshār voices reservations about some compositions, primarily basing his judgment on scribal marginalia, contradictory attributions in other sources, or content inconsistent with Shushtarī's thought as he understood it, he chose to cast as wide a net as possible in compiling his edition of the *Dīwān*, including some rather doubtful poems. Corriente uses philological criteria to assess their authenticity, evincing skepticism about poems whose stylistic and metrical characteristics he adjudges typical of later periods, but he nonetheless transliterated and translated into Spanish all the strophic poems collected by Nashshār. While I have chosen poems that I judge to be of reasonably certain attribution, this sampling is in no way intended as a judgment of which poems are "most certain." The variations, corruptions, interpolations, and omissions so prevalent in certain later manuscripts and especially in songbooks are powerful evidence of a robust oral tradition, unfortunately impossible to address in such a brief study. I have focused on the most frequently attested poems; I have also included several poems that have become quite central to the received *persona* of the poet, even though some copyists and modern scholars have speculated that they may actually be the work of later admirers and imitators. Ultimately, however, the overriding factor in my choices was the extremely personal judgment of poetic quality and/or doctrinal significance.

While the establishment of a sound reading of the Arabic original is, of course, a crucial first step in preparing a good English translation, the act of translation inevitably introduces a new order of semantic shifts, distortions, and unavoidable transformations. Perhaps the most serious problem is that the English perforce clarifies what was never meant to be clear, fixing one meaning, one reading, to the exclusion of several others possible in the original—that is, when the English does not inadvertently introduce new shades of meaning. While this is inherent in any literary translation, it is especially true when working with mystical poetry, which in attempting to explore the limits of the inexpressible, deforms language and violates its grammatical conventions. In the case of mystical poetry in Arabic, the famous ambiguity and semantic plasticity of the Arabic language are pushed to their extreme. Take, for example, the opening line of Shushtarī's "I sang to the moon":

> To me, from me; He's the goal.
> "Hey me, what's up with you?"

The poem begins with a logical and grammatical contradiction. After the first prepositional phrase, one expects a verb and a subject, either stated or implied. Instead, the prepositional phrase is followed by another, signaling movement in the opposite direction. The pronoun that follows, *hu*—a dialectal shortening of *huwa*—can be read as "he" or "it," but in mystical texts it often means God, as in the One who needs no qualifiers or descriptions, the One who is beyond and above language. *"Wuṣūl,"* a verbal noun from a verb meaning "to join," "to unite," "to connect," or "to arrive" (among other things), could then, depending on how one reads *hu*, denote a dizzying series of possibilities. One variation might be "it (meaning that implied journey from myself, to myself) is the joining, a sublime union"; another, "He (meaning God) is the arrival that is the goal of that inner journey." The second hemistich adds a lighthearted contrast to the obscurity of the first, while still echoing its circularity. The poet addresses himself, *Fayā ana,* that is, "there I am," or "hey there, me," and asks, as if greeting a friend at the market, *aysh khabarak*? that is, "what's up?" Needless to say, beneath the veneer of this informal verbal play lie serious theosophical propositions about mystical union, the search for knowledge of God, and the essential oneness of God. This is but one example of the many different types of semantic and lexical ambiguities found in the majority of Shushtarī's poems.

Another unavoidable consequence of translation is the loss of much of the tension and play between linguistic registers so prominent in the original. Shifts between standard Arabic usage and highly informal colloquial diction were negotiating a gap analogous to that which separated classical Latin from vulgar Latin and the emerging romance vernaculars at about the same time. Modern English offers the translator no parallel or equivalent that is not encumbered with class or racial overtones.[23] Take, for example, the first line (divided into hemistiches) of "My lover is second to none":

> My lover is second to none,
> and no spy watches over him.

The first hemistich literally reads: my lover (or my beloved, *ḥabībī* can have either meaning), to him there is no second (*thānī*). Of course, this is a clear declaration of the incomparability or peerlessness of the beloved and—understanding that beloved as God—the line is also a proclamation of absolute monotheism. The line's informal diction—in some manuscripts reading *mā lū thānī,* rather than the more standard, yet still informal, *mā lahu thānī*—tempts me to translate it as "ain't no one like my baby." Yet out of fear of appearing to disrespect or belittle this or similarly informal compositions, I have avoided nonstandard or ungrammatical usage. While my renditions in some cases flirt with the informal registers of English, to push any further would be distracting, focusing attention on the translation itself rather than on the material being translated.

Translation across cultures also obscures intertextual references and allusions, as one moves from a language that reverberates with

Qur'ānic usage and an Islamic worldview to one in which much of that context needs considerably more glossing. Despite my best efforts at documenting the most important of these in the notes, many layers of meaning will doubtless be lost. Let me offer another example. A bit later in the poem "My lover is second to none," the phrase "sūrat al-ʿuqūd" or "sūra of the necklace" or "sūra of the covenants" presents an enigma: there is no Qur'ānic sūra by that name. Perhaps this is why in some manuscripts sūra becomes ṣūra, that is, "picture" or "image" (even though that change hardly results in a better reading) and in one very late (and extremely defective) manuscript, the line becomes "sūq al-ʿuqūd" or the "jewelry market." However, if we remark that the word *ʿuqūd* appears only once in the Qur'ān, in the opening line of Sūrat al-Mā'ida [sūra 5, The Feast], the reference to that particular sūra becomes clear. With this in view, the persistent echoes and allusions to that Qur'ānic sūra become readily apparent, confirming that the poem as a whole functions as a mystical gloss on its deeper themes. Rather than focusing on the dietary restrictions and the warnings to those who violate God's covenant—the aspect of the sūra most insistently highlighted by the legalists—Shushtarī emphasizes the bounty and grace that is also promised by God in those verses. Thus, the Andalusian poet sings:

> I am content in the Creator, upon Him I rest.
> In Him I am joined, in Him I am separated,
> in Him I desire Him.
> In Him I see, in Him I hear and my soul is in His hands.
> He bestows on me his favor. My life in Him is sweet.

The current volume presents a selection of Shushtarī's vernacular and classical lyric, his longer doctrinal poems, and a brief prose treatise, *Risāla al-Baghdādiyya [Baghdad Treatise]*, all of which are rendered in English for the first time. The lyric poems are organized thematically into six chapters, each preceded by a brief introduction. Notes keyed to verse numbers follow at the end of the volume. The poems in "Intoxicated by the Divine" take up the theme with which Shushtarī is now most closely associated: the celebration of the ecstatic wine of the mystics. The songs in "Love-crazed" include some of his most lyrical and appealing compositions, which explore the paradoxes of union in and separation from God using the language and conventions of classical Arabic love poetry. "Denudatio/Stripping bare" explores the seeker's relationship to all that will pass away, from the riches of the material world to the comforts of the familiar. "Deciphering the signs of God" presents poems dealing with interpretation and mystical hermeneutics. One of Shushtarī's persistent themes is the complex interrelation between divine signs in their myriad forms: as letters of a divine text or as the grand patterns of creation. The poems in "The night journey" wed the imagery of classical Arabian desert odes—the desert encampments, the yearning and recollection of blissful union with the beloved, the long and lonely night trek of the suffering lover—to a mystical understanding of *miʿrāj*, Muḥammad's ascension to heaven.

In the poems of the subsequent chapters, aesthetic and poetic values are overshadowed by a more explicit engagement with doctrinal concerns. "At the monastery" foregrounds one of the most controversial aspects of Shushtari's work: his explicit invocation of Christian imagery and scenes and his exploration of how a mystical approach might transcend confessional divisions and unify believers. In Shushtarī's longest and most-commented poem, the *Nūniyya*, he explores the multifaceted and often paradoxical relationship of reason to the mystical pursuit of knowledge. Wrongly labeled a spiritual *isnād* (or chain of authorities) by Massignon, this work is far more complex, exploring the role of human reason (*ʿaql*)—in both its positive and negative aspects—in the thought of a long line of philosophers and mystics, from Hermes to Socrates to Ibn Rushd (Averroes) and Ibn al-ʿArabī. The poem's vast chronological sweep has inspired an influential tradition of commentary that is explored in the section introduction and in the notes.

The prose selection *Baghdad Treatise* is a brief and animated rebuttal to those who criticized the mystics' embrace of voluntary poverty and their wearing of wool and patchwork cloaks as religious innovation (*bidaʿ*) and ostentation of piety (*shuhra*). Shushtarī repeats the traditional justification, found in Sufi manuals such as Kalābādhī's tenth-century *Doctrine of the Sufis* or Qushayrī's *Risāla*, that the *ḥadīth* bear ample witness to the Prophet's wearing of woolen garments and his disdain for material goods. Likewise, he points to the example of many pious Muslim forbearers in their embrace of extreme poverty.

What is novel in our poet's treatise is the argument that because intention (*niyya*) is not discernable through externals such as clothing, one cannot form judgments about others. Reminding his readers that the Qur'ān calls believers to respect each other and refrain from criticizing and casting blame—"some suspicions are sinful" (49:12)—he defends the idea that one should act guided by conscience, neither condemning nor being condemned by others. This work can be read as a succinct introduction to many of the debates surrounding thirteenth-century Sufi practice, debates that echo those surrounding the creation of the mendicant orders during the same period in Christian Europe.

"My time is a wonder": The rising tide of Islamic mysticism in the thirteenth century

Shushtarī's art flourished in a time when Islamic mysticism enjoyed unprecedented growth, diversification, and cross-fertilization between its Eastern and Western practitioners. The efflorescence of Sufi institutions in the thirteenth century—including increasing numbers of dedicated centers of communal religious life (often called *ribāṭs* in the West and *khānaqāh* in the East) or retreat houses (*khalwas* or *zāwiyas*) and the advent of formal mystical schools (*ṭarīqas*), carrying the name of a prominent mystic and serving to propagate his views and mystical practices—greatly increased the number of adepts and the varieties of mystical life.[24] Widely divergent views on theology, daily spiritual praxis, and the believer's relationship to the material world are reflected in the wealth of appellations mystics used to describe themselves and differentiate themselves from others: *Ṣūfiyya*, *Mutaṣawwifa*, *Malāmatiyya*, *Fuqarā'*, *Qalandariyya*. The lines separating these groups —if we can even speak of lines—are often quite fuzzy. Indeed, the use of these labels is frustratingly inconsistent, even within the work of a single author. In his own writing on the subject of the varieties of mystical practice, Shushtarī expresses a preference for the way of the *fuqarā' al-mutajarradūn*, who, he explains, practice the most rigorous form of poverty, but the poet is careful not to denigrate other approaches, saying "all of them are paths to God Almighty."[25]

The early history of Islamic mysticism in Spain, Shushtarī's place of birth and where he spent his formative years are neither well documented nor well understood.[26] Nor is there any clear consensus on the reasons for the striking efflorescence of Sufism there in the twelfth century.[27] The Sanhāja Berber–led Almoravid dynasty, which ruled over the Maghreb and al-Andalus from the late eleventh-century until the mid-twelfth century, vigorously promoted strict religious observance and received enthusiastic support from the clerical class, the *fuqahā'*, who saw its power and influence rise dramatically during that time. These rigorist rulers and their local allies viewed Sufism with suspicion, as a source of *bidaʿ*, or religious innovation, and as a threat to their authority. Their concern grew such that in 1106 the Almoravid Amir ʿAlī ibn Yūsuf ibn Tāshfīn called for the public burning of Abū al-Ḥāmid al-Ghazālī's tremendously influential *Iḥyā ʿUlūm al-Dīn [Revival of Religious Sciences]*, a book widely perceived as bringing Sufism heightened legitimacy and acceptance in other parts of the Islamic world. As the Almoravids struggled under military threat, both in Morocco and from the Christian kingdoms to the north, the regime lost popular support, and critics increasingly voiced resentment of the ruling Sanhāja Berbers and their alien customs, exemplified by the veils worn by their men. Ethnic and religious tensions increased. Jews were denied important posts they had held under previous governments and were increasingly victims of violence and extortion. The situation of the Mozarabic Christian communities became increasingly precarious, for they were seen as potential allies and collaborators with their correligionists to the north. As society unraveled, the suppression of Sufism, clearly perceived as both politically and doctrinally threatening, intensified. The influential Sufi leaders Ibn al-ʿArīf (d.1141) and Ibn Barrajān (d.1141), both based in Almería, were arrested and brought to Marrakesh.[28] Ibn Barrajān was murdered in prison, while Ibn al-ʿArīf died shortly after his return to Almería, allegedly the victim of a poisoned eggplant. The outrage over the fate of these two revered teachers is thought to have been a major factor in impelling Ibn Qāsī (d.1151), a Sufi leader in the Algarve (the south Atlantic coast of the Iberian Peninsula, now part of Portugal), to launch a serious, though short-lived armed revolt against the Almoravids.[29]

The mid-twelfth-century rise of the Almohads, another Berber-led movement that toppled the ruling Almoravids, first in North Africa and then in Spain, signaled a very different climate for mysticism, as well as for philosophical enquiry. Both groups were motivated by religious zeal, but their ideological differences were profound. The Almohads (*al-Muwaḥḥidūn*, literally, "those who assert the oneness [of God]") distrusted the complex edifice of juridical decisions and kalām that were the stock-in-trade of the *fuqahā'*; instead, they advocated a direct engagement with the Qur'ān and prophetic tradition. Al-Ghazālī's work was promoted under the new regime; legend has it that Ibn Tūmart, the founder of the Almohad dynasty, met al-Ghazālī when he traveled east as a young man.[30] The works of other eastern Sufis circulated freely, as did works by earlier Andalusian Sufis. By early in the thirteenth century, Islamic Spain and North Africa not only had burgeoning communities of mystics but also had begun to produce towering theosophical thinkers and Sufi leaders—such as Ibn al-ʿArabī, Ibn Sabʿīn, Abū Madyan, al-Shādhilī, and, of course, Shushtarī—whose impact would reverberate throughout the Islamic world.

Ironically, the declining fortunes of the Almohads in the first half of the thirteenth century may have contributed to widening the scope of influence of these Andalusian mystics by forcing their emigration eastward. As military pressures, famine, and heavy taxation eroded support for this second Berber-led government, the fortunes of the *fuqahā'* began to rise anew. Sufis, philosophers, and others suspected of heterodoxy faced increased scrutiny, accusations of impiety, and persecution. The eastward exodus of many prominent Andalusian and Maghrebī Sufis and the resultant contact and interchange between Eastern and Western mystical currents profoundly marked the development of Sufism, precisely at the time of its institutionalization and the formation of a canon of theoretical, literary, and poetic texts in a variety of languages.

Writing the mystic's life

There is relatively little reliable biographical information for Shushtarī. Over the centuries the scant details about his life provided by early biographers have been supplemented by myth, legend, and a considerable amount of surmise predicated on the assumption that his poems are autobiographical and refer to actual lived events. For example, some have argued that the poem "Little shaykh from Meknes" indicates that the poet resided for a time in that Moroccan city; others have opined that "*Maknās*" simply provided a fortuitous rhyme.[31] None of the early biographies puts him in Meknes. As the stories about the poet's life acquired more dramatic flourishes—whether the stories were derived from the text of his poems or those falsely attributed to him—commentators began to use them to explicate the meaning of his poems. This clearly circular procedure obviously does little to further our understanding of the historical events of the mystic's life; moreover, it results in a problematic foreshortening of the interpretative horizon of the poems, diminishing, if not—at least in certain cases—eliminating, their characteristic ambiguity and enigmatic qualities.

What is known with reasonable certainty is this: Abū al-Ḥasan ʿAlī ibn ʿAbd Allah Numayrī al-Shushtarī was born in 610 AH/1212 CE to a prominent family in Wādī Ash (Guadix), a town cut into the steep hillsides of the towering Sierra Nevada, northeast of Granada. The family's *nisba*, or appellation, derives from Shushtar, the district of Guadix where they resided. Shushtarī's birth coincided with the crushing defeat of Almohad forces in the battle of Las Navas de Tolosa by the combined armies of Leon, Castile, Aragon, Navarre, and Portugal. The Moroccan-based Almohads would maintain a precarious hold on power in Islamic Spain through Shushtarī's youth, but by the time he was thirteen, the Muslim population of neighboring Seville and Murcia would be decimated by Christian incursions. Conflicts over dynastic succession in Marrakech, the seat of Almohad power, proved to be a distraction for much of the ruling class, which shifted its attention southward rather than to military threats emanating from the north. In the years between 1225 and 1236, when Cordoba fell, life in much of al-Andalus was marked by internal divisions, plague, and drought.[32] A number of local Muslim rulers in the crumbling kingdom entered into pacts with the Christians, either in the form of alliances to gain advantage over political rivals or in the payment of tribute to avoid conquest and dispossession. The extra burden of taxation required to pay these tributes only served to fuel popular resentment and rebellion. Not a few observers saw the mounting crisis as divine punishment for either the sins of the rulers or for the general sinfulness of the populace; many pursued religious renewal, either in the form of rigorous enforcement of religious law or a turning away from political solutions to embrace asceticism and ecstatic spirituality.

Shushtarī was among the large numbers of Andalusians who opted for the latter course. As a Sufi, he led a peripatetic existence; his earliest biographer, writing in the late thirteenth century, places him in Tunis, Qābis (Gabes, also in Tunisia), Malaga, Bijāya (Bougie, now part of Algeria), and Damietta.[33] Other sources mention travels to Damascus and several pilgrimages to Mecca.[34] Almost all of Shushtarī's biographies repeat a memorable anecdote about Shushtarī's premonition of death on 17 Safr 668 AH (October 15, 1269 CE). Arriving at a barren, salt-encrusted plain in the sub-Sinai near the Mediterranean, he asks the name of that place. When told "Ṭīna," he replies with an untranslatable play on words, "*ḥannat al-ṭīna illā al-Ṭīna*" (my clay [ṭīna] longed for Ṭīna").[35] His followers, numbering in the hundreds, carried his body to the nearby town of Damietta for burial in more solid ground.

Our poet's most influential biographer is Ibn Luyūn (1282–1349); his account forms the basis for most subsequent accounts, including those of Ibn al-Khaṭīb and al-Maqqarī.[36] Ibn Luyūn was a mystic and expert on poetical matters hailing from Almería, a longstanding center of Sufi thought.[37] The Almerian took a special interest in Shushtarī, writing a summary of his *Risāla al-ʿIlmiyya,* which he prefaced with an account of Shushtarī's deeds and qualities. According to this biography, the young mystic studied with Andalusian followers of Abū Ḥafṣ ʿUmar al-Suhrawardī[38] and with Ibn Sabʿīn. Ibn Luyūn further recounts that Shushtarī met the Syrian mystic and poet Najm ibn Isrā'il al-Dimashqī (1206–78), who said: "He came from a line of emirs (*umarā'*) and he joined the ranks of the poor (*fuqarā'*)." This corresponds to a motif commonly found in Sufi hagiographies: the sons of privilege who turn their backs on riches, status, and book learning and embrace higher forms of perception (*dhawq*) in the quest for spiritual illumination. There is ample material in Shushtarī's poetry to lead us to believe that there is more to Dimashqī's account than mere convention. Lines like:

There is no one in richness like You
  and in poverty there are none like us.
We see You manifest in everything;
  nothing is ours.

might be read in the sense of a kind of metaphorical "spiritual poverty." Yet others like:

> I clothe my body
>   in cords and needles,
> bits of discarded wool;
>   I beg a bit of bread.

speak of a poverty that is in no way abstract. Shushtarī's prose works make his embrace of extreme poverty even clearer and more explicit. In fact, in the *Risāla al-ʿIlmiyya* he treats the subject at great length, arguing that poverty is a good not only for the virtuous or outstanding, but even for the evil, for they are thus stripped of their ability to do harm unto others. Nor does he make any distinction between voluntary and involuntary poverty, declaring 'the poor man (*faqīr*) is outstanding whether he renounced the world by choice or by necessity."[39] Although we will examine this question in special detail in the chapter devoted to renunciation, "Denudatio/Stripping away," Shushtarī's championing of the popular classes is a theme that runs through all of his work, animating the songs that directly reach out to the excluded and the marginalized.

The most vexing and controversial question confronting Shushtarī's modern biographers has been establishing a chronology of his thought and his relationship to Ibn Sabʿīn. In the century following Ibn Sabʿīn's death, attacks on the Hellenizing Murcian philosopher intensified. The Hanbalī scholar Ibn Taymiyya wrote at length against his ideas; some biographers began circulating the charge that, like Socrates, Ibn Sabʿīn had died a suicide—a somewhat doubtful charge, given the fact that the earliest biographers make no mention of this. As Ibn Sabʿīn's reputation declined, the idea that Shushtarī ultimately broke with his revered master and rejected his teachings appeared to take root. Of course, Shushtarī's earliest biographer reports no such break. He does acknowledge the fact that Ibn Sabʿīn was, by all accounts, a difficult personality, mentioning that many seekers or scholars (*ṭalaba*) preferred Shushtarī to Ibn Sabʿīn. However, Shushtarī is presented by him as Ibn Sabʿīn's defender, replying to his master's critics, "if they say that, then it is because of their lack of familiarity with the master and shortcomings in their own character"[40] (4:31–38). Writing biographical sketches of both Ibn Sabʿīn and his most famous student, the polymath Ibn al-Khaṭīb mentions the controversies and accusations that followed the Murcian philosopher and, as further proof of his arrogance, relates that when the young Shushtarī met the even younger Ibn Sabʿīn, the teacher said to him with his characteristic haughtiness, "if it is paradise you seek, then go with Shaykh Abū Madyan, if it is the Master of paradise, then let's get going"(4:206). Yet Ibn al-Khaṭīb speaks of no rupture between the disciple and his master, instead claiming that Shushtarī took over the leadership of a group of some four hundred followers of Ibn Sabʿīn after the master's death. Furthermore, in both the *Iḥāṭa* and *Rawḍat al-taʿrīf*, Ibn al-Khaṭīb reproduces the complete text of Shushtarī's *Nūniyya*, a work that strongly identifies the poet as an unabashed follower of the Murcian philosopher-mystic.

The earliest account of a break comes at least a century and a half after the poet's death in a brief biographical note by Ibn Ḥajar al-ʿAsqalānī (1372–1449).[41] Later biographers, such as Aḥmad Zarrūq (d.1493) and Ibn ʿAjība (1746–1809), claim that Shushtarī did indeed repudiate the problematic aspects of Ibn Sabʿīn's thought, including "divine union (*ḥulūl* and *ittiḥād*) and a tendency towards deviation and heresies."[42] Ibn ʿAjība, who clearly holds Shushtarī in high regard, frequently citing the Andalusian's verse in his writing, is especially concerned with rescuing his memory from the heterodox taint of his master. Yet there is still the matter of whether the writings that predate this return to orthodoxy contain objectionable ideas. Ibn ʿAjība clearly rejects any attempt to pass judgment on individual poems or treatises; instead, he urges readers to recognize the contributions of these controversial mystics and employ *ta'wīl,* or figural interpretation, to come to what is sound (*ṣaḥīḥ*) in the writings of both men. Ibn ʿAjība thus squarely places interpretation, evaluation, and personal decisions about faith and conduct on the shoulders of the reader, and does much to remove the pall of suspicion cast over the writings of master and student.[43]

Ultimately, the various perspectives offered on the possible rift are most instructive on the much larger issue of the evolving reception and status of the "radical Sufis"in mainstream Sufi brotherhoods. If, as Alexander Knysh so clearly demonstrates, "Ibn ʿArabī's posthumous image was molded largely against the backdrop of the theological controversy over his intellectual legacy,"[44] Shushtarī's reputation was molded in the tension between a similar controversy over Ibn Sabʿīn's theological propositions and the widespread admiration for the poet's beautiful and well-loved verses.

Indeed the question of Shushtarī's relationship with Ibn Sabʿīn is just a part of larger questions surrounding the intellectual climate of the period and the relationships among many of the key figures in that extremely fertile time that coincided with the institutionalization of Sufism and the rise of mystical brotherhoods. Shushtarī's poems and prose works—and those attributed to him—reflect such a broad spectrum of ideas that commentators have been unable to agree on the trajectory of his thought and whether or not he later abandoned some of the controversial positions he once espoused. According to some accounts, he was first invested or initiated in the Sufi order (*ṭarīqa*) of the Andalusian-born Abū Madyan (1126–97), a key figure in promoting a moderate and accessible practice of Sufism largely modeled on the ideas of al-Ghazālī.[45] He was also said to have studied with followers of Shihāb al-Dīn al-Suhrawardī (d.1234), the author of the influential Sufi compendium, *ʿAwārif al-Maʿārif.* Suhrawardī represents a middle ground between the ethical Sufism of Abū Madyan and more speculative and philosophically tinged currents. Shushtarī's *Risāla al-ʿIlmiyya* draws heavily from Sarrāj's *Kitāb al-Lumaʿ.*[46] Additionally, Shushtarī's writings reflect admiration for the Sufi "martyr" al-Ḥusayn ibn Manṣūr al-Ḥallāj (857–922), executed for his public declarations of radical monism.

A more difficult matter is determining how well Shushtarī knew the work of his fellow Andalusian Ibn al-ʿArabī. To be sure, the teachings and writings of the Greatest Master, as well as his personal contacts with mystics from a broad swath of the Islamic world, were so influential that they have colored the interpretation not only of the mystics that followed him, but also, retrospectively, some who preceded him, such as the poet Ibn al-Fāriḍ. Indeed, this becomes a major hurdle to elucidating the philosophical specificities of certain currents of Sufi thought, especially those of contemporaries or near-contemporaries—like Shushtarī. To begin with, we cannot be sure how complete a knowledge of Ibn al-ʿArabī's writings and teachings he might have had. It would seem that our poet knew at least some of the work of his fellow Andalusian; he mentions him in the *Nūniyya* (lines 60–61) and also composed a series of short odes (*qaṣā'id*) apparently in response to poems in al-Shaykh al-Akbar's *Interpreter of Desires* (these poems can be found in Chapter 6, *Desert Wanderings*). Shushtarī is also credited with writing a type of poetic gloss, known as a *takhmīs*, on a poem found in Ibn al-ʿArabī's *Kitāb al-Isrā'*.[47] (By the same token, Ibn al-ʿArabī had composed a *takhmīs* on a poem of Abū Madyan.[48]) In fact, given that Ibn al-ʿArabī initiated the use of Andalusian strophic forms for mystical verse, it is tempting to read Shushtarī's career as deeply marked by an unspoken competition with the Greatest Master, whom he mentions directly only in the *Nūniyya.*

It is also unclear how well our poet knew the work of the Egyptian poet Ibn al-Fāriḍ (1181–1235), widely considered the most masterful Arab mystic poetic and legendary for the difficulty and dazzling artifice of his compositions.[49] Some of Shushtarī's classical odes certainly appear to echo those of his Egyptian predecessor, yet because Shushtarī's style and diction are so radically different, it is hard to discern more than general thematic similarities. Given that Ibn al-Fāriḍ reworks tropes coming out of the highly stylized tradition of pre-Islamic desert odes, Shushtarī's embrace of similar motifs is suggestive but not in and of itself convincing evidence of an artistic link between the two men.

Shushtarī's thought is further marked by many lesser-known mystics, such as the twelfth-century Andalusian Ibn Qāsī, who, in addition to leading a short-lived Sufi revolt against the Almoravids, was also the author of an influential treatise, *Khalaʿ Naʿlayn [The Shedding of the Sandals].*[50] Our poet also admired the enigmatic tenth-century Iraqi mystic Niffarī, whose work was heavily influenced by al-Ḥallāj.[51] Shushtarī's interest in Ibn Qāsī and al-Niffarī once again raises the question of how to distinguish between the general intellectual milieu in al-Andalus and the Maghreb—were these figures well known there at that time?—versus a possible (unacknowledged) intellectual debt to Ibn al-ʿArabī, who wrote extensive commentaries on their work.

If Shushtarī's verse clearly engages with (and raises questions about) the mystical currents of his day, it is equally immersed in secular literary traditions, from classical Arabic poetry to the popular vernacular culture of the Andalusian *muwashshaḥ* and the *zajal.* As we shall see, Shushtarī quotes or alludes to the verses of many secular writers, from Abū Nuwās (d.813), celebrated for his wine poems and his irreverent wit, to Ibn Zaydūn (1003–70), the Cordoban poet whose ill-fated love affair with the princess Wallāda provided him with material for his most-admired odes and her with material for devastatingly satirical poems. But Shushtarī's most striking references may be those to the work of Ibn Quzmān (d.1160), the self-proclaimed bad boy of Andalusī letters and master of that most informal of Andalusian verse forms, the *zajal*. In poem after poem Shushtarī appears to have borrowed the celebrated rake's colloquial diction, his irreverent attitude, and his tone of self-parodying boasts, recasting them and imbuing them with religious and metaphysical significance. Thus, Shushtarī's engagement with his diverse poetic predecessors indexes multiple levels of meaning, a dizzying polyvalence that annihilates the simple dichotomies of classical and vernacular or sacred and profane.

Shushtarī's prose writings

Although he is remembered primarily as a poet, Shushtarī also composed a number of prose treatises on a wide range of subjects, from practical matters of *ḥadīth* criticism and controversies regarding Sufi practice to extremely esoteric approaches to cosmology and ontology. Most of his surviving treatises remain in manuscript, often in unique copies.[52] Among the texts that have been edited is Shushtarī's *Risāla al-ʿIlmiyya*, extant only in the summary version of Ibn Luyūn. In this treatise the poet defends the customs and practices of the *fuqarāʾ al-mutajarridūn*, literally, the "poor dispossessed" or the "poor stripped [of everything]." *Fuqarāʾ* (singular, *faqīr*), in the sense of "those who live for God alone," is a term commonly used by Sufis to define themselves, yet in his treatise Shushtarī claims the term for a subset of Sufis, those following the strictest rule of poverty; he calls them "the heirs in rank to the people of the bench" (*ahl al-ṣuffa*)."[53] The text covers many of the usual topics of Sufi manuals, enumerating how their custom (*sunna*) is rooted in the example of the Prophet and his Companions. It also carefully examines many aspects of communal religious life, from the relationship between master and student to proper manners at table and to the use of musical instruments to accompany poetry and song at mystical sessions. The book closes with a brief meditation on the understanding of *tawḥīd* (the oneness of God) and a glossary of about 250 mystical terms and expressions.

Many topics of the *Risāla al-ʿIlmiyya* are also discussed—more succinctly, however—in the *Risāla al-Baghdādiyya* [*The Baghdad Treatise*], translated in this volume. This text focuses on several controversial questions of Sufi practice: the use of distinctive Sufi dress (particularly the *muraqqaʿ* or patchwork cloak), the practice of extreme voluntary poverty, and begging. Although it is quite brief, it is a fascinating (and spirited) rejoinder to the very vocal critics of "immoderate" Sufism. *Al-Risāla al-miʿrājiyya* is found in an undated manuscript containing writings of Shushtarī's student Aḥmad Yaʿqūb Ibn al-Mubashshir, including a commentary on the opening sūra of the Qur'ān, the *Fātiḥa*, a copy of Ibn al-ʿArabī's *Kitāb al-Isrā'*, and several anonymous poems and text fragments.[54] From its title, one might expect *al-Risāla al-miʿrājiyya* [*Treatise on Ascension*] to follow the pattern of numerous other Sufi treatises that interpret the theme of the Prophet's night journey to Jerusalem and to heaven as an allegory for the soul's quest for the divine. Shushtarī's text dispenses with allegory, instead tackling sweeping and abstract cosmological and ontological questions through an extended meditation and explication of the Qur'anic passage: "He runs everything, from the heavens to the earth, and everything will ascend, and everything will ascend to Him in the end, on a day that will measure a thousand years in your reckoning" (32:5).[55] Bypassing any "creature-centric" vantage point, the treatise explores the interrelated ideas of creation and time, asserting that neither of those concepts has any meaning in the eternity that is beyond time.

Singing at the crossroads of cultures

While Shushtarī's prose treatises help flesh out our understanding of his mystical philosophy and its relationship to the broader intellectual and religious currents of the time, it is his poetry and its groundbreaking use of Andalusian vernacular poetic forms that are of enduring resonance and of primary interest to us here. The issue of language is paramount indeed given the cultural imperative to protect and preserve *fuṣḥa*, the clear, pure Arabic of the Qur'ān, of classical poetry and erudition, from contamination by the *laḥjāt* or local vernaculars. That concern is reflected in numerous grammatical treatises written to correct local pronunciation and usage. In the introduction to his *Laḥn al-ʿAwwām [Grammatical Errors of the Commoners]*, the Andalusian grammarian al-Zubaydī (918–89) explains his concern that those errors have crept into the usage of the elites: "these incorrect usages have infiltrated into the works of poets, and the most eminent scribes and functionaries include them in their correspondence and make use of depraved expressions in their conversations."[56]

Dialectal slips and even "depraved expressions" did indeed occasionally creep into the writing of the literate classes, despite the best efforts of Zubaydī and other grammarians to prevent this. As a result, medieval copyists routinely corrected colloquialisms, seen as embarrassing lapses on the part of an author or prior copyist. Indeed, many modern editors of medieval manuscripts continue to make such corrections *in silentio*, regarding the footnoting of each corrected "misspelling" or colloquialism as pedantry. During the first centuries of Islam, it was simply unthinkable to *purposely* write in an Arabic language as distant from "pure" or "clear" Arabic *(fuṣḥā)* as the medieval Romance languages were from the Latin of Cicero.

It was thus quite revolutionary when, around the tenth century, secular poets in Islamic Spain began composing poems that not only broke the rules of meter, but also cast aside the traditional stately monorhyme for much lighter strophic rhyme schemes and also incorporated the much-castigated vernacular. These poems, called *muwashshaḥāt* and *zajals*, sung to characteristic Andalusian melodies, quickly gained admirers throughout the Arab world, even if most anthologists and poets remained reluctant to commit them to writing.[57] Many prominent Andalusian poets composed *muwashshaḥāt*; however, those poems, considered a light and perhaps ephemeral form of diversion, were often excluded from their *dīwāns*. For example, there are no *muwashshaḥāt* in the manuscript copies of the *dīwāns* of Ibn al-Zaqqāq (d.528 AH/1133–34 CE) and al-Aʿmā al-Tuṭīlī (d.519 AH/1126 CE),[59] despite the fact that these authors figure prominently in collections devoted to popular strophic poetry. Ibn Bassām, author of *al-Dhakhīra fī maḥāsin ahl al-jazīra* [*Treasury of the Merits of the Andalusians*], an early twelfth-century compendium of the writings and biographies of Andalusian notables, describes this type of poetry and even mentions the names of several poets who composed it, but he balks at recording these verses in his anthology. It was not until late in the twelfth century or early in the thirteenth—precisely when these forms were first adopted by Andalusian mystics—that compilations of these poems began to appear. The first known anthology is *Dār al-Ṭirāẓ*, a collection made by the Egyptian poet Ibn Sanā' al-Mulk, an admirer of this style of poetry who had never traveled to al-Andalus. By this time, these Andalusian songs had found enthusiastic audiences throughout much of the Arab world.

The *muwashshaḥ* and *zajal* not only flouted the grammatical rules that occupied al-Zubaydī and the other guardians of *'arabiyya,* but they went even further in effecting a startling bilingualism. Early examples of *muwashshaḥāt* juxtapose verses in classical Arabic with final verses, known as *kharjas* or *markazs*, in Romance or the Andalusian vernacular Arabic. Such bilingualism is even more apparent in the *muwashshaḥāt* of Jewish poets, who punctuated verses in Hebrew with *kharjas* in Romance or colloquial Arabic (written using Hebrew letters). Although later writers—no doubt coming out of much less polyglot environments—often did without such linguistic contrasts, the association of the *muwashshaḥāt* with bilingualism persisted, as evidenced by the *muwashshaḥ* with a Persian *kharja* that Ibn Sanā' al-Mulk composed for his anthology. Even the sixteenth-century Spanish Moriscos preserved examples of bilingual *muwashshaḥāt* and coplas in honor of the Prophet Muḥammad.[60]

The *zajal* (pl. *azjāl*), written entirely in colloquial Arabic, is similar in rhyme scheme and meter to the *muwashshaḥ*, but its length is much more variable, running as long as twenty stanzas in contrast to the *muwashshaḥ's* three to five strophes. Later poets, including Shushtarī, blur the distinctions between the two poetic forms, writing poems that follow the strophic conventions of the *muwashshaḥ,* but rather than juxtaposing classical usage with the colloquial phrasing of the closing couplet, they employ a highly vernacular diction throughout. While some Western scholars have argued about how to classify this and other hybrid forms that emerged later—many adopted the term *zajal-like muwashshaḥ*—Arab scholars, perhaps more keenly aware of the myriad problems arising from such taxonomic impulses, have generally avoided making these sorts of classifications.

Much of the popularity of both of these forms is doubtless due to their increasingly complex strophic rhyme schemes, which makes them especially suited for singing. [See the examples below.] These stylistic innovations appeared to give new generations of Andalusian poets license to undertake thematic experimentation. Thus the poems not only engaged in linguistic code-switching, but they also juxtaposed—or *sampled,* in the modern parlance—tropes and motifs drawn from disparate genres in such a way as to defy or even ridicule the well-defined thematic conventions of more "serious" poetry. The *muwashshaḥ,* always linked to al-Andalus, became the first "foreign" poetic innovation to gain acceptance in the cultural centers of Baghdad, Basra, and Damascus, yet it never gained the prestige of the traditional Arabian forms. And perhaps most suggestively, the earliest attempts to collect and preserve secular Andalusian strophic poetry coincided with the mystics' appropriation of these forms. Was it that the mystics started composing such informal verse because it had already gained some measure of prestige that had earlier been denied? Was it that those verses, and indeed the cultural legacy of al-Andalus itself, was finally perceived as gravely endangered and in need of preservation? Or did the mystics themselves contribute to improving their reputation? The one thing that is certain, however, is that once these poems became incorporated into the devotional rituals of a number of Sufi orders, their preservation and propagation was assured.

The Lover's visit

Below are sample transliterated strophes of a *muwashshaḥ*, "The lover's visit." Note that the rhyme of the first and second hemistiches of the first two lines (called the maṭlaʿ, literally, the "opening" or "rising" of the poem) will be repeated after each strophe and corresponds to the rhyme of the *kharja.* Not all *muwashshaḥāt* exhibit the same degree of internal rhyme.

zāranī ḥibbī waṭābat awq**āti**	wasamaḥ li-lḥab**īb**
waʿafā ʿan jamīʿi zall**āti**	ʿalā ghayẓ al-raq**īb**
zāranī mūnyatī wazāl albās	*wasamāḥ bilwisāl*
waḥadār ḥāḍrati wadār alkās	*wabalāgtu l'amāl*
washaribna waṭābati al'anfās	*min mudāman ḥalāl*
āmla kāsi fafih mizāti	*nāshrubū ya labīb*
waḥabībi ūnsi wamishkāti	*māʿi hādir qarīb*
āy mudāma, wāy khamrā, wāy khammār	*wāy(u) tarāb, wāy ghinā*
fi riyādan tafāttaḥat azhār	*wa'anārat lanā*
waṭṭuyūr fi manābir al-'ashjār	*takhtatāb baynanā*

Below are sample strophes of Shushtarī's *zajal*, "My art." Note the repetition of the refrain, and how the final (single-hemistich) line of each stanza repeats the rhyme of the refrain.

Qulū li-lfaqīh ʿannī *ʿishq dhā-l-malīh fannī*
wa-shurbī maʿū bi-l-kās
wa-l-ḥadra maʿa al-jallās
wa hawlī rifāq akyās
qad shālū al-kalif ʿannī
Qulū li-lfaqīh ʿannī *ʿishq dhā al-malīh fannī*
ayya madhhab tadrīnī?
al-sharīʿatu tuhayīnī
wa-l-ḥaqīqa tufnīnī

"Loving the Beautiful One is my art"

Tell the faqih on my behalf:
loving the Beautiful One is my art.

Shushtarī appropriates these colloquial song forms to transform their message, but perhaps most radically, to suggest a new reading of all the ordinary elements of everyday life. "Loving the Beautiful One is my art," he proclaims in catchy, insistently rhymed verses, self-consciously echoing poems of the scandalous Ibn Quzmān in which *dhā al-malīḥ* meant "that handsome (beardless) lad." This poem presents a clear example of a composition that can easily be read as either profane or mystical. Just like Niẓāmī's poem about Majnūn Layla, it is basically the willingness of the reader to apply a mystical hermeneutic that makes this a religious poem. Is the "Beautiful One" God? Could loving a beautiful person be a metaphor for loving God, a way of loving God? On many levels the poem quite pointedly refuses to answer the question, and leaves the translator with the dilemma of whether or not to capitalize "beautiful one" or "him." How does one faithfully preserve the edge that many of these poems have while not causing offense or breeding misunderstanding in that treacherous passage across time, and across linguistic, cultural, and religious boundaries?

Throughout the poem, Shushtarī pursues that flirtation with the illicit that makes this poem such a powerful challenge to his self-righteous critics. The choice to use the sexually-charged word *ʿishq* ("passion, ardor")—rather than any one of dozens of other words for love, and especially when speaking of "the beautiful one"—heightens the aesthetic affinities with the work of Ibn Quzmān. By Shushtarī's time there was already a long history of controversy among Sufis as to which words for love were appropriate in referring to humankind's love for God, or God's love for God's creatures. Abū al-Ḥasan al-Daylamī (flourished 1000) begins his *Treatise on Mystical Love* (*Kitāb ʿatf al-alif*) with precisely this question.[61] In Shushtarī's poem, the defense of the Sufi way against the implied criticism of the *faqīh,* the jurist who represents a legalistic interpretation of Islam, is joined to a self-referential wink at the *zajal* itself. Shushtarī's *fann*, his art, his artistry, is the poem itself, which revels in its bold informality. The message of love and annihilation in the beloved (or the Beloved) is here unabashedly expressed in the language of the market and the home. The poem is itself an act of devotion. Yet at the same time, the life of the seeker is *fann*, a field of work, a specialization, an all-consuming "art" in its broadest understanding.

Here, as in other poems, an intimacy with the listener is enacted not only in the striking informality of the diction, but also in the imagined confrontation with the *faqīh*, the stodgy jurist who understands worship as a set of legal requirements rather than as an exuberant passion. In this repeated refrain the listener is tacitly asked to take the side of the poet in conveying an increasingly bold—if not downright insolent—message to the jurist. He continues to grow bolder as he approaches the point at which the conflict between a juridical and a mystical interpretation (of the poem, of life) will be made explicit:

The law revivifies me
and the truth annihilates me.

Legal scholars would certainly argue that the *sharīʿa*, the law, infuses man with life, gives him the guidelines to follow the righteous path, but the next line throws the interpretation of the previous one into question, at least for the listener who has been initiated in the conventions of Sufi exegesis. The truth, al-*ḥaqīqa*, for the mystics refers to the received or intelligible knowledge of al-*Ḥaqq*, Truth with a capital T, which is one of the names of God. If in the Sufi hermeneutic the highest good is effacement, annihilation—for it is when the self is completely emptied of the self that God's presence is complete—how then to understand the "revivification" referred to in the previous line? Is it a question of reversed dualities, in which death is understood as the key to eternal life? Is life, then, death? Is he really saying the law is deadening? Or is he asserting that the law, while life giving, is completed, made more perfect through the knowledge or experience of God? Or is he more slyly proposing a hermeneutic that allows the assertion of apparently contradictory propositions? Once again, the poem admits multiple readings.

In any case the poet proclaims, "know then, that I am a Sunni," that is, know then that I am the one who follows the *sunna* or the practice of the Prophet. In the context of this one-sided dialogue with the critic of Sufism, Shushtarī is saying: "No, no, I am not the one who has strayed from the path." The confrontation grows even bolder:

> If you could see me at home
> when I raise the curtains
> and my love is naked with me…
> In union with him, I am made glad.

The poem finds the dangerous place where raising the curtains or the veil, a common topos of reaching a higher degree of mystical understanding, retains the outrageousness of making visible, making public, that act of union. Here, the poet does not use a conventional mystical term like *tajrīd*, meaning "to strip bare" (metaphorically "to abstract, to get to the essence of"), but rather *ʿārin* literally, "nude" or "naked," a shockingly blunt way to speak of mystical union. Naturally, the Arabic has no capital letters, and the lines would readily admit a profane interpretation were it not for the saintly reputation of the author.

"The world is your boudoir," he continues, accusing his critics of seeking union with things of *this* world. (Thus explaining why they cannot understand his meaning.) In this poem—as in many others—Shushtarī uses the confrontation between *faqīh* and *faqīr*, between jurist and Sufi, to explore a complete reversal of conventional meaning. I suggest that the reading of the poem depends on the line "the truth annihilates me," because *that* line only makes sense when read mystically; it then proposes new meanings for every other line.

If in "My art" and "Let them criticize me" and the many poems in which he describes himself as "wanton," "unrepentant" and having "cast off all restraint" Shushtarī seems defiantly unconcerned with the possibility of being condemned by the defenders of orthodoxy, in other poems he is quite preoccupied with the real dangers of being misunderstood and even the impossibility of communication itself. In "Just understand me" the insistent refrain highlights this concern:

Listen to some words select,
just understand me, just understand me.
What did someone say to me perchance?
(Understand how I explain my meaning):
What is your beloved's name? I said: him.
There is no confusing the name of the beloved,
just understand me, just understand me.
My beloved encompasses all existence.
He is visible in white and black
in Christian and Jew,
in the letters and their points,
just understand me, just understand me
in the plants and in the minerals,
in black and in white,
in the pen and the ink.
In this there is no mistake,
just understand me, just understand me.

The deeper message of this poem, repeated over fifteen strophes, appears, just as the Muslim profession of faith "there is no god but God," to be simple, incontrovertible: God encompasses all existence. The poem becomes an extended meditation on the experience of that overwhelming totality that Shushtarī describes (as did Ibn al-ʿArabī before him) as "an ocean with absolutely no shore." Yet how to encompass that totality of existence in just a few words, how to be understood? Therein lies the difficulty.

Shushtarī is acutely aware of the insufficiency of language to express concepts that are beyond human language, yet he rejects the approach of other Sufis who choose to make the impossibility of communicating a central theme of their work. In this he is quite unlike Ibn al-ʿArabī, who wrote many perplexingly esoteric verses, utterly absorbed in the problematic of language, such as this short poem:

Here, what the mind denies is witnessed
through the sign of revelation: there is no other-than-You.
And it has no likeness to bring You its image,
except prayer if I pray with other-than-You.
But, I erred in saying that it was through other-than-You;
the Real is with him who prays through other than
other-than-You.[62]

While the English translation cannot replicate the multiple levels of syntactical and epistemological ambiguity in this passage, it should be clear how forbidding it would be to a reader unschooled in the conventions of mysticism and an understanding of negative theology. While Shushtarī does occasionally make declarations of anxiety or frustration about language, even those are expressed with diaphanous clarity:

I translated an illegible letter.
Will anyone understand me?

Shushtarī's songs continued to speak to generation after generation of Muslim mystics who were unlikely to be willing or able to ponder the erudite word plays of Ibn al-Fāriḍ, the opacity of so many of the poems of Ibn al-ʿArabī. Moreover, they proudly embraced the cadence and diction of the common man to promote voluntary poverty and simplicity as a clear path to salvation. Shushtarī's brilliant combination of Andalusian popular song and his joyful mystical vision have made his poetic corpus one of the most vibrant and enduring elements of the legacy of Islamic Spain. His simple, direct, and hauntingly beautiful songs, still very much a living part of Sufi practice throughout North Africa, continue to impart their hopeful message, speaking of the divine in the mystical language of everyday life.

PART TWO

Poems and Songs

Chapter 1

INTOXICATED BY THE DIVINE

Introduction

The poems and songs in this first section highlight the theme with which Shushtarī is now most closely associated: the celebration of the ecstatic wine of the mystics. Throughout much of his poetic corpus, Shushtarī sings of wine (*khamr*) or cups (*akwās*) or drunkenness (*sukr*). While in the selection presented here, this symbolic wine and its myriad symbolic attributes are foregrounded, the reader will note the theme throughout many poems in this volume.

Newcomers to Sufi poetry might be surprised to find devout Muslims singing the joys of the grape; however, Sufi poets had long written of mystical extinction or *fanā'*, that is, the loss of self in the overwhelming infinity of the divine as an intoxication. The vocabulary and expressions used by Shushtarī were part of the widely accepted lexicon of Sufi terminology, a mystical vocabulary that predated even tenth-century mystics like al-Ḥallāj (d.922).[1] In some cases Sufis simply borrowed preexisting secular wine poems (which remained quite popular despite Islamic strictures against wine) for their devotions, making perhaps minor lexical changes to point toward a spiritual interpretation. For example, verses of the great ʿAbbasid wine poet Abū Nuwās are unapologetically and unself-consciously cited in al-Qushayrī's famous eleventh-century manual of Sufi practice. As Th. Emil Homerin points out, the substitution of the word *nushwa* (inebriation) by the conventional Sufi term, *sakra* (intoxication) and the interpretative context of a Sufi handbook transform the verses of the famously dissolute poet into a meditation on an ineffable state.[2]

By the same token, the *Wine Ode* (*al-khamriyya*) of the Egyptian poet Ibn al-Fāriḍ might be read as nothing more than an exquisitely classicizing poem extolling wine and its pleasures. However, because of the poet's pious reputation and his well-known *Poem of the Sufi Way*, the poem is understood by readers as speaking in an esoteric register.[3] Dozens of commentaries have offered detailed mystical interpretations of *The Wine Ode*, and this dense and challenging work is routinely reprinted with extensive notes drawn from these commentaries. Thus it is entrenched as a classic of Sufi literature, even more firmly cementing the poetic link between bacchic and mystical verse. What Shushtarī—coming perhaps a generation or two after the Egyptian poet—contributes in his own wine songs is an exciting and groundbreaking directness; his verses eschew high-culture artifice. They proclaim their message boldly, in readily accessible language. With rare exceptions (which will be treated in the next section), the reader need not appeal to the author's biography or apply recondite exegesis to apprehend the mystical intention of the poem. The distance between secular and religious expression is erased, not in the reader's imposition of a mystical interpretation, but in the poem's narrative trajectory, moving modally, as is proper of song, from one register to another, from secular to religious, and in the process challenging the distinction between them. Perhaps this helps explain why throughout North Africa, Shushtarī is considered the foremost bard of the divine cups, even if Ibn al-Fāriḍ is held to be more polished as a stylist.

The compositions in this first section—and in many other sections of this book—deploy the common tropes of secular Arabic poetry, from the sweetness of the wine secretly shared between lover and beloved to the boisterous conviviality of drinkers gathered late at night, and from the intimate conversation during the nocturnal visit of the lover to the poet's refusal to give up the all-consuming love, even when that love leaves him bewildered and confused. Just as Jewish and Christian mystics read the sensual yearning of the bride and groom in the lyrical love poetry of the *Song of Songs* as an allegory for Israel and God or the individual believer and God, so too Muslim mystics saw in Arabic love poetry a form in which to express or give shape to an ineffable and ultimately incommunicable experience.

Like the secular *muwashshaḥāt* and *zajals* of an Islamic Spain regularly portrayed as libertine—often by the clerics and social reformers who saw material splendor and cultural refinements as the roots of al-Andalus's decay and weakness—Shushtarī's poems delight in recreating the glowing joy, the complete abandonment, and the loss of self-consciousness in the grape. These poems are sheer exuberance, making do without the finely wrought details of the cut of the crystal goblet or the vagaries of light as reflected in the "ruby red liquid" that mark the more elevated registers of classical wine poetry (*khamriyyāt*).

The section opens with "How I began." Tradition has it that this is the first song that Shushtarī composed. According to the twentieth-century Moroccan Sufi scholar ʿAbd al-ʿAzīz ibn al-Ṣiddīq, when Shushtarī decided to follow Ibn Sabʿīn, the master told him to sell his goods and abandon all rank and honor. After changing his clothes for humble woolen attire, he was to take a *bandīr* (a sort of tambourine) and sing among the lowly and the scorned of the souks. Over and over, he recited as instructed: "*badaytu bidhikr al-ḥabīb*" [I began with the invocation of the beloved], unable to add any verse to that opening line. Finally, after three days of recitation, inspiration came to him and the rest of the now well-known song poured out: "*wahimtu waʿayshi yaṭīb/wabuḥtu bisirrin ʿajīb*" [I fell head over heels/life became sweet, a wondrous mystery revealed]. In a song marked by insistent internal rhymes, that wondrous mystery is then described as "a cup of contentment" passed around among the drinkers, joined together in the knowledge of God's forgiveness.

In its declaration that this ecstatic illumination comes through the invocation of the name of the Beloved, the song asserts the power of *dhikr*, a term that can be understood as "remembrance," "recollection" or "invocation." *Dhikr* is a key aspect of Sufi devotional practice, in that context specifically referring to the rhythmic repetition of the name of God or a religious formula such as "there is no god but God," or simply "Him" (*hu* or *huwa*) while focusing intensely on its meaning, shutting out consciousness of all else. Sufis often cite the Qur'ānic injunction "Remember your Lord often" (3:41) as justification for these informal litanies. Just as al-Kalābādhī proclaims, "Real recollection consists in forgetting all but the One recollected,"[4] the poem links invocation, remembrance, *dhikr*, with the intoxication and self-effacement of those sharing the cup, reiterating the symbolic connection even more clearly in the lines that follow: "their spirits are revived/their problems disappear."

The *qaṣīda* that follows "Licit to drink?" opens with a celebration of the drinking of mystical wine. From the beginning the poetic voice declares a reversal of conventional Islamic morality, explaining that *this* wine is not forbidden; rather, what is forbidden is its abandonment. The contraposition of legal strictures and mystical ethics is even more pointedly explored as the poem moves into a dialogue between a jurist (*faqīh*) and the speaker who asks for a *fatwā*, or legal verdict, on the permissibility of drinking while performing various ritual acts, primarily connected to the Pilgrimage. The literal-minded jurist fails to understand the nature of the question and the allegorical meaning of "wine." The Sufi's reply, "if you would but taste it," seems to admit ruefully that the jurist is bound to reject his view, and yet the mystic will continue to assert the primacy of experiential knowledge, the knowledge that leads to a reckoning of the limits of literal or surface interpretations.

Like the preceding *qaṣīda*, the *zajal* "My art" (discussed in the Introduction to this book), dramatizes the contest between the religious outlook of the jurist and the mystic. "My art" (*fannī*) defines the poetic act itself and the poet's mystical approach to life as ways of loving the Beautiful One. The relatively short *zajal*, "Many a cup," presents another variation on Shushtarī's bacchic theme. To the familiar images of brilliance or luminosity that are intertwined with the ecstatic wine, the poet here adds the idea of vastness, from the sun to the depths, a heart that can encompass mountains stretching into the horizon. This wine makes the poet lose all shame, that is, abandon all consciousness of the self and its limitations and imperfections in pure contemplation of the divine. As in other poems, he proclaims himself "unrepentant," urging the listener to look for him in the tavern, "slumped among the wine jugs," in a self-conscious echo of the proclamations of famous wine poets like Abū Nūwās and Ibn Quzmān.

"Wine from no wine press" adds to the initial praise of this life-giving beverage a warning to conceal the secret from those who are unprepared to understand it. The Muslim mystics, like many philosophers and esoteric thinkers, stressed the importance of shielding the uninitiated from secrets that they are not ready to grasp. Such revelations can harm either the hearer, who may take away the wrong message or reject the message entirely due to misprision, or they may harm the revealer, who could face persecution or even martyrdom because his message is misunderstood. Shushtarī's own proclamation of secrets and his warnings to protect may seem paradoxical. Do not his own poems, addressed as they are to those unversed in the ways of the mystics, violate the warning he just gave? Or is this a clever rhetorical device (and psychological stratagem) for creating a bond between the poet-narrator and the listener? Of course, the same apparent contradiction obtains in a vast tradition of classical Arabic poetry and European courtly love lyric in which a poet-lover draws the listener into the intimacy shared between lovers while reviling the *raqīb*, the spy.

The short *muwashshaḥ* "At your service" presents an interesting twist on the usual scene of the Sufi castigated by the jurist for his wantonness. Here the "friends," perhaps those who would prefer "real" drink and savory delights, apparently criticize the poet for his worship and supplication—his Path to the most brilliant of wine. The last two lines speak of the confusion of self and divine, as the one who calls out is, at the same time, the One who responds. The *muwashshaḥ* "Love crazed for God" is an affirmation of the pious observance of those who are head over heels for God; here Shushtarī clearly distances himself from those who might claim that the mystic is not bound by the religious duties of ordinary people. Lines 8–18 focus on solitary prayer (*wird*) and meditation, devotions that go beyond the five daily obligatory prayers. The final section of the poem is a glimpse of that meditation itself, reflections on God through God's names, through the descriptions that men must use to understand God's greatness and perfection.

"Oh, perplexed heart" presents a less-prominent facet of the poet's work. While the vast majority of his poems focus far more on the ecstatic dimension of the spiritual path, here in memorable lines Shushtarī speaks of fear: "You flung your spirit into an overflowing sea, a sea of passion,/yet you are afraid of a sprinkle" (lines 3–4). In opening "*yā qalb, yā qalbī*" [Oh, heart, oh, my heart] he leaves open the possibility that he is addressing himself, his own fear and regret, or a beloved friend, for in Arabic (as in Spanish and other languages) it is not unusual to address someone dear as "my heart." (To this day, addressing the beloved as "my heart" or "my eye" remains very common in popular Arabic music.) But for the declarations that the wine of which he partakes "was not pressed by the presser/or harvested from a trellis," one might even read the poem as a rather conventional *muwashshaḥ* in which a lover urges a reluctant or standoffish beloved to end the suffering of the lover. In any case, in this intimate conversation, with another mystic, with a reluctant beloved, or with his own momentarily fearful heart, the poetic voice urges oblivion in the rapturous love-madness, "for everyone is confused in your love."

The final poem of this section, "I'm on my way," circles back to the idea of beginnings seen in the first poem of the collection and is itself the opening poem of most of the Eastern recensions of the *dīwān*. While we know nothing about how or when this *dīwān* was compiled or organized, one can discern a certain ordering of poems by content. The most difficult and equivocal poems are generally grouped at the end of the collection. By contrast, this opening poem explicitly refers to *starting* on the path. Unlike other poems that speak of a marvelous mystery unveiled, here, "the secret meaning opened *a bit* (*shuwaya*) for you" (lines 38–39). That is to say, the journey has just begun; there is still a long way to travel.

How I began

I began by invoking my beloved.
Head over heels, I fell, life became sweet,
  a wondrous mystery revealed.

The cup goes round
  those gathered together;
spirits revived,
  their problems disappear.

Pouring their draught of contentment,
  God forgives what's past.

Drink up, my companion, be content.
Live in the peace of the beloved.
  achieved through a wondrous mystery.

Go on, drain the glasses,
  drink them up.
May your innermost self benefit
  in the station of the saints.

Lightning lit up the sanctuary.
  God forgives what's past.

Oh, cupbearer, have pity on us;
the master forgives our transgression.

Pour wine for us,
bring us happiness and peace.
For we are passionately in love,
just as the noble saints.

Make the vastness open to us.
God forgives what's past.

Licit to drink?

How good to drink wine in the Sufi retreats.
My friend, pour me some cups
of that wine we are forbidden to abandon.
There is no sin in it, not even a shadow of suspicion.
Aged in jugs since before the time of Adam,
its source is the utmost goodness.

O *faqih*, give me your verdict, tell me,
is it licit to drink on Mount Arafat?
Is it permissible to perform the circambulation and
the *sa'y* with it?
to announce our service to God, to throw stones at
the devil?
Are the Qur'an and *dhikr* allowed under its effects?
or may one glorify God in prayer?

The *faqih* answered: If this wine
is of the grape, an intoxicating drink,
then certainly we deem it forbidden to drink;
it is more than just dubious.

O *faqih*, if you would but taste it
and listen to the melodies in the Sufi gatherings,
you would give up this world and everything in it
and live love-crazed until the day you die.

My art

Tell the *faqih* on my behalf:
loving the beautiful one is my art.

My drink, with him from the glass,
and the *hadra,* with those gathered round,
Close by, good companions.
they lifted the weight from me.

Tell the *faqih* on my behalf:
loving the beautiful one is my art.

What kind of believer do you take me for?
The law revivifies me
and the truth annihilates me.
Know that I am a Sunni.

Tell the *faqih* on my behalf:
loving the beautiful one is my art.

And know that there is no one home
except you, so let's get to the point.
Enter into the arena with me.
Have faith. Don't push me away.

Tell the *faqih* on my behalf:
loving the beautiful one is my art.

If you could see me at home
when I raise the curtains
and my love is naked with me…
In union with him, I am made glad.

Tell the *faqih* on my behalf:
loving the beautiful one is my art.

So leave me be and spare me your delusions,
for you lust for yourself
and this world is your boudoir.
Wake up, you will see my beauty.

Tell the *faqih* on my behalf:
loving the beautiful one is my art.

Timeless love

I was poured a cup
of timeless love,
not of this world
nor of heaven.

In it, I became
unique in my time,
bearing my banner
among men.

Mine is
an amazing path
of love unsurpassed.
How lucky I am!

You who love him,
the beautiful one has many followers.
If you are unkind to them,
what misfortune!

Far be it from you,
dear ones of Najd,
to cut the ties of
hope between you and me.

Let go of Zayd and Mayya

I drink wine from the goblet
and from myself I come closer to myself.
In myself it is myself I love.

For he is my essence, my true soul,
the fine wine that fills me and quenches my thirst.
I care not what others may say.

I seek in myself what I already have.
Drink up in good health
the vintage mellowed and pure!

My allusions are from me and for me, so learn.
Don't resist me, understand.
I am everything, the center of totality. Accept this.

Forget about him and her,
let go of Zayd and Mayya.
Take pleasure in loving sincerely.

What's temporal will pass away—my life remains.
My being is not separated from my life
for my essence is my wholeness and my wholeness
my essence.

My essence radiates like the sun
and from myself, I draw near myself
in myself, it is myself I love.

Many a cup

Your love has served me many a cup.

Its light-brightness has illuminated my senses.
My night has turned to day.
The sun is mine and the stars.

My dominion encompasses the depths.
   My heart is the Atlas mountains.

Your love has served me many a cup.

When I looked away from myself,
I saw myself, the writing of my being visible to me.
What had been hidden
appears to me,
   its meaning beyond ordinary wealth.

Your love has served me many a cup.

I'll tell you true, if I may:
I am a *faqir*, indeed,
and wanton. Shushtarī is unrepentant.
   I drink with my companion from the cup.

Your love has served me many a cup.

Look for me in the tavern.
You will see me
slumped among the wine jugs.
I love—without restraint—the one
   who revives the spirits of those who join with him.

Your love has served me many a cup.

Wine from no wine press

My beloved plied me with glasses
   of a wine from no wine press,
the drink of the pure.
   In it, all things are made manifest.

I took a swig
   and I fell passionately for you, O majesty!

My bride was revealed to me;
  I saw only perfection.
My drunkenness inebriated me,
  as it had others.

This drink brings souls to life
  whoever drinks of it is intoxicated.
Unveiled to me like a bride,
  I saw the sun and the moon.

Pay heed, my brother, don't be loose-tongued.
  Hold fast to the marvelous secret,
so the cloak may be lifted,
  and you see the beloved.
In you and through you, he is everything,
  if you are discerning or sensible.

Return to your essence, dive in.
  Careful! No stopping on the rugged terrain.
The masses will languish in ignorance,
  while you openly see your beloved.

You who are unversed in this,
  admit what you see:
The wine is passed round
  and every one of us is drunk.
See the men here
  with hearts abrim?

See them all dancing?
  The secret is manifest in them,
for this they gave their lives
  and their night has become day.

At your service

My savories and drink are delightful
My beloved provides for me.
So my friends, forgive
my worship and supplication.

Finely scented wine,
its brilliance pure light.
The cupbearer saw to its pouring,
may it be my salvation.

I am drunk from his love.
There is no wine but him.
Whenever I call out: Oh Lord.
My response is: at your service.

O perplexed heart!

O heart, O my confused and perplexed heart,
  how you cling to this amorous passion!
You flung your spirit into an overflowing sea, a sea
    of passion;
  yet you are afraid of a sprinkle.

Persist in your ardent wish, don't regret it
  because you were right.
Die for love and you will live carefree,
  obtaining everything you desire
Don't complain of the distance,
  you know your beloved is not far away

Anyone whose beloved is always present,
  tell me, how could he be lonely?
For his eyes constantly reap beauty, the fulfillment
    of desires.
  He is refreshed.

That love erases my erasure.
After my obliteration, I come into being.
People wonder at my survival.
With the love of the one I love, I prevail.
My drink comes from a cup
but it tastes as sweet as roses.

Wine that was not pressed by the presser
nor harvested from a trellis.
How it has intoxicated great men before us!
One thirsts for this kind of drink.

O utmost beauty! How wonderful you are!
Your beauty frees me from the world of forms,
I am extinguished in your love, lose control.
O you, who are sight and sound,
You made every heart your abode
and concealed your beauty from sight

For the mind is enraptured by your love, the heart is perplexed,
in you, it is baffled.
Everyone is confused in your love,
yet they circle the sacred space in pursuit.

O desire of the one mad with love,
by God, I love no one but you
In you, I made my heart's abode.
Make my eyes see you.
I may pretend to love Lubna,
Saʿda and others

despite all that, your lover is here,
submitting to the humiliations of love's ardor and refreshed
upon seeing the secret marvels,
becoming intimate with the mystery, despite his fears.

You, a suffering lover like me,
desire only a beautiful union.
Be true in your love as I am.
Don't listen to the words of the censurers.
In the religion of love there are timeless covenants,
always kept,

confirmed through the power of the heart,
written and engraved deep within.
When what is secret is put to the test, there you will read:
"Here lies the faithful one, slain by love."

I'm on my way

I'm on my way to find myself
banish the delusion within
and join myself in myself.

Those who plunge into the meaning
will see the secret in it.
They'll see the one with the wine jugs.
Tell the sensible ones, who understand.
You there, wake up,
knock on the door and be proud.

In order to see every thing,
you must not be afraid of your appearance,
envelop the whole of the universe.

You, listen to yourself speak,
you to you, my friend.
When your drink is pure,
pour it for the sick.
Lift your veil now
pray and live righteously.

Nothing will escape you
none of these concepts,
if you polish your mirror.

O critic, don't reproach me
   for it's no use to blame.
You always want me
   to abandon what I want.
By God, leave me alone. Enough!
   I remain alone, solitary.

I won't listen to temptation, no.
   Because as I have it
   whoever dies will live forever.

If you want to endure, efface yourself.
   Concentrate your thought on yourself.
Cling, O tired one,
   to those who favor you
and understand the meaning from us
   at the door of the king.

After the cloak was lifted,
   the door of the secret meaning
   opened a bit for you.

O *faqih*, speak of me,
   I consider you distinguished.
No one will approach
   union with the beloved
except those who sing,
   those who are close to us.

Those who aspire to partake of learning
   the secret meanings,
   garb themselves with us.

Chapter 2

LOVE-CRAZED

Introduction

When the great Andalusian mystic Ibn al-ʿArabī wrote his most famous collection of poems, *Interpreter of Desires* [*Tarjumān al-Ashwāq*], he was met with skepticism and doubt. What was mystical or religious about these poems that apparently celebrated earthly, erotic love and furthermore did so in the style of the classical Arabian ode? Responding to this criticism, Ibn al-ʿArabī wrote a commentary on his poems, a detailed explication of how they speak of "mystical sciences and realities."[1] Thus, "fair-complexioned and coy virgins" are said to represent the "divine sciences embodied in the world of similitude," "the blackness of hair on her brow" represents "the mysterious sciences of which she is the bearer," and so on.[2] While the commentary may have satisfied at least some of his critics, as Stetkevych observes, it results in "a hermeticism that is dense in symbolic texture but restricted in experiential scope."[3] That is to say, the mechanistic X-stands-for-Y "interpretation" effectively deprives the reader of imaginative license and denies the polyvalence that lies at the heart of poetic symbolism. Furthermore, Ibn al-ʿArabī's commentary dodges the essential questions: What makes a work of poetry mystical? Where does its mysticism reside?

Shushtarī, who addressed many of his compositions to audiences unschooled in mystical hermeneutics, took a different approach to these questions. While his poems are steeped in pre-Islamic or secular Andalusian poetic traditions, they are rather clearly marked as religious either through the use of Qur'ānic vocabulary or mystical terminology or through rhetorical techniques, such as the circular use of pronouns (see, for example "Let go of Zayd and Mayya"). The first five poems in this section—all of them monorhyme classical poems, it should be noted—are something of an exception, however. While they certainly admit mystical readings and are in fact read as religious poems, like those of Ibn al-ʿArabī's *Interpreter of Desires*, they are not explicitly marked as such. The last three poems in the section—which use popular strophic forms—move toward a more unambiguously spiritual message through the introduction of a religious vocabulary of sin, redemption, and salvation; through Qur'ānic allusions; and even through directives and admonitions addressed to the listener.

The selection begins with the beautifully lyrical ode "Layla." The quintessential beloved of Arabic poetry, the figure of Layla becomes in the hands of Sufi poets from Niffarī to Niẓamī to Ibn al-Fāriḍ a symbol for divine Beauty. This poem focuses on her omnipresence, her myriad manifestations, and her ephemeral nature. These are explored in a lovely series of similes: "She is like the sun, its light radiant,/yet when you seek it, it turns to shadow,/.../She is like the eye which has no color/yet in it appear colors in every hue." If the poetic voice in this poem is identified with Layla's lover, Qays, as he enumerates the qualities of his ever-elusive beloved, the poem closes with a startling inversion that expresses the paradoxical confusion of identities inherent in divine unveiling and mystical union. Layla unveils for Qays, who exclaims: "I am Layla and she is Qays. What a wonder!/How is it that what I seek comes to me from me?"

The next four compositions offer striking and diaphanous images of the lover overwhelmed and bewildered by love. The poet-lover loses himself: "all of me is stolen/and your beauty the thief" ("Torments of love"). He wastes away: "consumed by weakness," ("Only love remains"); he is "withered because of love" ("My heart resides in the east"). He pays no mind to the critics and finds sweetness in the anguish of love, even when such suffering is incomprehensible to others, for, he concludes: "To efface yourself in it is to live./So efface yourself, if you wish to endure" ("My heart resides in the east").

Just as the preceding *qaṣīdas* employed many of the common figures of classical Arabic poetry, the *muwashshaḥ*, "The lover's visit" revisits many of the standard tropes of Andalusian popular song: the night visit between lovers eluding the spy, the garden setting, the sharing of wine between the lovers, and love as a cause of madness. The poem signals a mystical interpretation primarily through its insistence on the symbolic nature of the wine, which first is described as licit (*ḥalāl*) (line 10) and then as neither from grape nor raisin (21). Read in an interpretative framework that understands wine as a symbol of divine intoxication, the references to the lamp (12), to birds singing from their "pulpits" (*manābir*) (18), and to the beautiful ones (*al-milāḥ*) (36) take on additional layers of meaning.

In the first six poems of this section love is presented as an overwhelming experience that comes about solely because of the irresistible attraction of the beloved and not because of effort expended by the lover. In his discussion of the Sufi doctrine of love (*maḥabba*), Kalābādhī begins by quoting the famous ninth- to tenth-century Iraqi Sufi al-Junayd: "'Love is the inclination of the heart,' meaning that the heart then inclines toward God and what is of God, without any effort."[4] "Robbed of my senses"echoes the tropes seen in the earlier poems in this section but goes beyond them in not only describing the annihilation of self in the ecstatic vision but also in the ongoing journey. "Robbed of my senses" moves into a more explicitly religious register, speaking, for example, of embracing "the image of a servant" and ascending "the staircase of the meritorious."The poet directly exhorts the listener to listen and learn and to avoid the company of the ignorant. In the final strophe he speaks of a search for meaning, "guided/by the star of our wisdom," a quest that calls for discretion and initiative on the part of the seeker.

In "Robbed of my senses" and perhaps even more explicitly in the closing selection here, "My lover is beyond compare," Shushtarī explores the relationship between the creature and the Creator. As Kalābādhī explains, "The seeker is in reality the sought, and the Sought the Seeker: for the man who seeks God only seeks Him because God first sought him."[5] As Shushtarī says, "He drew close to me and drew me close to Him." Everything that man does is through God's will, "I am content in the Creator, upon Him I rest./In Him I am joined, in Him I am separated, in Him I desire Him./In Him I see, in Him I hear and my soul is in His hands."

Layla

There is no life but Layla. 1
When in doubt ask everything about her.

Her mystery emanates in everything 2
and because of that everything praises her.

Her beauty is widespread, its fullness, concealed. 3
The witness says:

She is like the sun, its light radiant, 4
yet when you seek it, it turns to shadow.

She is like the mirror in which images appear 5
reflected, yet nothing resides there.

She is like the eye which has no color 6
yet in it appear colors in every hue.

Hers is the right course, even if I suffer, 7
her evidence is in the removal of the cloak.

Her injustice is just. As for her justice, 8
it is grace; my brother ask for more.

In her meadow, there is none but her 9
so she alone is invoked.

A wonder, she remains distant, no where. 10
Then union draws near, hands full.

And union with her brings us fullness, 11
distance from her, division; both are mine.

In union, there is no difference between us. 12
In division, confusion upon me.

In her raiment, her ambiguity is displayed 13
for everything is mirrored in her.

She unveiled one day for Qays and he turned away, 14
saying: O people, I loved no other.

I am Layla and she is Qays. What a wonder! 15
How is that what I seek comes to me from me?

The torments of love

My neglect of you, reprehensible, 1
your love, binding.
My craving, everlasting,
   union, elusive.

Your love put its mark 2
on the slate of my heart.
My tears are the ink,
   beauty is the writer.

The reader of my thoughts 3
would constantly recite
lessons on the signs
   of the beautiful one.

My gaze meanders 4
in the heaven of your beauty;
its penetrating star
   pierces my mind.

Prattle about others— 5
listening to *that* is forbidden,
for all of me is stolen
   and your beauty the thief.

They said to me: repent 6
of loving the one you love.
So I replied: I am repentant
   of my negligence.

The torments of love 7
are sweet for every lover

even if, viewed by another, they are hard
and never-ending.

Only love remains

You, present in my heart, 1
thinking of you makes me glad.

The visitor may be invisible to the eye, 2
in my view, the heart stands in.

I haven't disappeared, yet my body 3
wastes away consumed by weakness.

The naysayer will not find me; 4
no spy will see me.

If destiny knew of me, 5
people would come.

Only love remains, 6
ask it and it shall answer for me.

My heart resides in the east

You who criticize, be kind 1
to the one withered because of love.

Censure doesn't kill love's ardor 2
but instead makes the craving stronger.

Indeed, he hears not. 3
So you take heed, lest you be disappointed.

Our love for things blinds 4
and deafens, I say in truth.

Everything you say resides in the west 5
but my heart resides in the east.

You won't see ardent love sinking; 6
in it the sensible one ascends.

Dear heart of mine, how sensitive you are, 7
Trembling from low thunder's rumble.

Everything in love is sweet, 8
even the pains one encounters in it.

To efface yourself in it is to live. 9
So efface yourself, if you wish to endure.

Before the morn

The one I love visited me 1
before the morn
and my shamelessness and infamy
became beautiful to me.

He filled my cup 2
and bid me sleep and forget.
There is no sin
against the one who loves us.

So pass round the cup 3
of the one I love and adore.
Adoring the beloved
is the essence of righteousness.

Serve it to the dead, 4
they'll return to life.
It is the joy
and the repose of souls.

Don't criticize me 5
for I will not bend to the critic.
No, not even if my bowels
were cut out by the clamor.

How sweet the praise 6
of my beloved
among people of purity
and salvation.

The beloved appeared 7
in the dark of night
and he gave me union
till the morn.

My time is sweet 8
and I have no more shame.
So give me the cups
and bowls of drink.

The lover's visit

My dearest one visited me. How sweet those moments!
  The beloved heeded me.
Generously, he forgave all of my lapses,
  infuriating the watchman.

My heart's desire visited me, darkness fell away,
  in that union, he was generous.
He attended my *hadra*, the wine glass went round,
  and my hopes attained.
In good cheer we drank
  of the wine that is not forbidden.

Fill up my glass, for in it is my joy.
  Let's drink, dear one.
My beloved is my intimate confidant and my lamp,
  present, so close.

What drink! What wine! What a vintner!
  What music! What song!
In a garden blooming with flowers
  that fill us with light.

From their pulpits in the trees
  the birds speak among us.

My bottles are full, yet in my cup
  there is no grape or raisin.
You who listen, understand my allusions.
  Truly my time is wondrous!

How fine is that wine, how excellent that drink
  in a place of joy.
Let me drink and love my beloved
  each day anew.
Foolish is the one who bids me repent,
  for I am wisely guided.

And should the naysayer come, I will say to him:
  Truly my time is wondrous!
I know what is past and what is to come.
  My illness is also my cure.

In that passion, I am the master of my time
  and I love without shame.
In the love of the beautiful ones,
  my life and my art are spent.
In the gloom of night,
  my moon came to me, invisible to the eye.

He illuminated my abode, my space;
  I almost lost my mind.
Present in my stillness and my motion
  He is always there.

My path brings me closer
  to the one I love passionately.
Present in my *hadra*, present in my intimacy,
  my time is illuminated through him.
When I encounter him, I exclaim:
  O moon! O sun!

My dearest one visited me. How sweet those moments!
  The beloved heeded me.
Generously, he forgave all of my lapses,
  infuriating the watchman.

Robbed of my senses

O you, who stole my heart from me,
your passion robbed me of my senses.

You hid me from myself,
  in myself, I am no longer visible.
I disappeared from my own sight,
  as if no longer there.
So I went searching for myself,
  that I might find me.

Then in my mind I said: "Enough,
my union with myself suffices."

He who wants to live forever
  dies to self-delusion.
He recasts himself
  in the image of a servant,
and ascends
  the staircase of the meritorious.

Like a king he lives, always at peace;
in his poverty, he is rich.

He who is contented,
  in this existence he is a sultan.
He does not tempt
  Satan to wish him ill,
for if he were deceived,
  he would again lose his way.

So understand, learn from me, my son,
and then join with me.

If you trust me,
  turn away from the naysayer and understand.
Lean toward me to listen:
  learn this knowledge.
Beware! Don't go near
  those whose ignorance is notorious.

They are known to be harmful.
Leave them and accompany me.

Where is the one who seeks
  and understands the meaning?
Let him then be guided
  by the star of our wisdom,
for when it appears, it approaches
  and lingers and declares to us:

Loving the beautiful one, my friend, is my art
  and I drink from my own jug.

My lover is beyond compare

My lover is beyond compare.
No spy watches over him.
He drew close to me and drew me close to him
present, no distance between us.

I am content in the Creator, upon him I rest.
In him I am joined, in him I am separated, in him
    I desire him.
In him I see, in him I hear and my soul is in his hands.

He bestows on me his favor. My life in him is sweet.
My brethren, I am happy in that marvellous mystery.

My allusions are to my beloved, understand my signs,
Teach the ignorant one who does not understand
    the meaning
From the others, conceal the mystery of love and
    deliverance.

For the secret of love is divine and its meaning is amazing:
I adore him and he adores me. I speak to him up close.

When I am alone with my beloved, I become absent
    from creation
I read the secret written for me in the covenant.
In him my drink is licit, in him I gather roses.

I roam in my fragrant and delightful garden.
My sadness departs and I have my way with my beloved.

He appeared and in my heart I saw him: the master
    of glory.
He called me and I answered. He bid me follow.
Mirrored in me—I saw him—his countenance like the
    new moon.

And he revived me and answered my call and said to me:
    Repent.
Brother, dwell like me in my welcoming abode.

O poet, take advantage, venture for your Lord's sake
    and boast!
Make those with discernment hear praise upon praise.
And say to the critic, to those present and absent:

I am the servant of my Lord until the day of Reckoning
May my Lord forgive me and may I not fail in my goal.

Chapter 3

DENUDATIO/STRIPPING BARE

Introduction

Like many ascetics before him, Christian and Muslim, Shushtarī held that renunciation of the material world was fundamental to advancing on the spiritual path. He would certainly have agreed with John Cassian, the fourth- to fifth-century French monk credited with bringing the rules of Eastern monasticism to the West, when he writes: "Covetousness cannot be overcome except by stripping one's self of everything. This is a sufficiently dreadful and clear instance of this tyranny, which, when once the mind is taken prisoner by it, allows it to keep to no rules of honesty, nor to be satisfied with any additions to its gains. For we must seek to put an end to this madness, not by riches, but by stripping ourselves of them."[1]

For Shushtarī, *tajrīd*—the process of peeling away what is superfluous or superficial—is the essence of the mystical path. *Tajrīd* is closely linked to *faqr*, poverty or renunciation, which he calls "a needfulness of God."[2] His elaboration of the stages of this shedding or renunciation shows it to be a constant and dynamic process, each layer uncovered reveals another to be peeled away:

> The first stage of *tajrīd* is the shedding of blameworthy qualities through garbing oneself in praiseworthy ones, then the *tajrīd* of this world by executing the command of the next, then the shedding of the cosmos through contemplation of the Creator, then the shedding of contemplation by extinction (passing away) in worship, then the shedding of extinction through extinction of extinction itself, then the shedding of these stages through the observation of existence, then the shedding of all of that in the Beneficent Presence (*sakīna*).[3]

POEMS AND SONGS

The songs in this chapter explore the seeker's relationship with all that will pass away, from the riches of the material world to the comforts of the familiar. For Shushtarī, poverty means renouncing home, family, and one's attachment to a self-concept that seeks the approval and respect of others. Some of these poems also address the contest between a conventional understanding of life, religious practice, and moral behavior, and the worldview of Shushtarī and his followers. The others are asleep, he sings. What they see is mere illusion; our poverty will become our riches.

The section opens with "Burning all discernment," a short monorhyme ode that explores the theme of resignation, the letting go of self and the acknowledgment of the omnipotence of the divine. Even the shedding of inhibitions, the letting go itself, is an act of God rather than an act that can be claimed by the believer. Poetically, this is expressed through the insistent use of negation, which is rendered even more prominent by the use of enjambment, letting the negation hang at the end of hemistiches and lines. The poem that follows, "Leaving my land," also speaks quite lyrically of the abandonment of the familiar, of every type of possession, "that I might see Your land."

The poems that follow treat themes familiar to Muslims and members of many other faith traditions. The poor will attain the loftiest station, "kings will desire their rank," he proclaims in "The Rank of the Poor." Worldly possessions are but a loan ("Borrowed goods"); nothing is truly in the possession of or under the control of mortal man. Not only is poverty an insistent theme in Shushtarī's poetry, but he treats the subject at length in his prose. Shushtarī repeatedly cites the tradition, "Poor Muslims will enter Paradise half a day before the wealthy, [a day] five-hundred years long."[4] Still the renunciation Shushtarī speaks of is never easy, especially the separation from family and loved ones, as he says in the closing poem:

> I weep—how could I not weep?—
>   for my dear friends.
> For I bid them goodbye and left,
>   riding away from them.

Burning all discernment

Truly, I shed my inhibitions 1
in your love
by your power, not
my power, nor my devices.

I leave behind being until 2
I do not see it, nor even
see it leaving,
receding behind me.

Creation is your creation 3
and all affairs are your affairs,
for what am I?
not even ruins.

I speak the truth: 4
there is nothing in the universe that is not you.
I seek refuge in God
from my knowledge and acts.

In your existence there is no place 5
for the veil but
in the secret of the letters.
Look toward the mountain.

You showed yourself, 6
then you hid yourself in your manifestation.
You pointed to yourself
and you pointed to me.

You show yourself 7
to yourself in yourself.
Continuity which bespeaks
the enigma of eternity.

You know yourself, 8
so who is it that knows you?
You are one and the life of love,
O my hope.

The ignorant cannot deny it, no, 9
for knowledge is your knowledge.
However, ignorance
occurs in what was created impatient.

In illusion man stands firm 10
and in certitude he is lost.
I am weak as a moth
to endure the fire.

The majesty of glory 11
has burned all discernment.
I confess I am powerless,
submissive and inert.

Leaving my land

I left my land
that I might see your land.

I left my abode,
my purpose, my self-determination.
In you, I dropped my pretenses.

I became strong in my dominion
when I became enamored of your dominion.

I disappeared in the meaning
until there was only me
and the meaning became dear to me.

I declared in my heart:
guard my secret in your heart.

I left my protection
and the world of forms
until I became present to perfection.

O repose for the love-mad one,
have mercy on one besotted with you.

I drew close—as a servant draws close—
to a secret manifest within me.
And my love-ecstasy increased.

For out of beneficence
you keep leading me to your beneficence.

You continue to weaken me,
you push me away and draw me near.
I cried out in the push-pull:

My palace lost its garden
when your garden appeared to me.

O you whose memory slays me,
union with you has brought me life.
O matchless king

forgive me my sin and disobedience
for your disobedience has harmed me.

The rank of the poor

There is a people of poverty. Follow them 1
and seek to love and serve them.

If your noble soul knows 2
what you seek, seek the grandeur that is theirs.

Take your place among those 3
at the head of the line on their day of fortune.

In the presence of our Lord—may He be praised— 4
  the ones whom He has raised.

That day, you will see no glory 5
  but theirs, lifting them because of their humbleness.

Whoever loves and respects them 6
  and follows their ways shall be with them.

Kings will desire their rank 7
  on seeing how lofty their station.

God decreed their fate long ago, 8
  so they end up with their share.

Purify the houses of God

In word and deed, strip away the others. 1
Bring the dispersed branches together in their roots.

Don't incline yourself to family, tell them to stay. 2
To bring fire, one must leave family behind.

Purify the houses of God of all images; 3
for if you are truly wise, His house is your heart.

Borrowed goods

How can anyone who doesn't see the signs
  aspire to glory?

I am your veil:
If you shut the door
(understand what's in your interest)
no visitor will call on you.
  If you understand what I'm saying, then listen:

Awaken from your slumber.
Prepare for your salvation.
And look where you rest your head.

Our attire is borrowed. What I have is on loan;
is anything *mine*?

If you understand what's been said to you…
This place is yours and yet this place is not yours.
You are but a servant of the Title-holder.

Do you propose to glean a profit
on borrowed goods?

Poverty and riches

We come to you in poverty, not riches, 1
for you are the generous one.

You accustomed us to every grace, may 2
your grace endure.

These poor disheveled souls of yours are drenched 3
in your love, because it is the utmost of desires.

There is no one in richness like you 4
and in poverty there are none like us.

We see you manifest in everything; 5
nothing is ours.

I hid your name out of jealousy. Look at me, 6
lost on a mountain trail and a slope.

Since you are always with me, 7
I have no need to carry provisions: I am rich.

For you, you are the truth, there is no other 8
and I—would that I knew—who am I?

Let go of delusions

My sweetest moments are when I am one with my essence.

When I am with my deepest self
my intimacy rises from me like the sun.
Poverty comes naturally to me.

Creation is revealed and man can see
the totality of being comes from my particles.
My sweetest moments are when I am one with my essence.

O *faqīr*, listen to what you will do:
Put yourself above the cosmos and enjoy.
Nothing is more beautiful than you.

Set aside the others, understand the secrets.
Enter the arena and you will see the past and the present.
My sweetest moments are when I am one with my essence.

Roam in your thought and stroll about;
for existence, all of it, is your garden.
If something is revealed to you, be happy.

Appearances are a delusion. Rise to the fore.
The signs are in you. To come near the king, diminish yourself.
My sweetest moments are when I am one with my essence.

Apply your intellect to what is rational,
the proof leads you to the proven.
You will see, the bearer is what is borne.

To say this is a mistake would be a mistake.
Music allows me to speak to the people.
My sweetest moments are when I am one with my essence.

Listen, O most amazing of creation.
Love the one you desire passionately and find enduring
contentment.
You are the lover and the beloved.

The journey is to yourself and you are the meaning of
the good.
There is nothing but you, O abode of essential poverty.
My sweetest moments are when I am one with my
essence.

Riding away

To be separated from you, my son,
is my greatest affliction.
For when I drew near you,
I gave up those close to me.

In you, I miss my superficiality;
that's how far I've gone.
I remember you
and my poor heart is perplexed.
Our intimacy presses me toward you—
yet fear grips me.

If things were
as I would have them,
and I had my chance with you
I would clutch you with my claws.

You poured me a bit
of your finest old vintage.
You accompanied me,
a companion in my drunkeness
In you, I was indulged.
Still, I wanted more.

I am not worthy
of your drink

and yet, through your generosity
   I fulfilled my desires.

Careful! Don't see double,
   don't listen to an error.
There is but one,
   you alone.
Understand these concepts,
   observe these points.

Be united in yourself.
   One seeks
only your qualities
   in those around you.

And you, who chatter to me about
   all the "beautiful people,"
do you really see the stars
   in the splendor of the sunrise?
I saw the absolute, so listen up
   and go back for clarification.

There is nothing but the one,
   understand this my friend,
multiplicity is like
   an abundance of peanuts.

This *zajal* has quickly come to its end
   and it's turned out, as you see,
a worthy composition
   Lawshī and *Shushtarī*
modeled on the *zajal* of a lover
   whose fame is well-known:

I weep—how could I not weep?—
   for my dear friends.
For I bid them goodbye and left,
   riding away from them.

Chapter 4

Among the Sufis

Introduction

The poems in this section all touch upon, in some way, life among the Sufi brethren. The opening and closing poems, "Little *shaykh* from Meknes" and "Poor like me/By God, natural" describe the itinerant life of the destitute Sufi, with a traveling bag on his shoulder and dressed in rags or, as in "Poor like me," in "cords and needles and bits of discarded wool." The simple devotional songs "In my heart so near" and "Remembrance of God" are marked by their insistent repetition. "In my heart so near" starts each line of the refrains with a repeated invocation to God or a repeated command to the listener: "let me speak," "listen," "witness" and "enter." In the next poem, "Remembrance of God," every line closes with Allah, God, and thus the poem is very consciously a form of *dhikr* or remembrance. Although I was strongly tempted to keep the rhyme in "Allah" for poetic reasons, ultimately I chose to keep it all in English to avoid the distancing effect that the Arabic may have on some readers. The strongly didactic "Shirts and caps" contrasts life in the Sufi lodges with the worldly life of honor and prestige enjoyed by the jurists.

The opening poem deserves special comment. The *zajal* "Little *shaykh* from Meknes" is among Shushtarī's most famous compositions; songbooks attest to the fact that it was so popular that it was adapted to several different melodies.[1] In many ways these verses have come to define a popular public image of the Andalusian poet: a wandering minstrel; a salty man of the people, detached from any desire for social status or favor; someone who rather jauntily dismisses his critics; a saintly folk hero warmly received by ordinary people. The idea of sanctity presented here is uncomplicated: "Do what's good and you'll be saved" (line 7). *Tawakkul* or absolute trust in God is exemplified in this wandering and carefree beggar.

It must be observed that *shaykh,* or as it is often rendered in English, *sheik*, is a word that not only has proverbially lost quite a bit in translation, but it has also acquired a good deal of highly negative baggage dating back to early Valentino films like *The Sheik* and *Son of the Sheik* and the pervasive modern image of the despotic "oil sheik." Yet the Arabic word *shaykh* essentially means an older person; the tribal or village *shaykhs* are respected or powerful because of their age. *Shuwaykh*—the diminutive of *shaykh* used in some but not all the versions of this poem—then, conjures up images of a wizened figure, perhaps a bit stooped over. To call this headstrong beggar a "little *shaykh*" is both warmly affectionate and a wryly ironic acknowledgment of the higher wisdom he embodies.

Little *shaykh* from Meknes

Little *shaykh* from the land of Meknes
   wanders the souks and sings:
What care have I for others?
   What care have they for me?

What care have I, my friend,
   for the rest of creation?
Do what's good and you'll be saved,
   Follow the people of truth.
My son, hold your tongue
   or be sincere.

Mark my words on a sheet of paper,
   write them like an amulet.
What care have I for others?
   What care have they for me?

What's been said is clear,
   it needs no explanation.
What need has anyone of anyone?
   Understand this advice.

Look, how I'm on in years,
  my walking stick and my sack.

That's how I lived in Fez,
  lowness my comfort.
What care have I for others?
  What care have they for me?

What beautiful words
  as he wanders through the souks.
You see the merchants
  turn toward him,
a bag around his neck,
  with walking stick and a palm basket.

The little *shaykh* stands on solid ground
  upstanding as God wills.
What care have I for others?
  What care have they for me?

If you could see that little *shaykh*,
  how fine his message!
He turned to me and said:
  I see you're following me.
I put out my basket
  may the one who has mercy on me, bless it.

And he puts it out
  and says: leave me be, leave me be.
What care have I for others?
  What care have they for me?

"My son, those who do good
  reap only what's good,
they contemplate their failings
  and denounce their shameful deeds.
Whoever is like me
  will remain an outsider."

Those whose spirit is sweet
can forgive the singer:
What care have I for others?
What care have they for me?

In my heart so near

God,
O God! How men wander seeking the love of the beloved.
God, O God, present in my heart so near!

Indulge yourself, my heart, be joyful for your beloved has come.
Enjoy praising your lord, follow the path.
Savor it and you will live the good life among men.

Let me,
let me speak of my beloved; mentioning him is so sweet.
God, O God, present in my heart so near!

What can I do in this condition? I am your servant,
You'll find me casting off my excuses because of your love.
My spirit—what else is left to me?—I give to you.

Listen,
listen, O people of love, for the beloved answers.
God, O God, present in my heart so near!

The one who gives his spirit to his lord benefits and profits
and ascends the heavenly staircase, and is exalted.
He holds fast to the Sufi mystics, finds refuge with them, and heeds them.

Witness,
witness the essence of beauty and the astonishing
 perfection.
God, O God, present in my heart so near!

I am that meaning of meanings and the secret of
 being.
Stroll in the grace of my creation, but guard the
 limits.
Abandon that which is not of me; you will enjoy the
 grace of contemplation.

Enter,
enter the pureness of my presence, beside the beloved.
O God, O God, present in my heart so near!

Remembrance of God

Oh, you who ask for God's forgiveness,
 hand over your cares to God.
Say with sincerity and seriousness
 God, God, God.
Savor him and be congenial
 for you are in the presence of God.
You have gained a treasure
 and every grace is from God.
Cling tightly to him
 for God's Name of Names is God.
You must be present in your heart
 when you mention God.
There is a mysterious intoxication in him
 known by whomever invokes God.
Greet the universe and dance
 while saying, "God, God."
Find ecstasy in that and drink
 the wine of your remembrance of God.

That's the life,
  there is no death in it, by God.
The master who brought this to you
  stood before God, through God.
So give yourself to him and you will live
  in his favor, may it please God.
And bless my master and preserve
  the guide to God,
Ahmad, the best of the messengers
  sent to creatures by God,
and his family and Companions
  and all of those who call upon God.

Shirts and caps

Tell me about the wearing of that *khirqa*
  and the meaning of that cap.

"O my Sufi brethren, you apprentices,
  you in seclusion or in *zawiyas*,
O Master, I want to leave you all
  and enter the sanctuary
to find happiness in the four schools
  and in the most distinguished station.
My longing increases, my eyes weep
  tears mixed with agony.
Pour for me the pure wine
  that quenches this fire,
that I may cure this love-ardor
  and live a contented life."

"O desirous one," the *shaykh* said to me, "How is that?
  Listen to my words and understand them:

Nothing will quiet your heart or your longings
  other than a tale you should hide.
Be like me, a passionate lover of the beautiful one.
  Gaze on his beauty and serve him.

Understand me. For those that understand will ascend
to the awesome presence.
Each *hadra* brings you closer
and you will see the meaning of the cap.
Since you ask about the secret of my poverty
and the cap, O seeker,
come and put your hand on my head
and the beneficial secret will appear to you.
Think twice about dressing haughtily
for this world shall pass away.
The symbolism of the way
makes shirts and caps superfluous.
In this abandonment, O my dear heart,
nothing of me remains."

Poor like me/By God, natural

Natural. Natural. Yes, by God, natural.
Natural. Natural. Yes, by God, natural.

He's poor—like me,
a traveling bag on his shoulder.
Unburdened by worries,
his chest carefree.
He is beloved
by those light of spirit.

The natural one's like that. Everyone's amazed by the natural.
Natural. Natural. Yes, by God, natural.

From the start of the day
when I set out to beg
I open my mouth
and stretch out my hand.
If only you could see my sincere effort
in my own fashion.

The unnatural one. Leaving him is natural to me.
Natural. Natural. Yes, by God, natural.

I clothe my body
in cords and needles,
bits of discarded wool;
I beg a bit of bread.
What's his name?
people are confused.

I'm staying natural. All the natural folk, I please.
Natural. Natural. Yes, by God, natural.

My head is shaved
I walk about in rapture.
I beg at the market
or the houses of luxury.
Barefoot, yet elegant
"Give for God's sake," I say.

Natural goodness from whom it's natural.
Natural. Natural. Yes, by God, natural.

When I am seated,
no thought of walking.
If I want to sleep,
the ground is my bed
I eat wild grass,
in Him my life is good.

The natural one. He pleases every natural.
Natural. Natural. Yes, by God, natural.

My sack has
an oyster shell.
There's a jug hung
from my walking stick.
My head is polished
like a plate.

Natural I walk. Imprinted by poverty.
Natural. Natural. Yes, by God, natural.

When I stop
at the market or village,
I see the Bedouin
come out toward me,
like brothers
their words are sincere.

The natural is welcomed by the natural.
Natural. Natural. Yes, by God, natural.

There's no artifice about me.
I have no secrets.
I desire neither food
nor clothing.
That's the condition
of the easygoing one.

Naturally poor. Every natural he pleases.
Natural. Natural. Yes, by God, natural.

I know no judge
or ruler
What's more noble
and more natural to my condition.
that's what characterizes
the rank of excellence.

The natural heart is marked like that.
Natural. Natural. Yes, by God, natural.

Wherever I go,
my house is there.
I cast off my protection
in the middle of the desert.
I chew the grass
of the open country.

Natural sustenance, what's inside me is natural.
Natural. Natural. Yes, by God, natural.

These practices,
  all others are deficient.
Whoever bows
  before a vizier or sultan
he's the arrogant one.
  Yes, he's confused.

His garment suits him, for it is imprinted with
    covetousness
Natural. Natural. Yes, by God, natural.

Cutting my sleeves
  I aim to find salvation
expelling both worlds
  from my heart at once.
I shed my sandals
  and I ascend to the mystical session.

Other than natural. Leaving him is natural to me.
Natural. Natural. Yes, by God, natural.

Those seated with me
  pure like my heart
The intimate session
  where I polish my drinking glass
A gathering of glasses
  and learned/well-bred Sufis.

Natural. Natural. Yes, by God, natural.
Natural. Natural. Yes, by God, natural.

Chapter 5

DECIPHERING THE SIGNS OF GOD

> Poets live and work at this margin of the inarticulate. Their work is visual at the edge of darkness, auditory in the cradle of silence. In this raiding of what we cannot speak, their vocation embodies a longing for, a reaching toward, what we cannot manage with our minds alone, the endless working with words which "after speech, reach/Into the silence."
>
> —MARK BURROUGHS

Introduction

This section presents poems that grapple perhaps more explicitly than others with matters of interpretation and mystical hermeneutics. One of Shushtarī's persistent themes is the complex interrelation between divine signs in their myriad forms: as letters of a divine text or as the grand patterns of creation. The poet often meditates on his own use of poetic signs and allegories to attempt to communicate mysteries that are inexpressible in human language and ultimately beyond human understanding.

The section opens with "Just understand me," a *zajal* marked by its insistent repetition of the injunction *ifhamnī qaṭ*, "just understand me." This refrain functions as a plea to the listener, as well as an acknowledgment of the limitations of the poet's own speech, of the poem's ability—of any poem's ability—to communicate a message that transcends human language. In the first five strophes especially, the line functions contrapunctually, interrupting the very lyrical evocation of the beloved as "him," the one who exceeds all boundaries and categories. Line 33 marks a turning point in the poem, as the poetic voice shifts from recounting his own delight in the Creator to addressing the listener directly with advice and instruction. Soon (line 43), the poem shifts from second person advice into the voice of God, who proclaims what appear to be antitheses: "My absence is My presence," "My veiledness is in My nearness." These statements might be taken as the culmination of all the prior assertions of God's boundlessness. Thus, the injunction to join in the activities of the Sufis (lines 53 ff.) raises a question. Is it Shushtarī now who is urging the listener? Or that earlier divine voice?

The *zajal* "I translated an illegible letter" is perhaps Shushtarī's most explicit and direct exposition of the problem of communicating a mystical vision using human language. The verb *tarjama*, which opens the poem and is repeated in each refrain, is defined in one Arabic dictionary as "to elucidate or explain (*fassara*) something in another language." What is translated or explained here, a *ḥarf*, the "letter" as I have rendered it, is itself a richly polysemic word. The verb *ḥarafa* means to turn a thing from its proper way; a related form, *ḥarrafa*, is used in the Qur'ān (4:46) in the sense of altering the divine word or perverting its meaning. Among the many meanings of *ḥarf* is the extremity, edge or border of something, a ridge, as in a mountain ridge, or the nib of a pen. It can also mean a letter, a word, a grammatical particle, or a dialect or idiom. Whether it is an edge, a ridge, a letter or a dialect, this *ḥarf* is always incomplete, the visible or perceptible sign of something more, something beyond: a river, a mountain, a sound and the meaning it conveys, the abstraction that is language.

The quest to find occult meanings in the letters of words gave rise to a number of approaches, such as using numerical values assigned to letters, or elements (fire, water, earth, and air) associated with them, the practitioners of the "sciences of letters" (*ʿilm al-ḥurūf*) would attempt to discern secrets or harness magical powers inherent in certain combinations of letters. Certain mystics became interested in applying these techniques to the names of God with the aim of achieving *kashf* or unveiling.[1] Rather than following either of those approaches, the poem "The letters of His name" is a more free-flowing meditation on the unique name of God, focusing on the imagery evoked by the physical shapes of the letters *Alif, Lam, Lam,* and *Ha.* The doubled *Lam* at the center of the word becomes a focus of the poem, the space between the two letters compared to a cleansed heart shrouded on two sides, a sun between two moons; that is, meaning, essence, resides in the blank space in the heart of the word, where the self has no marker against which to locate itself.

Just understand me

Listen to some words select,
just understand me, just.

What did someone say to me perchance?
(Understand how I explain my meaning):
What is your beloved's name? I said: him.

There is no confusing the name of the beloved,
just understand me, just.

My beloved encompasses all existence.
He is visible in white and black
and in Christian and Jew,

and in the letters and their points,
just understand me, just.

in the plants and in the minerals,
in black and in white,
in the pen and the ink.

In this there is no mistake,
just understand me, just.

There is no one like my sweetheart.
I know this without a doubt.
He is not veiled to those who know.

In everything he is comingled,
just understand me, just.

I have known him for all time,
present to me each moment
in the waters and the valleys

in the the rising and the falling,
  just understand me, just.

In my love, I am joyful.
Everything makes sense.
He appears, there is no doubt,

in vastness and boundlessness
  just understand me, just.

Take leave of the world of the imagination
lest you think you see an equal to him,
for what you see is chimera.

Your existence is connected to him
  just understand me, just.

My friend, my friend,
don't pay attention to my form.
Look and you will see my marvels.

In an ocean with absolutely no shore,
  just understand me, just.

The secret of existence is in my totality
my absence is in my presence.
My veiledness is in my nearness.

Listen to these points,
  just understand me, just.

If you are absent to existence
and annihilate yourself in contemplation,
there is no trace and no boundary

and no end and no middle
  just understand me, just.

Open your heart gladly to men
in the *hadra* is union
clothe yourself in the clothing of perfection

and take a seat on the carpet,
just understand me, just.

The stars appeared to the blind.
That's not what commoners mean by "taste."
Nor those not yet mature,

the meaning has escaped them
just understand me, just.

The remedy comes in a spoonful of honey.
Hope is its sign.
The condition is that you understand this lesson.

Take it from me,
just understand me, just.

In that station speech is annihilated,
so too, the purpose of the ecstatic states,
for there is no union and no division.

Nor is there excess in what I say
just understand me, just.

If you wish to understand these words
and ascend to that station,
break with the fantasies of the commoner.

Say only: he is God
just understand me, just.

I translated an illegible letter

I translated an illegible letter.
Will anyone understand me?

From the dot of *ba*, I was lifted
to *alif*, a more brilliant rank
where one forgets what is near.

What perplexity there! What confusion!
I repose with the one who mentions me.

I translated an illegible letter.
Will anyone understand me?

Among us any mention of the mentioner is hidden.
Effaced, he effaced thought.
it disappeared before the eyes of the gazer.

In the secrecy of the mystical session, a cry goes up:
"O Lord, make me many or make me one."

I translated an illegible letter.
Will anyone understand me?

Save me from the ocean of oneness
and display me on the shore of individuality.
Disrobement is in the eye of man.

In that way, I went beyond
the others and exceeded my vision.

I translated an illegible letter.
Will anyone understand me?

I can't find the one I flee.
If you see me, I am ascending.
My wine is mixed in every glass.

I am the bottle. I am the wine.
  You cannot keep me from my intoxication.

I translated an illegible letter.
  Will anyone understand me?

  I am the drinking companion. I am the cupbearer.
  My yearning is increased by the company of others.
  I am annihilated in the eternal meaning.

What is news other than what is veiled?
  In every letter, I am translated.

I translated an illegible letter.
  Will anyone understand me?

  On my tablet appeared writing,
  the secret of the lover for the beloved.
  So understand and you will find that you are sought.

In every glance or gaze
  it's you who is the object.

I translated an illegible letter.
  Will anyone understand me?

  I drowned in an ocean of names
  in the midst of gloom and blindness,
  until Salma appeared to me.

Why, when I thought you had abandoned me,
  did you, O beautiful one, appear to me?

I translated an illegible letter.
  Will anyone understand me?

The letters of His name

الله

Alif before double *Lām*
and *Ha*—delight of the eye.

Alif proclaims the name
with two incorporeal *Lāms*
and *Ha*: the written sign.
Secret is spelled with two letters.
There is a name with no place.

Read these letters together.
You will see that in them, the heart is cleansed,
forgets its past trials
and advances shrouded on both sides
by two delicate symbols.

My crazed passionate love became public.
Dawn appeared after my night
and I became a light unto creation
a sun between two moons:
I know not where I am.

My most pious love means
to be extinguished in Him like a slave
and truly, in the extinguishing I am extinguished
for the finding is between losing and losing
and life is in two deaths.

My darling, the one I passionately love,
and when I die, the sustenance of the soul.
Fearing separation, I sing:
"When, O apple of my eye,
will I find union without place?"

Master of illusion

Turn away from fantasy and delusion,
put thought and discernment to use.
People are but shadows,
so look to the master of the images.

Contemplate, contemplate in earnest,
you will confirm the truth in what you see.
Picture this—may you succeed— existence is its own veil,
so look to the one who made it come into view.
The universe was there to him even before he made it.
The most auspicious [star] is the one that ascends.

He who rises from lowliness to the heights
he shall see the essence in the trace.
People are but shadows,
so look to the master of illusion.

The weak one, like a child, first perceives embodied forms.
Crude things from crude matter,
but they admit polishing.
To the essence, he attributes to deeds and words [he sees]
no matter [how refined] his analysis.

He mistakes the source for the copies
he perceives with his eyes.
People are but shadows.
So look to the master of illusion.

Then, when day breaks
and the child, rightly guided, reaches his prime,
he sees the essences that moved
appear lifeless and petrified.

Through them the one who molded them is veiled,
hidden in them, just as he appears through them.

A drink that had gleamed like icy water,
the wellspring overcame it and engulfed it.
People are but shadows,
so look to the master of illusion.

I am amazed, his mystery is amazing,
His judgment, how it is carried out!
This one—as he wishes—is close,
and that one, distant from union
This one is innocent and that one suspicious,
like the will of the magician.

You see him appear but he pays no mind,
in every condition, he has a purpose.
People are but shadows,
so look to the master of illusion.

He dresses them, draping their costumes,
an outfit for each one.
Their limbs suspended with string,
unseen by people, when they forget.
For to be conscious there are hurdles,
the first is to abandon appetites.

For invoking [him] is the first perfection
which nurtures the perpetual vision.
People are but shadows,
so look to the master of illusion.

Pierce the surface of things,
what is hidden within appears in the depths.
Those veils are themselves veiled,
they are known when transformed into letters.
Clear is the eye of whoever uses them to see,
for the one who forgave has triumphed.

My friend, accept [what I say] about the stations,
for sobriety is more appropriate for the inebriated.
People are but shadows,
so look to the master of illusion.

The heart is unseen and so too the master.
What is unseen befits the unseen.
Stop, you superficial one, next comes the best part.
So seek it, for it is the fruit you seek.
Underneath the outer layer is the drink of
the cupbearers
and he who drinks it sings:

Stop speaking of the impossible
whether it be hidden or manifest.
People are but shadows,
so look to the master of illusion.

Don't say He forgot you

Gaze in your mirror.
Gaze in your mirror.
The one you see there,
that is you.

Raise the mirror and look.
Everything is there.
You will see open space and dense civilization,
death and life.
What is veiled you see
only in the mirror.

Your cloak is removed.
Your cloak is removed.
You will endure in oneness
and see nothing but yourself.

Don't seek the blemishes of others
for you too have blemishes.

Every blemish is yours—
turn away and repent.
If your heart were to open,
the veils would be lifted.

You would see this and that
You would see this and that
You would delight in the knowledge of the unseen
and thank the one who gives.

All words are yours
and speech.
Accept the essence of beauty
and cast wickedness aside.
Tell the ignorant:
in your ignorance you are blinded.

Had he wished to guide you
Had he wished to guide you
You would have carried out his orders
and avoided what was prohibited.

Know O humble servant of God,
the truth of this knowledge.
Knowing that God
loves the pure,
hope only in God,
be satisfied in Him.

Don't say He forgot you.
Don't say He forgot you.
In what is hidden and what is visible,
He always sees you.

I'm a sight to see

Indeed, I'm quite a sight
for whoever might see me.

I am the lover and the beloved.
There is nothing else.

O seeker, the heart of the matter
is cloaked by your eye itself.

Return to your essence and proclaim
there is nothing outside of you,

for the good comes from you and the knowledge,
and the secret is in you.

You are the mirror of the glance,
the axis of time

Encompassed in you is what is dispersed
throughout time.

Listen to my words and take them in
so you may understand.

For your treasure is stripped
of all talismans.

He is what is spoken and the speaker,
at the summit of understanding.

Listen to my call, up close,
not with your ears:

The sun of my essence is everpresent
to the eye.

Gaze at my beauty, manifest
in every human being.

Like water that seeps into
the roots of the branches,

although watered with the water of oneness,
the flowers are multicolored.

So reverently worship the Lord of majesty
as you draw near to each other.

And read the verses of perfection,
the seven oft-recited verses.

I sang to the moon

To me, from me; he's the goal.
"Hey me, what's up with you?"
You'll find me running and the course
leads to me—so I might see you.

I am never away from my presence.
I see no veil before me.
The height of presence is my absence.
I wish you could see me and the truth.
All truth is in my hiddenness
for if not, I would not be found.

For I continued and continue
setting up snares for my soul.
I ensnared myself and thus I see
I am alone in the battlefield.

I have no like and no equal
I say to myself without cease:
I am the signifier and the signified,
in me, it's proven, no doubt.
I am rich and at the same time poor.
Garments of clay veil me from myself.

Shadows, those are the ruins.
My garment is mine alone.
I shed it, for nakedness suits me
And I'll accept the consequences.

I seek myself in myself,
absent to myself, I search asking:
My beloved, tell me true,
do you see me and not an illusion?
I said to myself: Indeed.
Yes, yes, I have no equal.

I have attained my deepest self
I have seen the one who shaped you.
You come back and tell me I invent things;
the others have changed you.

My wine is a fine wine,
it intoxicated me long ago
So good, I shatter open the cache
but its breaking is not in vain.
My story is all marvels
I am the tablet and the pen.

My essence was so divided:
"Me? I don't recognize you."
When I cast aside the mirror
and everything in your image,

I felt in myself and the feelings
were manifest from me to me.
The names were for me a shell,
my essence is the heart of the matter.
While hidden from view,
I sang out to the moon one night:

O night, whether long or short,
watch you I must,
but if my moon spent the night with me,
I would not stay to watch yours.

Breaking the talisman

He who breaks free of the talisman 1
is, in this world, the master of self-knowledge.

The hidden treasure appeared to him. 2
Let him praise God, who made him understand.

You will find him suffering among men, 3
some may even despise him.

You see people flee when they meet him 4
like the wild ass from a lion.

The Beautiful Ones served him—actually, all of them, 5
by them I mean the luminous seven.

He opened the lock that man had locked. 6
O friend, how powerful he is!

He unlocked the secret of the names, 7
the caliph of God who provided for him.

In my heart's eye

O hidden one—eternal
How clear you are, how manifest!
You may have disappeared from my sight;
in my heart's eye, I see you.

You never hide from me.
Nor is your mystery hidden from me.
Your command, your judgment and your decree
proceed upon the dead and the living.
I look at things and I see
your kindness present in everything.

For you are eternal with no end,
your judgment triumphs over humanity.
The criminal among us and the innocent,
how can they escape your command?

O you who wish to see God,
look at the totality of being,
silent or speaking or still,
animal or plant
in everything you will see God
with no divisions and no dimensions.

With no dimensions and no divisions,
you will see the God that provided for you.
All of Him is scattered.
He wants to test you.

One. He has no equal
and no peer and no likeness.
Invoking the beautiful one,
I shortened the long night.
Forgive the singer who exclaims
and the one to whom he sings:

O night, whether you are long or short,
watch you I must,
but if my moon spent the night with me,
I would not keep watch over your moon.

Hidden in plain sight

You, who appear visible when concealed,
hidden when in plain sight

You are manifest,
hidden from no one
And absent,
visible to no one

For you are the one;
there is no other.

Absolute oneness. The message is true.
What is added to the oneness emanates from you.

Listen, you'll see what I say
is marvelous to say.
To whom do I say "listen"?
For you are the listener
It is you who speak
and you who listen.

Just when do you think what is absent will appear?
God is the One with no other.

There is nothing like me,
I am one.

And the very notion of place, in truth,
is trouble.
When you let go of "whereness,"
you will find us.

So repent or cut it short.
Deep in your heart you will see the meaning of my message.

Tell me, who is a devil
or an angel?
Or Adam or Eve
or a star?
Who is saved? Tell me,
who is damned?

Who bowed before the sun or the moon?
Who worshiped fire or stones?

The sensible one will understand,
   become discerning,
read and learn
   and become a *faqih,*
know the road of truth
   and follow it.

If he understands his erudition, what is he waiting for?
Leave those worlds, you will see the moon.

Stop tiring yourself

Add not one verse. *Add not one verse.*
I achieved my goal: the beloved. I saw him.

Who was it that became known
   through his generosity in creation?
How can you ask him: How?
   The mass of men is oblivious.
In that place, the penstrokes disappear
   and the boundaries.

Wherever I walk. *Wherever I walk.*
From him, to him, in him, I walk. Let go of this
      and that.

The *samāʿ* is all you need. Listen
   and abandon everything other.
For creation is, if you analyze it:
   o-t-h-e-r.
So take your name from the one you love,
   and stop tiring yourself.

In the other you were lost. *In the other you were lost.*
If you flee from fantasy, you cannot escape createdness.

To flee is the height of illusion itself
   that is the obstacle

said to be swept away
   wherever it is imposed.
Who will return to fix it in place
   after it already disappeared?

Say to him: "I have plunged"—*Say to him: "I have*
      plunged"—
"in the sea diving for pearls; through the diving,
      I ascend."

If you feel, it is yourself you feel,
   you yourself are the feeling.
If you perceive nearness or distance
   or darkness or light,
that's you, taking place in you,
   revolving around you.

Everything I see. *Everything I see.*
You are in the unfolding, but you have forgotten.

Why does he forget? Why does he say:
   "I wonder, why this?"
He knew and yet he asks:
   "What is that called?"
Here, the situation itself declares:
   "What on earth caused him to do this?"

How?—and I engulf   How?—and I engulf
everything that is manifest and in Him I am hidden.

You are my deeds. You are my name.
   You are the letters.
In you the seer translates
   what he sees when he sees me.
One thousand like you,
   like thousands they seem.

If you are denied, *if you are denied*
You are him, and I, what remains hidden in plain sight.

Chapter 6

Desert Wanderings

Introduction

The poems in "Desert Wanderings" use the imagery of classical Arabian desert odes—the abandoned encampments, the yearning and recollection of blissful union with the beloved, the long and lonely night trek of the suffering lover—to speak of spiritual journeys. Many of these poems are set in the stylized poetic desert mapped by Ibn al-Fāriḍ and Ibn al-ʿArabī as a mystical space. Shushtarī invokes their familiar signs and images—the topography of dunes, ruined abodes, and frightening expanses—not to surpass his predecessors in elegant description or poetic conceits, but to elucidate more clearly the moral lessons of that desert. In the poetry of the Arabs the desert is always represented as a place of bewilderment, where the correct interpretation of signs—the fading traces of an encampment, a distant light, or a lightning flash—carries vital consequences.

Place names abound here: Najd, Ḥima, Salʿ, Kazima, al-ʿAqīq, Wadi al-Qarī, Mina, Khayf, and Mecca. Each of these is richly allusive, some to the poetry of Imru' al-Qays and other towering figures of pre-Islamic poetry, others to the sacred landscape traversed by the Prophet and his Companions. The mystic resonances of the pre-Islamic place names flow out of a powerful combination of geographical realities and poetic tradition. For example, the Najd, a highland plateau near the Red Sea favored with cooling breezes and magnificent vistas, came to represent a privileged destination. Ibn al-ʿArabī defines Najd in his desert odes as representing variously, "God on his throne," or "divine knowledge," and also speaks of "the gazelles of Najd" defining them as "the exalted spirits."[1] Likewise, Khayf and Minā resonate as places of prophetic history, commemorated in the repetition of the sacred rituals of the Pilgrimage.

In Shushtarī's mystic desert odes, like those of Ibn al-Fāriḍ and Ibn al-ʿArabī, those two sets of toponymic symbols are brought together. As Jaroslav Stetkevych observes, speaking of Ibn al-Fāriḍ, "[The many place names] move between remote dunes, hills, and valleys where ancient, pre-Islamic abodes once stood abandoned, from which so many tribal caravans departed, and those newer places, with their newer names and echoes, full of the sweetness of ritual, of faith, of ineffable gnostic essences, of loss in the fold of the Mother of Cities."[2] All of these nostalgic signposts mark the spaces in which the soul wanders searching for welcome, for hospitality, and for the rewards that follow the arduous journey. Following in the wake of his two poetic predecessors, Shushtarī works in an almost telegraphic mode, condensing and synthesizing their use of symbol, evoking a similarly elegiac and nostalgic mood in a very economical style.

The section opens with a very brief poem, "The night's journey." While it is not explicitly set in the desert, it is linked to the poems that follow by the idea of a night journey, a journey in which fantasy and illusion are abandoned in the quest for self-knowledge and knowledge of the divine mysteries. The idea that self-knowledge is central to mystical gnosis is a crucial theme in the works of most Sufis. Many mystics, including Shushtarī, cite the maxim (often attributed to Muḥammad despite the objections of *ḥadīth* scholars) 'he who knows himself, knows his Lord."

The next poem brings the reader/listener fully into the poetic world of the desert ode, from the flashes of lightning that illuminate the sky to the closing reference to the famous lovers Qays and Layla. Addressing the listener in the second person and frequently using imperatives, Shushtarī bridges the distance between those timeless images, collapses time, and places the listener in the desert. The poetic voice instructs the listener to speak—as the Qur'ān tells Muḥammad and his followers to recite or proclaim—"say I was happy when I saw the lightning." That "I" collapses and confuses the poetic voice and the voice of the listener who does as he is bid. Thus poet and listener, master and student are joined in recitation, describing illumination as it gives way to intoxication and then purification. Thus the *moment*—a term often used by Sufis to refer to a brief, and potentially disorienting, flash—is purified. The idea is reiterated and reinscribed through the reference to 'the builder of the wall," that is, the unnamed figure in the Qur'ān 18:60–82 generally identified as al-Khidhr, who meets Moses and then tests his patience by performing a series of odd and initally inexplicable actions, including repairing the wall of a town that had refused them both hospitality. At the end of their meeting the stranger tells Moses the meaning of the things he had not been able to bear patiently. Among Sufi mystics, al-Khidhr is seen as a prototypical *shaykh* or teacher who leads the student from bewilderment to understanding.

The following poem, "Pay no attention,"contrasts "the One/loved by others for His dazzling beauty"(5) with a list of conventional poetic symbols of beauty, grace, and yearning. Like Qays, who wanders the desert in a love-crazed fog, and poet-lovers in countless other poems, Shushtarī here speaks of being "disheveled and dusty,"and yet he celebrates being "enamoured and confused."

The short poem "But you are in the Najd"seems to be a reply to a poem of Ibn al-ʿArabī, hinting perhaps that Shushtarī found Ibn al-ʿArabī's esoterism needlessly complicated. Here wanderings between the familiar stations of the desert become a cause for confusion, disorientation.

The *qaṣīda* "Drop all pretense of shame"celebrates the end of the journey: rest, a warm fire, water, music, and drink. Unlike the poems of wandering, in which the place names of Arabian poetic landscape mark loss, nostalgia, and confusion, gesturing toward the rich tradition of elegiac musings, here the destination is nameless. This is a distinctly Sufi idyll, in the sense that it extolls the delights of Sufi practice: music and communal ecstasy. Shushtarī calls on the listener to abandon the pretense of shame (*ikhlaʿ ʿidhāraka*), to cast off the self-consciousness that would prevent the traveler from losing himself in the delights offered in that place where desires are fulfilled.

The night's journey

You who look 1
in the mirror.
Do you see
whom you see?

Is the looker someone 2
other than you,

or a reflection
of your fantasy?

Turn your glance toward 3
the glance itself,
for it holds wisdom
concealed from the others.

When day breaks, 4
may
peoples praise
the night's journey.

When lightning flashes

Whether lightning flashes at al-Himā 1
or you watch for it, cast off restraint.

Say to whomever finds in it a bad omen: 2
I was happy, when I saw the lightning.

When it appeared over the high place of worship, 3
it taught the morning to shine.

When a wanderer came in the darkness, 4
it turned his night to day.

His sun rose from his deepest self to the summit 5
of perfection, leaving him perplexed.

Drunkenness afflicted him, from what he saw and 6
the kindness of the cupbearer rounding toward him.

He poured for him a convivial old vintage, 7
the choicest wine, an overpowering drink.

His intoxication made him stagger, and he called out: 8
"Friend, don't abandon the great ones.

Be wanton, like me. 9
Drinking this has left me with no choice.”

Through it, the moment is purified, since it passed ’round 10
to the builder of the wall.

How odd: Qays of Layla, 11
complains that the one who visited him fled.

Layla did not leave him, 12
instead, she put a veil on her face.

When she came before him without it, 13
her mad lover called what he saw a disgrace.

Pay no attention

By God, O gazer, pay no attention 1
to the one slender like the green branch.

A flock, a ban tree, Laʿlaʿ, 2
Khayf, the gazelle of Bani Amr, what are these?

O heart, turn away from the delusion of the sand dunes 3
and abandon the flock of the forbidden sanctuary.

The beauty you mention will not last, 4
what need has the wise man for what is mortal?

Rather, he seeks the one 5
loved by others for his dazzling beauty.

The disheveled and the dusty are like me, 6
extinguished on account of the first and the last.

He bestows brilliance on the sun. 7
He lends radiance to the moon.

In him I became enamored and confused, 8
how good to be enamored and confused.

But you *are* in the Najd

How confused you are by two paths and the mountain 1
when the matter is clearer than fire on the mountain.

You traverse from Salʿ and Kazima, 2
from Zarūd and the neighbors of the people of Mecca.

You keep asking about the Najd. But you already are 3
    in the Najd.
and about Tihama—this behavior is suspect.

There is no life but for Layla. Go on, ask 4
about her—your questions are a delusion, they bring
    a void.

Say what you will about her, for she is pleased 5
either way, whether it be silent or spoken.

Desire drives the camels

Desire drives the camels on the night journey 1
  when sleep calls out to their eyelids.

Slacken the reins and let them lead, for they 2
  know the abode of the Najd as well as anyone.

Prod the mounts, for Salʿ is just ahead 3
  and dismount just right of the path to Wadi al-Qari.

When you get there, smell that soil; 4
  it will smell of musk, pungent.

When you reach al-ʿAqiq, say to them: 5
  the heart of the enthralled is back at camp, worn out.

If no one is there, embrace their habitations 6
and be satisfied, for earth stands in for water.

Oh, people of Rama, how I long to join you; 7
for that I would sell my life, if anyone would buy.

With a lover's hand, I hold fast to the bond of your 8
closeness
even as fate sunders the bond to which I cling.

I bid you welcome, for everything that pleases you 9
pleases me, and what you want for me, I want.

Drop all pretense of shame

Let the camels set down in the courtyard. 1
Dismount there, for you are protected.

Oh, friend, let the beasts rest from the fatigue of the 2
night's journey
and know that your travels are over.

Look toward the singer before us 3
near the stream to the right of the fire.

This land is theirs but the fire 4
was kindled for passersby.

Those lost in the gloomy darkness are guided by it, 5
guidance for the confused and lost.

Oh, Saʿd, joining them will do you good, 6
for you have arrived at the dwellings of the pious.

Abandon your wandering; you have attained your desire. 7
You reached the priestly monastery through the
scriptures.

So drink of the wine that welcomes the newcomer 8
to the echo of the flute.

Quicken to the melodies and abandon yourself to them; 9
sway to the ecstasy of the strings.

Adopt the manner of the drinkers 10
while guarding the secret of the mysteries.

Drop all pretense of shame at your eternal love for them. 11
Don't you see that I have lost my shame?

He who is called Sabʿīnī repents 12
in his self-effacement, and he awakes serene.

If the scold could see

If the scold 1
could see
what I have experienced,
how confused he would become.

And the next day he would say 2
to his friends, if you
deny what is in me,
you will have done an evil deed.

The tribe 3
has broken with custom.
That's why they called
them conjuring tricks.

Chapter 7

AT THE MONASTERY

Introduction

A blazing light atop a monastery—resembling a glowing chalice of wine—guides and beckons weary travelers during the arduous night journey. This suggestive image opens one of two highly unusual *qasidas,* unusual not only in Shushtarī's poetic production but also within Islamic mystic tradition, for they rehearse encounters between Muslim pilgrims and the Christian monastics who receive them. In the case of the first poem, "Is that a lamp?" it is a priest (*quss*) who welcomes them. The second poem, "The monastery door," speaks of monks (*ruhbān*), a priest (*qissīs*) and an acolyte or sacristan (*shammās*). In addition to depicting the intercommunal sharing of wine that is explicitly marked as sacred, Shushtarī's poems point toward sacrament, ritual, sacred space, and religious attire as points for discussion and interchange between the Muslim pilgrims and the Christian monastics. Whether the poems are read as literal descriptions of meetings or as symbolic theological encounters, the rich array of intermingled signs—including an abundance of Christian terminology, Qur'ānic allusions, Sufi expressions, the vocabulary of hermetic alchemy, metaliterary self-consciousness, and the curious apparition of a grail-like glowing chalice—opens up a host of interpretations. Unlike the desert poems with their more familiar poetics of the wandering and bewildered lover, the monastery poems, as I shall call them, have no prior models in Arabic or Sufi poetry. Nor are these monasteries to be confused with the monasteries commonly cited in Arabic wine poems and drinking songs.

The monastery (*dayr*, pl. *diyarāt*) was a familiar element in the life of travelers—irrespective of their religion—throughout much of the Islamic world during the first centuries of Islam. Ranging from hermitages to larger complexes with a church, monks' cells, shops, and inns with attached vinyards and olive groves, Christian *diyarāt* provided waystations frequented by rulers and princes, merchants and ordinary folk. These monasteries—and more specifically the taverns attached to them—are frequently depicted in poetry, perhaps most famously by Abū Nuwās, but they are also a common element in Andalusian poetry. In the Arab poetic imaginary, the monastery was, of course, a place for drinking, but also a safe, enclosed space where the poetic "I"could meet people from a variety of social classes, engage in suggestive banter with Christians (of both genders) and proclaim secret longings and forbidden desires.

We see an example of this in a *muwashshaḥ* by the twelfth-century Andalusian Abū al-ʿAbbās al-Aʿmā al-Tuṭīlī, in which the flirtatious conversation between the Christian maiden and the Muslim drinker is quietly suggestive of the emotional state of the narrator:

> And I said to her: "O most beautiful creature,
> What do you [Christians] hold about partaking from
>   the cup?"
> She said "We have nothing against it.
> That is what has been passed down to us in the
>   commentaries of monks and the bishops."[1]

The drinker asks what he already knows—he is, after all, sitting in a Christian monastery—to make conversation, perhaps to fill in the painful silence, or simply to break the ice until the wine takes effect. It is then that he confesses his passionate, but unrequited, love for Aḥmad, who, it seems, not only disdains the affection of the narrator but also that of a good number of young girls. The religious terminology in the poem (the Gospels by which the maiden swears, and the writings of monks and bishops, the confession) is invoked in a lighthearted way, the object of puns and word play. Satire is further suggested by the abrupt shift into pathos and the concatenation of poetic clichés. While in some of his vernacular poems Shushtarī plays on this poetic tradition, grafting mystical meanings onto scenes in similar monastery-taverns, the monasteries in these two *qaṣīdas* are clearly religious—rather than recreational—spaces, peopled by priests, chanting monks, and crucifix-carrying deacons in procession. Let us begin with "Is that a lamp?"

before moving on to "The monastery door," where the Muslim-Christian encounter is much more clearly enunciated.

Is that a lamp?

The poem is structured around three major themes or narrative elements. The first is the night journey guided by a mysterious light, which leads to the encounter at the monastery and the drinking of wine. The second is a lengthy meditation on the quest for knowledge, and finally, a self-referential section takes up the question of the poet's acknowledgment of his own ego in versifying and his exaltation of the purpose of the poem. Analyzing the poem's structure in terms of the classic divisions of the Arabian ode, one might understand the first section as having dispensed with the customary *nasīb*, or remembrance of the beloved, and plunged the narrator and the audience directly into a journey, or *raḥīl,* to the primordial wine. The second section extends and complicates the notion of the journey, repeating the exploration of the notion of quest or journey in a series of images that problematize the metaphorical representation of the search for knowledge as a linear process. The desert trek upon a camel or riding animal that is characteristic of the *raḥīl* in the classical *qaṣīda* and that conventionally serves in mystical *qaṣīdas* as a metaphor for the soul's journey is referred to only once—rather obliquely—in this section: "our *mount* to the spacious abode is our patience." Other codes, metaphors, and symbols of quests of knowledge are piled up: ships plying the ocean of knowledge, truths revealed through alchemy, an unveiling found in asceticism. Poetic and religious syncretism are pushed to their expressive limits here. The final section, echoing the *madīḥ*, the poetic boast or praise of the powerful or generous patron that customarily closes the *qaṣīda*, acknowledges that the questions of language, authorship, praise, and pride become confused in mystical union: "Didn't you see the flash of "self"-ness/you felt in composing poetry?/For you are me but you are You, the One/who says "I" (35–38). In that confusion of pronouns, can the poet claim to compose verse? Who can say "I"?

Returning to the beginning ot the poem, the glowing chalice and the timeless talismans sought by the travelers in "Is that a lamp?" invite comparison with certain aspects of the grail legends, raising questions as to whether Shushtarī might have come into contact with some European version of the story brought back to Syria or Damietta during the Crusades, or whether perhaps he was familiar with other material that is sometimes proposed as an Eastern source for the tales. But the philological issues of transmission are tangential here; Shushtarī is interested in poetic images, symbolism, and the reworking of commonplaces to gain access to uncommon knowledge. If the grail legends can often be understood as enacting a symbolic encounter between Christianity and paganism or pre-Christian belief, here Islam faces Christianity.

Two curious metaphors describe the transformation—not just of the self but of the consciousness of all being—wrought by that primordial wine shared in the pivotal lines of the poem. The poet exclaims, "He continued serving us graciously, adding *until the multiple became single*" [*jā' bi-l-shafi'i fī al-watr*] (11). This ambiguous expression echoes an oath found in *surat al-fajr*, "by the even and the odd" (89:3). This phrase has been understood in many ways; al-Ṭabarī alone lists more than a dozen different interpretations. Because the two preceding Qur'ānic verses ("By the Daybreak, by the Ten Nights" [89:1-2]) have been understood by many commentators to refer to Islamic calendar—although there is no agreement about *which* ten days are in question—"the even and the odd" might refer to certain dates during that period. Others have suggested that "the even" refers to creatures, because creatures come in pairs, and "the odd" refers to God, who has no peer. Still, what is most striking in Shushtarī's verses is the logical paradox: the idea that addition could turn multiplicity into oneness.

In the next line the idea of transformation is expressed anew, now using the language of alchemy. The poet exclaims: "When we became substance (*tajawharnā*) and our souls were content, we feared boisterousness in our drunken state." *Tajawhara* is a somewhat unusual verb deriving from the nominal root *jawhar*, "intrinsic, essential nature or substance" (as opposed to form). After the poet's intoxication and annihilation, the journey, the knowledge of the divine secrets, and the poetic imperative itself are evoked, as memory and future knowledge are collapsed in the totalizing perspective of divine illumination. Enlightenment erases the division between the *faqīr* and the *faqīh*, that is, between exoteric approaches of the law and esoteric truths hidden within it (17). The next hemistich elaborates on the implications of this unification of religious knowledge or perspectives. I have translated

Fakka min al-qahr as "brings a release from subjugation," and there is no doubt that Shushtarī, like many Sufis, saw blind adherence to the letter of the law as a regrettable subjugation. Yet the verb *fakka*, which means literally "to separate," "to sever," "to dismantle," is—in addition to the sense of ransoming, redeeming, or emancipating—also used to refer to solving a puzzle or a riddle. In another poem ("Breaking the talisman") the same verb is used in the sense of solving or dismantling the puzzle of the Names of God. Freedom is linked to that release.

One of the essential elements of that transformation is renunciation: the "shedding of the sandals," the giving up of family and of "boorish habits." Asceticism as a path to knowledge, as a means of removing the deceptive veil of the material, is a common theme in the poet's work. Yet the unveiling is never definitive, the journey can have no fixed destination, for God's power is called "the ship of meaning that encompasses all that can be known./It sails in the sea of being and its vastness"(18–19). Learned men "plunge into that sea [of meaning]," "perplexed, they become confused in the enormity of the wave."

The language of magic and alchemy adds another way to conceptualize power, knowledge, and the perfection of matter. This is one of several poems in which Shushtarī speaks of talismans; his exact meaning is never fully clear. Amulets were—and continue to be—a part of popular religious practice in Islam. Talismans might be engraved with short sūras from the Qur'ān, divine names, the names of angels, astrological symbols, or magic squares. The Greek origin of the word *ṭilasm* and an abundance of texts attributing rules for their creation to Hermes Trismegistus link the notion of talisman to late Hellenic gnosticism. Many of the mystic thinkers who helped to shape Shushtarī's thought, from Suhrawardī al-Maqtūl to Ibn Sabʿīn, expressed a lively interest in hermeticism.[2] The term as used by Shushtarī does not seem to refer to a charm or amulet but is used instead metaphorically. Ibn al-ʿArabī's more discursive treatment of the subject may provide us with some clues as to how Shushtarī understands the term. He calls practices or objects that hold power or control over human beings and prevent them from perceiving the fullness of reality "talismans."[3]

Shushtarī's short poem "Breaking the talisman" calls the destruction or shattering of the talisman the key to "self-knowledge in this world." In that poem, just as here in "Is that a lamp?" the talisman is linked to treasure (*kanz*), but the meaning of *ṭilasm* itself remains elusive.

The "shattering," or *kasara*, of the talisman is here etymologically linked through word play with *iksīr*, a substance thought by alchemists to be crucial to the transformation of matter. Ibn al-ʿArabī uses "elixir" metaphorically to refer to the divine truth that transforms the unbeliever into a believer.

As the poem moves to its close, the narrator tells of a joining together that will allow those learned men to travel "on the ship of reverence that approaches landfall" (33). While I have rendered *tafrīq* here as the "dispersed," a more precise translation might be division, separation, distribution, or dispersion. In certain contexts this verbal root is closely associated with the division of sects and religious groups; ʿAbd al-Kathīr al-Baghdadī's famous heresiographical treatise is entitled *Al-farq bayna al-firaq* (*The Differences between the Sects*). After using a series of images and metaphors to describe the search for divine meaning, this union or joining together suggests the syncretism enacted by the poem's enunciation and articulation. The poem links the question of enunciation then to the metapoetic awareness of the final verses. "Let the names (al-asmā') be understood." Is this a reference to the Beautiful Names of God, one of the great sources of confusion and bewilderment for the believer?

The monastery door

"The monastery door" (*Ta'addab bi-bāb al-dayr*) is more easily interpreted as a narrative poem than "Is that a lamp?" and its structure is more readily discernible. The first cluster of verses, all addressed in the second person (lines 1–8), contains a flurry of commands or directives (lines 1–3), guiding the listener on how to behave in the monastery and in the presence of the monks, deacons, and priests, followed by a series of warnings (lines 3–5) about the bewitching nature of their voices and their wisdom. Lines 6–8 delineate the rewards for meeting the requirements or conditions expressed in the earlier lines. Thus this entire opening section takes on a clearly didactic tone, echoing the words of a *shaykh* or master to a student. Beginning on line 9 the poem shifts into the first person. After acknowledging the advice he has been offered ("everything that you said to me—I listened to it"), the narrator begins to recount his negotiations with the priest for the wine, a theme that recalls the much less contentious bartering found in lines 8–9 of the first monastery poem. Even though the traveler is willing to exchange the possessions he is carrying, the priest avers "our wine is more precious than what you have mentioned."It is then that the traveler proclaims the value of his *khirqa*, the robes that symbolize the Sufi's initiation into the mystical path. The *khirqa* demands sacrifice; the priest must give up his own robes and his family in exchange for it, that is, he must abandon the life he knows to seek the enlightenment of the mystic. The symbolic exchange, effected with the priest's acceptance of the *khirqa* as a bond with the traveler, and his sharing of the wine, results in disappointment. The traveler realizes that although this wine is very old, it is not the wine he seeks. It is a moment of crisis, for while the Sufi pilgrim and the priest have shared the same language, have spoken of the same wine, they each attribute rather different symbolic associations to the word.

The poem closes with another command, to make a profession of faith: "Confess that there is no master but God/and the prophet of God is the best of messengers." The addressee for that final command remains ambiguous, and the overall interpretation of the poem depends on whether the reader understands that directive to be directed to the master in reply to his initial series of instructions, as a response to the priest, or as concluding moral for the reader. We will return to this question shortly.

Moving from this preliminary narrative-structural analysis, ʿAbd al-Ghānī al-Nābulusī's (1641–1731) commentary on this poem provides a useful starting point for understanding some of the complexities involved in the mystical symbolic interpretation of either of the monastery *qaṣīdas*.[4] As with any mystical commentary, especially one written nearly five hundred years after the text it glosses, the Syrian's treatise must be approached with caution. As Stetkevych observes, medieval critics were distrustful of poetry's multiple levels of meaning, of its self-contained aestheticism. "Much critical effort was therefore exerted to somehow neutralize the attractive illusoriness of the externality of poetry, concentrating subsequently, with an even more unchecked zeal, on the rationally obtainable and meaningfully usable elements in poetry."[5] As in his other commentaries, here Nābulusī aims to resolve the poem's ambiguities, "constructing meaning through extrapoetic equivalences"; his commentary is what Stetkevych calls an anti-poem.[6] Yet the Syrian's commentary is important precisely because he highlights the most controversial aspects of the poem, oftentimes heroically trying to make the poem *not* say what it rather plainly says. While he is a keen, if idiosyncratic, reader of Shushtarī, Ibn al-ʿArabī, and Ibn Sabʿīn, there is an evident tension in his analysis between his desire to save Shushtarī from the charge of heterodoxy and his discomfort with the self-conscious universalism of Shushtarī's poetic imagery.

Nābulusī's treatise crafts an audacious justification for Shushtarī's use of Christian and biblical terms such as *monk, monastery, priest, church, crucifix,* and *baptism*, terms that must be rescued from their association with the "polytheists." The critic's own anxieties about maintaining denominational boundaries are made plain when he cites, at the outset of his treatise, his own verses against the "deniers," that is, those who deny the truth of Muḥammad's revelation:

> O deniers! you will burn in the fire
> your intentions have transformed your acts into serpents.[7]

Nābulusī's hermeneutic strategy is to establish symbolic equivalences, generally either through etymology or analogy, that effectively redefine each of the suspect terms in a way that divorces it from its conventional Christian meaning, attributing the different understandings of the terms to problems of translation from the Syriac.[8] He explains that the deacon (*shammās*) is thus named because he gives witness to the sun (*shams*) of eternity; the monk (*rāhib*, pl. *ruhbān*) is known for his fear of the truth of the Judgment Day (*khaufihi ḥaqīqata al-qiyāmi alayhi*), a formulation rooted in *rahba*, which means "fear," "terror" or "awe." The church (*kanīsa*) is the place where the pilgrims sweep away (*kanasa*) impurities. Nābulusī's procedure is by no means unusual; there are clear echoes of Ibn al-ʿArabī's attempt to affix spiritual and metaphysical meanings to the desert landscapes of *Tarjumān al-Ashwāq* in his later commentary.

The Syrian writer stresses that the central issue underlying Shushtarī's poem is that of Islam's relationship to the earlier revelations of Judaism and Christianity. Nābulusī reminds the reader that because the religion of God is Islam, all of the prophets of God, even those who preceded Muḥammad, are Muslims. Thus Abraham, while Jewish, was also a Muslim because he had submitted to God. In no way was he an infidel (*min al-mushrikīn*). The question then becomes how to apprehend the true meaning of Jesus' message, which, while identical to that of Muḥammad, has been recorded—through inspiration rather than revelation—in *Suryāniyya* (Syriac), a language whose spiritual secrets were rendered unintelligible when its evangelical vocabulary was translated into Arabic. While Muḥammad's revelation abrogated earlier religions, this applies only to their legal codes, not their religious truths; Nābulusī claims that Shushtarī, although a devoutly "Muḥammadan Muslim," is a disciple of Jesus.

Is that a lamp?

O Saʿd, ask the priest in the monastery: 1
is that a lamp or a glass of wine?

We set out for it at night, it looked like fire on a 2
mountaintop,
until the first blaze of dawn appeared.

I say, my friends, the fire is gone. It appears 3
and then disappears. Why does it do that?

A star would keep moving. 4
That confused me and I was confused

till I arrived at the monastery and above it 5
I encountered a goblet. I didn't know what was inside.
Didn't know.

"By what's due the Messiah, tell us true, what does it 6
contain?"
He said, "The wine of passionate love. Guard the secret.

For it was raised since before Seth for the night visitor 7
seeking the monastery in dark-cloaked night."

So we said to him, "For those who desire intoxication, 8
what is its price?" He said to us, "We can sell it,

however, in exchange for the soul and the wealth that is its due, 9
with humility, praise and thanks for the vintner.

So we said to him, take us in and pour us some; 10
anyone who criticizes or insults us [for it] must be borne with patience.

He continued serving us graciously 11
adding until the multiple became single.

When we became substance and our souls were content, 12
we feared boisterousness in our drunken state.

The vintner took note of us and said, "Drink 13
and be content, for there is no one in the monastery but me.

If you wish, go and guide others 14
to us, but hide this affair from the unwise."

Shushtarī grew anguished because of the secrecy 15
but the brightness after the obliteration eased him:

Leave me be—I drag my coattails proudly before mankind 16
and I aspire to the likes of Abi Bakr, the *faqih*.

The *ha* of the *faqih* has become one with our *ra,* 17
leading to a release from subjugation.

For His power, which encircles all power 18
is the ship of meaning that encompasses all that can be known.

It sails in the sea of being and its vastness 19
on an easy wind, swayed by horizons of knowledge.

That is our goal, what captivates us; 20
the lost cannot attain this, no matter how diligently
they journey.

Our mount to the spacious abode is our patience 21
in adversity. Indeed, the benefit is in that patience.

To aquire the fire of Moses, there are conditions: 22
one must leave family out of obedience and obligation.

That is our practice. The obstinate ones veil Him; 23
to rip [the veil], one breaks with custom.

In the shedding of sandals there is, as you heard, 24
a station, however it comes with morals and dictates.

The talisman of creation's treasure releases our 25
bondage
to reason and its benefits are eternal.

For you to break the talisman through humility is its 26
transformation,
that elixir known as "the breaking,"

which is the key to the secret of the letters and their 27
symbols;
the meaning of suffering is unraveled with ease.

The clever ones are sundered out of love of rank, 28
from that lower world, they are taken away, as if
by magic.

Our delight is in the upper world 29
which we now discuss, and life is in the searching.

Divestiture's hand raises the veil 30
behind which those beauties appear.

The secrets appear to you, sovereignty and riches. 31
Oh, how many learned men have plunged into that
ocean!

Perplexed, many a man becomes confused in the 32
enormity of the wave,
in the ebb and flow, not comprehending its meaning.

When he joins together what divides, they will travel 33
on the ship of reverence which approaches landfall.

Having understood the names, he becomes [both] ruler 34
and his lieutenant; bringing forth knowledge while
pulling [believers].

Didn't you see the flash of "self"-ness 35
you felt in the midst of composing poetry?

For you are me but you are You, the One 36
who says "I." Fantasy is what proceeds to multiplicity.

Those who see not, are they poor? 37
It is right to surrender and to compose verse and prose.

The monastery door

Go through the monastery door, shed your 1
sandals there,
greet the monks, mingle and dwell among them.

And glorify the priest if you seek grace 2
and praise its sacristan if you wish to rise.

Before you: the voices of the deacons. Listen 3
to their melodies and be careful lest they steal
your reason.

They appear like suns rising 4
in procession with crosses. Beware of being bewitched.

Take heed when you listen to their wisdom 5
and be careful about joining in with them.

If you respect this requirement with sincerity 6
and do not break your pacts or promises,

they shall name you a priest and call you a monk 7
and show you the secrets and approve of your deeds.

They will give you the key to the church in which 8
the image of Jesus is found in the form of the monks.

Surely, everything that you said to me—I listened to it. 9
I don't desire favor or affection for doing so.

When I came to the monastery, I became a master, 10
so proud, I drag my coattail.

I asked where I could find the winemaker: 11
"Is there a way to him or not?"

The priest said to me, "What do you want from him?" 12
And I said, "I hope for wine."

And he said, "By my head and Jesus son of Mary and 13
my religion,
[not even] if you trade jewels for it."

So I said to him, "I will add gold to the jewels." 14
He said: "No.
No matter how much."

I said to him: "I give you my sandals and my book, 15
and I give you my staff with which I have
traveled afar.

Here, take my knapsack, here, take my turban, 16
here, take my sash belt, and my beggar's bag and
my blade.

And here's the secret of my meaning and my toothpick 17
and the lamp that accompanies me at night during my
sessions."

He said, "My drink is beyond what you have described, 18
and our wine is more precious than what you have
mentioned."

So I said to him: "Stop exaggerating its description. 19
For if your wine is more precious, our *khirqa* is higher.

We saw our masters wear it 20
and in it our masters passed on our discipline.

In it we have the secret we pass round among us 21
and the secret of the secret that manifested itself.

The critics castigate us excessively for it; 22
our ears cast aside reproach for our garb.

For when we cloaked ourselves in it and became
enamored of it, 23
we left lands and property and family."

He said, "Perhaps you could give us those robes, 24
for it is proven to me that there is sincerity and justice
in them."

So I said to him: "If you wish to wear my robe, 25
purify yourself and become fit for it.

And trade all of that garb for it, 26
and for it, shred that belt and renounce your habit."

And he said: "Yes, for I have become enamored of it. 27
I shall make it a link between you and me."

So he gave [the wine] to me. "I have revealed its 28
secret to you."
He handed it to me in a jug.

So I said to him: "This is not the wine I seek 29
And I don't wish for this wine.

However this wine is very old 30
for it has not been described and not been
known before."

Confess that there is no master but God 31
and the prophet of God is the best of messengers;

upon him the peace of God wherever it lights 32
as long as the remembrance of God is recited among
mankind.

Chapter 8

ODE RHYMING IN NŪN

Introduction

The *Nūniyya*, that is, the "Ode Rhyming in Nūn," is Shushtarī's longest and, in many ways, his most enigmatic poem. Beginning with its examination of the goals of the mystic and moving on to probe the role of human reason, logic, and intellection in the apprehension of the divine, the poem concludes with an enumeration of—and brief remarks about—an eclectic list of philosophers and mystics. These thinkers, ranging from Hermes, Socrates, Plato, and Aristotle to famous Sufi mystics and others considerably more obscure, are often taken to represent the enormously diverse influences that shaped Shushtarī's thought. It is a bold declaration of a theosophical approach that attempted to wed a Hellenic—and pagan—intellectual heritage with the work of later Islamic philosophers and mystics. The central question here is epistemological, how can the believer come to know or understand what is beyond human comprehension?

At a superficial level, what is most striking about the poem is its uncharacteristically difficult style, surprising for a poet so well known for his bold expression and clarity. Ibn al-Khaṭīb notes the poem's "linguistic irregularities" and its "poetic shortcomings," suggesting that the style of the poem is derived from that of Ibn Sabʿīn.[1] The suggestion is certainly plausible. Ibn Sabʿīn has a well-deserved reputation as a difficult and extremely hermetic writer. Furthermore, the poem certainly presents Shushtarī's master in terms we might expect of a new adept under the spell of powerful personality: as a uniquely insightful figure who has overcome all the pitfalls that trapped his predecessors. The suggestion that this was a very early poem might also be a way to account for its absence from Eastern recensions of the *dīwān* despite its widespread survivals in Maghribī sources.

The initial verses treat the goals of the mystic, asserting that the mystic aims beyond a heavenly prize. The importance of sincerity (*ṣidq*) in religious practice, the idea that the believer should be motivated by the pure desire for God, with no thought for any other reward, is a recurrent theme among Sufi mystics. The twelfth-century Andalusian Abū Madyan is said to have exclaimed: "How great a difference there is between those whose high ambition is wide-eyed virgins and castles and those whose lofty goal is the lifting of the veil and [attaining] the Eternal Presence."[2] A tale told about the famous Sufi woman, Rābiʿa al-ʿAdawiyya (d.801) neatly exemplifies this virtue:

> One day some friends-of-God saw Rabiʿa running along with fire in one hand and water in the other. "Lady of the next world, where are you going and what does this mean?"
>
> Rabiʿa replied: "I am going to burn paradise and douse hell-fire, so that both veils may be lifted from those on the quest and they will become sincere of purpose. God's servants will learn to see him without hope for reward or fear of punishment. As it is now, if you took away hope for reward and fear of punishment, no one would worship or obey."[3]

Shushtarī highlights the virtue of *ṣidq,* speaking of seeking "not the reward, but something more,/inspired by a thought that shot an arrow surpassing Eden" (line 1). This is an allusion to Qur'ān 10:26: "Those who did well will have the best reward and more besides." Ibn ʿAjiba explains "something more" as "gazing with an everlasting vision (or knowledge) on the countenance of God (al-Karīm)."[4]

Perhaps the most basic task of the believer is to proclaim *tawḥīd*, God's absolute oneness, yet even in this seemingly straightforward proposition there resides an unfathomable mystery. How can man assert the oneness of God, if the act of assertion itself implies separateness from God and the very multiplicity that is being denied? Logic offers no escape, and thus the first half of the poem becomes a sustained critique of reason (*ʿaql*): "You are bound in conjecture which has overcome you; the light of reason has conferred upon you a prison" (line 8). The Arabic language itself asserts a semantic association between *ʿaql* (reason, understanding, discernment) and *ʿiqāl* (the cord used to bind the feet of a camel). Shushtarī plays on this association, calling his own advice "a binding-cord on reason"(line 19). While he does admit the intellect's necessity in attaining a certain level of understanding, he proclaims, "Our goal is the rejection of reason"(line 21). That is to say, the path of the mystic eventually transcends the bounds of reason and human intellect. Shushtarī makes several key points. One is that reason is the self-contained system upon which humans must rely to know themselves. Anticipating Descartes' "I think therefore I am," the Andalusian poet observes that humans are manifest to themselves through reason. At the same time, it is reason that "confines eternity within time," placing limits on what is limitless and defining all reality from its own restricted perspective. He likens reason to a sort of cocoon: "For we are like a silkworm, enveloped by what/we fashion, in pushing back the encirclement, we are imprisoned by it"(line 38). The intellect, thus, is incapable of transcending its own limitations.

Just as the process of shedding (*tajrīd*) was seen to be continuous and dynamic, so too is the quest for knowledge. (Indeed the two are metaphors for the same process.) Shushtarī warns against the distractions found along the Way:

> Don't stop in any station, for they are a veil; be earnest in the journey and seek aid.
> No matter what levels appear before you, let them go (15–16).

The believer cannot remain attached to any station or level, for otherwise rather than a step on the Path, it becomes an obstacle, a veil.

The second half of the poem, verses 39–69, is devoted to listing major intellectual and religious figures. It is introduced by a verse that speaks of the diverse benefits and pitfalls of *ʿaql*: "How often it destroys the bystander, and how often it rightly guides the traveler./ How often it reveals wisdom and how often it enriches the poor" (line 39). In a sense, this final section can be understood as a *madīḥ*, that is, the conventional praise and/or boast that closes the traditional Arabian ode. The poet acknowledges his predecessors in the journey, recalling their contributions or alluding to a noteworthy trait or action of theirs.

The *Nūniyya*

I see those who bid us seek not the reward, but 1
something more,
inspired by a thought that shot an arrow surpassing Eden.

Our bidder is what we seek, within our own existence; 2
through it we disappear to ourselves when lightning hits.

We abandon our inclination to the pleasures of the low 3
places,
deserting the distant purpose for the most brilliant quest.

And we find the existence of the cosmos to be but 4
delusion.
Nothing is fixed. This is the essence of extinction.

The rejection of multiplicity is a duty for us, 5
because our creed is to obliterate polytheism and doubt.

But how to reject [multiplicity], 6
for those who reject are [themselves the] rejected: us
and we are not.

So you who speak of union while at the station that 7
is veiled from [union]; listen well, as we have already
done.

You are bound in conjecture that has overcome 8
you; the light of reason conferred on you a prison.

You fell in love with the lights; we understood their 9
source,
the fountainhead from which they came into being.
We did not fall.

The lights can veil [reality] from the servant, just as 10
darkness binds the soul filled with spite.

What kind of union can be claimed in this case, 11
if the most perfect of men did not claim certainty?

If God's mystery could be known in this way, 12
would the commoners say to us: "Look, we do
not fail"?

How much strife and toils before reaching it 13
and how many [wildernesses] have we traversed?

On the journey, pay heed to nothing else, that is, 14
nothing but
God alone. Hold fast to His remembrance as a
fortress.

Don't stop in any station, for they are 15
a veil; be earnest in the journey and seek aid.

No matter what levels appear before 16
you, let them go. Those we abandoned were much
the same.

And say: I have no desire but Your essence. 17
Therefore, no image appears, no rare treasure
is collected.

Go toward the banners on the right, for they 18
are the path to good fortune. Do not abandon
good fortune.

Great horror lies before you; listen to my advice, 19
a binding-cord on reason, indeed, we have turned away
from it.

It destroyed mankind with difficulties, and before them 20
it destroyed with conjecture the Jinn and the Binn.

Our goal is the rejection of reason, and this 21
is our pilgrimage
and our proof; what follows is the "b" in which we are
enraptured.

[Reason] impedes our ascent because 22
it would that we stay here, rather than attain
the highland.

Among [reason's] aspects, three are manifest to us: 23
as seers, as seen, and in the seeing of which we speak.

Reason views man as a slave in his permanence. 24
he returns a lord through extinction, and [reason] has
no extinction.

As tablet, if the lines of our being are manifest 25
to it, through it, [reason] is the tablet and the small Pen

sketching out the lines of time. From its perspective 26
its comprehension is the utmost, and in it we are
manifest.

It established the lotus tree of its essence beneath 27
dahr
We and description of totality confused ourselves in
describing it.

[Reason] confines Eternity within time just as 28
from its essence it fashions joints for bodies.

It fashions the Throne, the Chair, the Orbit, and the 29
celestial bodies;
its ocean is that in which we swim.

It fashions the innermost of the body of totality, 30
the secret of the letters through our letters.

In appearance it divides the whole of matter 31
and diversity is made whole because our triumph has interlocked it.

It made multiple that which was but One 32
by pronouncing names through which meaning is dispersed.

It ascends, and the ascent is from itself to its essence; 33
to get to its highest stage we must use imagination.

And it creates a lowness and makes us imagine a descent, 34
forcing our souls to go down.

It ordains union after its own separation 35
and imposes distances that must be traversed as if a wilderness.

The stage of plurality reveals to us its uncertainty, 36
when [plurality] flashes from it, the falsehood catches up with it.

It attains the level of the polytheism of the dualists. 37
Reason is made apparent through them.

For we are like a silkworm, enveloped by what 38
we fashion, in pushing back the encirclement, we are imprisoned within it.

How often it destroys the bystander, and how often it rightly guides the traveler, 39
how often it reveals wisdom and how it enriches the poor.

It enthralled the hearts of all the Hermes, 40
and it sufficed for Socrates to dwell in the barrel,

and to abstract all the forms of the world 41
and reveal Plato in his ultimate beauty.

And Aristotle became enamored until he became 42
peripatetic out of his love,
and spread his ideas and did not withold anything.

It helped Dhu al-Qarnayn in his achievements, 43
for he was the one who sought the spring of life.

and he searched for the origin of what you know, 44
and in searching he overlooked the well when
prevented by clouds.

And it made Hallaj enjoy the taste of unity 45
so he cried out, "I am the one uncircumscribed by
meaning."

He was told to retract what he said and he said, "No. I 46
drank the wine that makes all those who taste it sing."

And it uttered through al-Shibli the union that 47
he referred to when he effaced the universe.

And it enraptured the essence of al-Niffari so that he 48
spoke of monotheism until it became his companion.

He was a speaker between two essences. He who is 49
Poor can see the ocean into which we have plunged.

It silenced Ibn Jinni in his "Tajrid al-Khalq"; 50
the matter was such it made his eloquence incoherent.

Qadib al-Ban was made drunk drinking its wine, 51
for he was like the others but he was dualist.

It made al-Shudhi leave his kindred, so he did not 52
incline toward friendship or to dwell in cities.

In it al-Suhrawardi became bewildered. 53
He shouted, but existence (*al-wujud*) did not listen.

Through it, Ibn Qasi, wrote "Khalʿ Naʿl wujudihi" and 54
"Libs Ihata,"
which made us repent of the forbidden.

Al-Masarra made pleasure the cupbearer, 55
represented the mysteries symbolically and bade
the rain to fall.

Because of his proximity to reason, the radiance of 56
lightning
gleamed upon Ibn Sina, and he thought what he thought.

Al-Ghazali imitated what I have mentioned 57
but he was inclined toward Sufism.

It awoke Ibn Tufayl and Ibn Rushd; 58
the Epistle of Awakening brought destruction.

It clothed al-Shuʿayb in the garment of unity of its 59
essence;
he dragged over those envious of him the trail and the
sleeve [of his garment].

And in it Ibn al-ʿArabi cloaked the simplicity of 60
his being,
in it the presence of the drunken profligate he removed
the weakness.

He publicly called himself spirit of the Spirit, and he 61
was not tested.
He saw no peer or equal in the mystical station.

In it [reason] ʿUmar ibn al-Farid, the poet who gave 62
himself over
to travel, eased what is difficult.

Ibn al-Harrali proclaimed it when 63
he saw his hiddeness was weakness and his
manifestation cloudy.

Al-Umawi had verse and prose on what 64
we mention and arguments like those we have.

Al-Ghafiqi revealed what was hidden [in it] 65
and revealed its levels, taking away the clouds and
the darkness.

He clarified the mysteries of worship 66
from their manifestation, which were not freed from
confusion and error.

We unveiled the cloak from its intermingling with 67
its secret
and what you saw hidden in it became visible.

He guided us to the creed of al-Haqq that caused us 68
to lose ourselves
by His power over our hearts and in Him we were guided.

Those who desire to go to the side of 69
holiness, let them accept it from us.

PART THREE

Prose

BAGHDAD TREATISE [ON SUFI CUSTOMS][1]

Introduction

The medieval critics of Sufism not only disapproved of its theosophical speculation and exegetical methods; but often their sharpest criticism was directed at issues of outward practice. Sufis were criticized for their wearing of wool, hairshirts, and other materials associated with ascetics and their use of distinctive clothing, such as the *khirqa* (a cloak of investiture in a mystical order) or the *muraqqaʿ* (a patchwork cloak symbolic of voluntary poverty). In *The Devil's Delusion* (*Talbīs Iblīs*), Ibn al-Jawzī (d.597/1200) categorizes the wearing of Sufi clothes as a misrepresentation, "exhibiting what is false in the form of truth," stressing that the outward piety of the Sufis misleads others and is calculated for notoriety and to gain the sympathy of others. He argues that the Prophet and his Companions favored austerity because they had no choice; they "patched out of necessity." To choose poverty voluntarily is, in his view, a deviation from tradition, a wrongminded "innovation" (*bidaʿ*) because "man is commanded to display God's bounty towards him."[2]

In this short treatise, Shushtarī rebuts many of the criticisms leveled at Sufis regarding questions of practice, or *sunna*. It is unclear if it is addressed to someone in particular, and if so, who that might be. The points covered correspond quite closely to the objections of Ibn al-Jawzī, who, though based in Baghdad, died before Shushtarī's time. Perhaps he is responding to one of his disciples; in any case, this list of objections was probably quite common. Shushtarī is adamant in asserting that the central issue at hand is how one determines and defines sunna, that is, the customs and habits of the Prophet and his Companions and by extension the proper practice of the devout Muslim. He appeals to the Qur'ān and the Ḥadīth to make his point. He frequently makes use of the abundant detail found in many *ḥadīth* to make points entirely unrelated to the central thrust of that particular tradition. For example, Shushtarī refers to the *ḥadīth* about how the Prophet once wrapped Fatima, ʿAlī, Ḥasan, and Ḥusayn in a cloak he was wearing and told them that God wished to keep them pure. This Tradition is generally interpreted as defining *ahl al-bayt*, that is, the family of the Prophet, yet here Shushtarī is more interested in the fact that the Prophet's cloak was made of black camel hair.

Shushtarī defends the Sufis' wearing of camel hair and wool, the patchwork cloak, and several other specific items of clothing. In this context his comments about the *khirqa* are quite noteworthy. He says that because so many people wear the *khirqa* the bad actions of just one person wearing it reflect badly on all Sufis. He seems to be making a distinction between the many people who had been invested as Sufis and a smaller group whose members have elected the way of voluntary poverty.

One particularly controversial practice of some Sufis was the contemplation of human beauty, especially in the form of beardless youth. Shushtarī argues that veneration or worship goes far beyond simply praising God (in speech). All five senses can become paths of veneration.

The opposition between legist (*faqīh*) and Sufi (*faqīr*) is among the most persistent themes in his poetry, and it is repeated throughout this treatise as well. As Shushtarī observes, the root meaning of *fiqh*—in a religious context taken to mean "jurisprudence"—is "understanding." He argues that Sufis are concerned with understanding only the Qur'ān and the Ḥadīth, implying, of course, that the jurist is more concerned with legalisms removed from those essential texts. His conclusion echoes that of Suhrawardī and others, that the *fuqarā'* are the real *fuqahā'*. Yet Shushtarī's final observation, that different schools of law offer different interpretations of sunna and that it is "obscure" reinforces a point he makes at the beginning of the treatise: people tend to think their own practice is *sunna* and that of others is bidaʿ. While he offers a spirited defense of the ways of the Sufis, ultimately it is up to God alone to judge a person's intentions; one should not question the practice of others, for casting blame on a fellow believer is a sin.

In the name of God, the Lord of mercy, the Giver of mercy

Greetings and peace upon our master Muḥammad and his family and Companions. And peace to whomever knows the Truth (al-Ḥaqq), for he serves Him; he distinguishes what is false and declares it to be so. "These are the signs of God. We recite to thee in truth" (2:252, 3:108, 45:6). "Alif. Lam. Mim. This is the scripture in which there is no doubt, containing guidance for those who are mindful of God, who believe in the unseen, keep up the prayer, and give out of what We have provided for them" (2:1–3).

Now then, you say the wearing of camel hair (*shaʿr*) is contrary to *sunna* and that the patched frock (*muraqqaʿ*) is a gaudy show [of piety] and that those seen in it are then treated deferentially by people. You also say that gazing upon the *fuqarā'* is an improper form of adoration, that veneration is saying "praise God" or words to that effect, and that *sunna* is the province of the jurists (*fuqahā'*).

To this we answer, and God is our refuge: Most people err in [the practice of] *sunna*, even though they profess it. For every member of the community claims that he is correctly practicing *sunna* and that others are duped by innovation. Thus, it is necessary for us in this work to study the righteous believers, and before God Almighty, defend against the fanaticism of those who err and the error of the innovators. The Prophet of God said: "Be guided by those who come after me: Abū Bakr and ʿUmar."

[The Prophet] said, "My Companions are like the stars, by any of them you will be rightly guided."[3] For *sunna* is the path, the following of the Prophet and his Companions. Whoever draws near to them and their way of life with respect to food, drink, clothing, shelter, completely in all his doings is *sunnī*. As for the custom (*sunna*) of wearing camel hair, it has come down to us through Muslim that ʿAisha reported: "The Prophet went out one day wearing a striped cloak (*mirṭ muraḥḥal*) of the black camel's hair. Fatima came, and he wrapped her with it. ʿAlī came, and he wrapped him in it. Then Ḥasan came, and he wrapped him in it. Then Ḥusayn came, and he wrapped him in it. Then he said, "God wishes to keep uncleanness away from you, people of the [Prophet's] House, and make you completely pure" (33:33).[4] This true *ḥadīth* can be doubted only by a heretic, whether or not you acknowledge it. The disapproval of the wearing of camel hair or of the other Sufi [practices] does not come from *sunna*. Their disapproval is because it is a "breaking of custom." If there is no text, neither the Qur'ān nor the Ḥadīth, to support their disapproval, then wearing it is permissible and acceptable. How could there be a prohibition? For we know from the texts that the Prophet wore it. The Almighty said, "[It is God who has given you a place of rest in your houses and tents, made from the skins of animals, that you find light to handle when you travel and when you set up camp;] furnishings and comfort for a while from their wool, fur and hair"(16:80).

As for the wearing of patchwork (*muraqqaʿ*), there is what is told in the *Muwattaʿ* on the authority of Isḥaq ibn ʿUbayd Allah Ibn Abī Talha. He said, "Anas Ibn Mālik said, 'I saw ʿUmar ibn Khattāb when he was the amir of Medina. Three patches were sewn between his shoulders, one patched over the other'."[5] It is also said that the Prophet wore sandals and a patched cloak. He once said to Aisha while she was patching with white and black fabric, "Don't discard a piece of clothing until you've patched it." Furthermore, several Companions said that they had seen Abū Bakr wearing patchwork. And the author of *Jawāhir fī al-taṣawwuf* claims that ʿAlī said, "I patched that coat of mine to the point that I became embarrassed by it. Someone said to me, 'Throw that out! The owner of a donkey would not give it to his donkey.' Thābit said on the authority of Anas: "I was with ʿUmar and he was wearing a shirt with four patches on the back and he was asked about that verse 'fruits and fodder' (80:31). This *ḥadīth* was related by the author of *al-Ṣafwa*.[6] Sufyan al-Thawrī said, "ʿUmar was wearing an *izar* with twelve patches." As for the (*abā'a*) [an outer garment or blanket] made of wool, the *Saḥīḥ* of Muslim has that Hudhayfa said, "The Prophet wrapped me in an extra *abā'a* of his." As for the *aqbiya*, the *ḥadīth* of Maymūn ibn Makhzum says, "One was presented to the Prophet, and he shared it with his Companions."

As for wearing narrow sleeves—which is known as *muzannad*—according to Muslim and Bukhārī and Mālik ibn Anas, Mughira Ibn Shuʿba, reported on his father's authority, that the Prophet went to relieve himself while on the expedition to Tabūk. Mughira said: "So I went with him, taking water. Then the Prophet came back and I poured water on his hands and he washed his face. Then he went to take his arms out of the sleeves of his garment but he wasn't able to [because of their narrowness]. So he took them out from underneath [his garment]."

On the wearing of wool, according to Anas ibn Mālik, "The Prophet accepted the invitation of a slave; he rode a donkey and wore wool." According to Abū Mūsā al-Asharī, "If you had seen us while we were with the Prophet and the rain had fallen on us, you would have thought that we smelled like sheep because we were wearing wool." Aisha said, "'Alī came to see the Prophet while I was mending with various patches."

As for needlework with a contrasting stitching, like white on black or black on white, Muslim has on the authority of 'Abd Allah Mawlā 'Asmā' bin Abī Bakr that she said, "I saw Ibn 'Amr in the market and he had bought an *izar* from the Levant and he saw a red thread in it so he returned it. Then I went to Fatima and mentioned this to her. And she said, "'Girl, hand me the Prophet's *jubba*,'[7] and she brought out a *jubba* with pockets and openings stitched with red brocade. All clothing is permissible except silk,[8] which is forbidden. Wool and camel hair are *sunna*."

As for those who claim, "you flaunt yourselves so that people will act deferentially toward you," none of that applies to us. The Prophet said, "Works depend on their intentions and to each affair what is intended." This applies to whomever seeks notoriety, whether he is a Sufi or a jurist, and it is God's affair. No one else should judge what is unseen in another or ask, "Why do your seek fame?" He sins in [judging] if that person did not intend fame, for he is slandering his fellow believer. This is not permitted. And God Almighty said, "some suspicions are sinful"(49:12). The Prophet said, "Beware of suspicion, for it is the most deceitful of speech."

Sulman Abū Darda visited the Levant from Iraq, and he was wearing coarse fabric draped around him (*kisā'un ghalīẓun maḍmūm mutawashshaḥun bihi*) and he was told, "You are showing off." He said: "what is good is the good of the next life. I am only a slave. I eat as the slave eats. I dress as the slave dresses. When I am free, I will wear a cloak (*jubba*) whose seams are not worn out."[9]

You should know that nowadays wearing the *khirqa* is an act of effacement (*'ayn al-khifā'*) because many people wear it and already there are negative impressions and ignorance about them. For someone wearing a *khirqa* is seen doing something despicable and that is then attributed to the Sufis (*fuqarā'*), so they are shunned on account of one man.

As for your claim that the Sufis' contemplation (*al-naẓar*) [of human beauty] is an improper devotion, to that we say, God Almighty said, "Do they not see (*yanẓarū*) the sky above them, how We have built it?"(50:6). And He said, "Has it not occurred (*anẓarū*) to them..." (7:184), and He said, "See (*anẓarū*) [what is in the heavens and on the earth" (10:101), [and] "Do they [the disbelievers] not see (*yanẓarūna*)?" (88:17). Thus He spurs us to gaze upon created things and these are the greatest proof of the greatness of the Creator. As God says, "We shall show them Our signs in every region of the earth and in themselves" (41:53). So there is praise [of Him] in mankind and in the regions of the earth. Gazing upon the countenance (*wajh*)[10] is to gaze upon the countenance or head or hair of a poor man or a rich man, or in general, upon animals, plants, and matter. The Almighty said, "Have they not contemplated the realm of the heavens and earth?" (7:185), and "on earth there are signs for those with sure faith"(51:20). Gazing on all of these is veneration. The Prophet said, "He who knows himself, knows his Lord."[11] For verily, man was created in the best form and honored above all else. [God] said, "We have honored the children of Adam" (17:70). He made the angels bow before him and teach Adam the names because of his specialness, and He specifically created him with His two hands."[12] Because of this man is greater than the animals and the plants and the minerals and gazing upon him is worship. In everything He has placed signs that He is one.

As for your claim that worship is praising God or similar invocations, we share [the praise of God] with inanimate things and the plants and animals: "There is not a single thing that does not celebrate His praise"(17:44). What man adds to this is [praise through] examination and thought. For the Almighty said, "We shall show them Our signs in every region of the earth and in themselves"(41:53). And part of the horizons is the face of man. Listening (*samā'*)[13] is veneration, as He said, "[My servants] listen to what is said and follow what is best" (39:18). Speech is veneration as long as what is said is good. Sensatory experience is veneration, all five senses.

As for your saying, "*Sunna* is with the jurists (*fuqahā'*)," to this we say, the word *fiqh* means understanding and our concern is only to understand the Qur'ān and the Ḥadīth. For it is incumbent upon whomever understands the book of God and the traditions of His Prophet to act in accordance with what is understood to be obligatory, and he who does this is by necessity one of the *fuqarā'*. For the book of God commands asceticism in this world and warns people against it [this world]. Thus He said to best of His creation [that is, Muḥammad], "Do not gaze longingly [at what we have given some of them to enjoy, the finery of the present life] (20:131). How much more so for anyone else? His understanding will make him flee all of his possessions. The exemplar in this is Abū Bakr or his justice (*naṣafuhu*) guided by ʿUmar or to be unto him a loan to the Muslims, like ʿUthmān and ʿAbd al-Raḥmān bin ʿAwf. Thus, the degree of sincerity is known in one's following of the Prophet. Imitate each [of his] actions.

If you say that the *fuqahā'*—those who are so called— have a certain *sunna* or that they practice a part of the *sunna*, we accept that. Farqad said to Ḥasan al-Basrī, "The *fuqahā'* are talking about you." He replied: "You have left your mother without child, dear Farqad. Have you really seen a *faqīh*? For a *faqīh* is an ascetic in this world, a seeker of the next."

And know that if you ask those who wear wool if that is *sunna* or not, then [also] ask those you judge to be Sunni. For we say—and trust in God for yourself—the Prophet never ate his fill of bread, and did not build brick upon brick or build up a house as people do. So who are they following in their building of homes and their ornamented doorways? It is said that Sufyān al-Thawrī averted his gaze when he passed by an ornamented gate. The clothing of the Prophet is known to have cost between five and twenty dirhams. The shirt that Uthman wore had mid-length sleeves, so by whom are they guided in their long, wide sleeves and their shawls (*tailasān*) and their turbans, which do not look like the turbans worn by the Prophet? And in this deviation by whom are they guided? The ancestors wore sandals.

In our view, the *fuqarā'* (the poor) are the *fuqahā'* (the ones who understand). For the source of their clothes is known, and their food is the food of the *ahl al-ṣuffa*,[14] and their dwellings are their dwellings, and their path is their path. They obtain what they need through the command of their religion. God Almighty does not impose on them *fiqh* with regard to divorce, manumission, oaths of condemnation, inheritance, sharecropping contracts, laws, precedence, and similar things. And these decrees are handed down from generation to generation because they are a collective duty (*farḍ al-kifāya*). But God asks of us sincere devotion: "All they were ordered to do was worship God alone, sincerely"(98:5). So how is it that you claim they imitate *sunna*? Do they follow it in food or clothing? Or in humility? Or in sharing with their slaves? Or in their mode of travel? Or in their wills? Or in their asceticism or their divestiture or in the paucity of what they have accumulated? Or in their visiting of poor sick Muslims and the unfortunate? Or in their morals?

In the *Saḥīḥ* of Muslim it says that the Prophet of God died leaving neither dinar nor dirham nor slave, just his white mule and his weapons. The land he left to charity. This is the custom among the *fuqarā'*. We know that he wore sandals and patched his gown and did the grinding [of food] with the servants. This is how the poor do things. It is said that marks of the mat were on his side and in this his practice was as that of the Sufis.[15]

It is said that once he said the afternoon prayer (*al-ʿaṣr*), then he entered his house and left quickly, and he saw people's astonishment at his rushing. So he said, "I remembered that some gold had been given to us, and I did not want it to stay with us overnight, so I distributed it." This is the custom among the *fuqarā'*. Patience, thankfulness, morals, bearing insult and other trials, these noble characteristics are the way of the *fuqarā'*.

As for the sciences (*ʿulūm*), know that in the time of the Prophet and his Companions there was not such fastidiousness (*tadqīq*) in the sciences, nor was there talk of personal judgment (*ra'y*) nor analogical reasoning (*qiyās*). For their sciences pertained to the hereafter: the oneness of God (*tawḥīd*), trust in God (*tawakkul*), asceticism, and faithfulness. For what is the *sunna* you seek if not the *sunna* in which most of the *fuqarā'* believe, whether you acknowledge it or not.

As for the *fuqarā'* staying in the mosques, according to the Messenger of God, in the *Saḥīḥ*, he had a delegation to *Thaqīf* dismount in one. He said, "It is dearest to their hearts." And the *Saḥīḥ* says that when Saʿd ibn Maʿadh was injured, [the Prophet] erected a tent for him in the mosque. The Banū Ghifar also had a tent in it.[16]

And it is said in the *Saḥīḥ* of Muslim that the Abyssinians (*al-ḥabsha*) stayed there and that they danced (*zafanū*) there. The Prophet watched and screened Aisha with his mantle while she watched them play. Abū ʿUbayd said, "the *zafna* is a dance."[17] As for their eating from charity, it has come down to us through al-Bukhārī in [the chapter on] the prayer of the two Eids that [the Prophet] walked through the rows of women commanding them to [give] alms. And Bilāl took in his gown what they gave him. And that *sunna* (practice) of the *fuqarā'* is the reason for the palm-leaf baskets we use. [The Prophet] gave alms only to the *fuqarā'* (poor) and the Ahl al-Ṣuffa, who were poor.

And as for earning little (*qillat al-kasb*), Bukhārī says in a *hadīth* attributed to ʿAbd al-Raḥmān ibn Abī Bakr that the *ahl al-ṣuffa* were poor men and that the Prophet gave to them and he entrusted their welfare to his Companions. He did not command them to aquire things. In Muslim it says that the *fuqarā'* were clothed and fed until the death of the Prophet. He did not object to their custom; rather, he loved them and praised their path. God Almighty entrusted them to him when he said, "Be steadfast along with those who pray to their Lord morning and evening" (18:28).[18]

And among the errors of people the most astounding thing is that they say that ʿUmar made the people leave the mosque and commanded them to seek earnings. If that is true then that would show—God forbid—that ʿUmar had a different view than the Prophet in a matter regarding the *ahl al-ṣuffa* and the *fuqarā'*.

Whoever says such a thing censures and criticizes what happened among the Companions out of his ignorance. The community is agreed that the *fuqarā'* will enter heaven half a day earlier than the rich (in the days of the next world). And the reason for the controversy in the Maghreb between the *fuqarā'* and the *fuqahā'* is that Imam Mālik believed that the unfortunate (*masākīn*) [those unable to make a living] were more deserving than the *fuqarā'*. This is the school of Abī Ḥanīfa and his followers. Al-Shāfiʿī thought that the *fuqarā'* were needier than the unfortunate because God said, "The boat belonged to some needy people" (18:79) and God mentioned the *fuqarā'* in his book, saying, "Alms are meant only for the poor, the needy" (9:60). And he gave precedence to the poor (*fuqarā'*), as the order in the book shows. The Almighty and All-powerful does not tell us that alms go to the blind and the infirm; instead we say, "For the chronically ill and the sick, their sickness is their storehouse."[19] As [Muḥammad] said, "It is not licit to give alms to a rich man, or to him who is perfect of form." Those alms are designated for the chronically ill and the sick, and otherwise the Qur'ān and the *ḥadīth* are flawed, for they say only "to the poor." And in the *Muwaṭṭa* of Mālik, the Prophet said, "Give to whomever asks, even if he is riding a horse,"and whoever has a horse is rich. This *ḥadīth* is [attributed to] Qabīṣa and others.

In general, *sunna* is very obscure, whether you admit it or not. Praise is to God alone, and may God bless and keep the last of the Prophets and his family and his Companions.

Commentary on Poems and Songs

The commentary and notes that follow give further detail about the poetic, religious, and linguistic dimensions of the poems in this collection. Many of Shushtarī's poems quote or allude to the Qur'ān or Ḥadīth, to earlier mystic poets, and to both formal and highly informal registers of secular Arabic poetry. Because the poet's unprecedented blending of disparate cultural, literary and religious references is central to his craft, these allusions are explored here. The reader will also find some explanations of Sufi technical terms (*iṣṭilaḥāt*) and concepts. Almost all of these technicisms are everyday words that have acquired additional layers of meaning when used in mystical contexts. These are glossed here with definitions taken from Shushtarī's own writings and from some of the well-known Sufi manuals, such as Abū Naṣr al-Sarrāj's *Kitāb al-Lumaʿ*, Qushayrī's *Risāla* and Kalābādhī's *Kitāb al-taʿarruf.* In any case, many of these poems are easily grasped and enjoyed as poetic compositions without this information, in part because Shushtarī targeted listeners unfamiliar with mystical hermeneutics.

An understanding of the multiple meanings conveyed by key vocabulary should aid the reader in apprehending the religious dimensions of the poems, especially those which on the surface seem worldly or perhaps even licentious. Rather than overburden the notes with copious detail on the technical aspects of the poetry—such as meter, rhyme schemes, or word play such as *tajnīs* (using two words with the same root letters but different meanings either in the same line or nearby in the poem)—these are limited to the relatively few cases in which such rhetorical flourishes contribute substantially to questions of interpretation. As with all poetry, many of the aesthetic pleasures of Shushtarī's songs are, sadly, untranslatable. As for the purely linguistic level, the dialecticisms and other features of the Andalusī idiom have been studied in detail by Corriente, thus my own comments on these issues will be brief.

1. Intoxicated by the Divine

How I began (*Dīwān* 339–40)

Line 1: *Dhikr*, literally recollection or remembrance. The Qur'an frequently enjoins Muslims to remember God, as in 33:41: "Believers, remember God often." For the Sufis, this meant the solitary or communal repetition of a word or phrase, such as the *shahāda* (profession of faith), "There is no god but God," or "Allah" or "Huwa [Him]." For an excellent brief introduction to Sufi approaches to *dhikr*, see Alexander Knysh, *Islamic Mysticism* (Leiden: Brill, 2000), 317–22.

9: The refrain "God forgives what is past" ("*ʿafā Allāhu ʿammā maḍā*," repeated in lines 18 and 26) is a paraphrase of Qur'ān 5:95: "God forgives what is past" ("*ʿafā Allāhu ʿammā salafa*").

17: The lightning flash, *barq* or *burayq*, was in traditional Arabic poetry a herald of rain as, for example, in this couplet of Imru al-Qays:

a-ṣāḥī tarā barqan urīka wamīḍahu	Look, that flash, now flickering there
ka-lamʿi l-yadayni fī ḥabīyin mukalli	like hands shot forth, in a towering cloud;
yuḍī'u sanāhu aw maṣābīha rāhibin	a shimmering light, like the lamp of a monk,
ahāna s-alīṭa li-dh-dhubāli l-mufattali.	fueled full for the twisted wick. (Translated by C. Greville Tuetey, 43)

Mystic poets borrowed the trope to symbolize mystical illumination, as in this example by Ibn al-Fāriḍ:

Is it a flash of lightning that shone over the mottled mountain,
  or do I see a lantern flickering in the hills of Nejd?
Or is that Laila of the Banū ʿAmir who unveiled her face at night,
  and converted the evening dusk into radiant dawn?
    (*Mystical Poems of Ibn al-Fāriḍ*, trans. A. J. Arberry
    [Dublin: Emery Walker, 1956, 34])

The idea of a sanctuary (*al-ḥimā*), a private, protected grazing area claimed by a ruler or tribal lord, dates back to pre-Islamic Arabia.

24: *Sādāt al-kirām*, the noble saints. This is a plural for the colloquial form *sīdī* used as an honorific before the names of saints, especially in the Maghreb.

Licit to drink? (*Dīwān* 35–36)

Line 1: *Fī al-khalwāt* can mean "in places of retirement or seclusion," but it also refers to the Sufi hermitages or retreats where Sufis might gather.

3: This line echoes a verse from Ibn al-Fāriḍ's famous wine-ode (*khamriyya*):

wa qālū: sharibta al-ithma. kalā wa innamā *sharibtu al-latī fī tarkihā ʿindī al-ithmu*	Then they said: "what you've drunk is sinful." "No, what I've drunk, in my view, would be sinful to shun." (*Dīwān*, 329, v. 33; translation mine)

Strikingly similar lines in the poetry of "bad boy" poets such as Abū Nuwās or Ibn Quzmān carry a far different meaning. For example,

lam qaṭṭ yabas lī min shārib *wa hadha huwa ʿindī baʿḍa-l-wājib* *wa man yaqul ʿannī innī tā'ib* *fa-hadhā shay lam yaqum fī bālī*	My moustache is never dry from it [wine] For me, it's like an obligation. Who says that I've repented? Why, that's never even occurred to me. (Ibn Quzmān, *Dīwān*, 164; translation is mine)

8: Mount Arafat is said to be where Muḥammad received his last revelation. As part of the Ḥajj, Muslims climb Mount Arafat and spend a day there in prayer. This is the high point (literally and figuratively) of the Pilgrimage.

9: The circumambulation (*al-ṭawāf*) of the Kaʿba in Mecca, done seven times, generally during the ḥajj or during the lesser pilgrimage or *ʿumra* which is optional and can be performed at any time of the year. *Saʿy* is the ritual of going back and forth between Ṣafā and Marwah seven times. This is done either during the *ḥajj* or the *ʿumra*. It is obligatory to do it upon arriving in Mecca and superogatory to perform once again when departing.

10: *Yulabbā* refers to the pilgrims' calling out "Labbayka" "Here we are, Lord," while performing various rituals associated with the *ḥajj*. *Yurmā bil-jamrāt*, the throwing of stones, forms part of the compulsory ritual of the *ḥajj* and symbolizes chasing away the devil.

11: *Dhikr*, see note 1, "How I began."

My art (*Dīwān* 276–77, Escorial 14v-15r, Yale 42v-43r)

Line 2: *Dhī al-malīḥ*, literally, the possessor of beauty, here, while clearly a reference to God also gestures to a rich tradition of profane poetry.

4: *Ḥaḍra*, which literally means "presence," is used by mystics to mean "being in the presence of God." The term also refers to ecstatic mystical gatherings.

9: *Madhhab* here refers to the schools of religious thought in Islam.

10: *Sharīʿa*: Although the word carries different meanings in different contexts, it generally refers to the rules and law codes governing the lives of Muslims, which are derived from the *Qur'ān* and *ḥadīth*. The study of *sharīʿa* is termed *fiqh*, whence the term *faqīh* for "jurist."

12: As Shushtarī repeats in the *Risāla al-Baghdādiyya*, a Sunni is simply one who follows the practice (*sunna*) of the Prophet and his Companions.

28: Literally the line reads "you are your own ephebe."

Timeless love (*Dīwān* 33)

Line 10: *Madhhab* is here rendered "path," in keeping with the poem's foregrounding of the personal. However, the original retains that tension between the idea of the traditional juridical schools and what Shushtarī offers: an amazing path of love.

14: *'Ahl*, literally "people," clearly referring to the "people of God," and, as I have rendered it here, to the idea that the mystical path is well traveled, that the believer is not alone on the path.

18: *Uhayl* (the diminutive of *Ahl*, "people"). The diminutive was a common feature of Andalusian Arabic, used to convey a range of meanings, from warmth and affection to dismissive disdain. I've translated it here as "dear ones." Najd is a frequent toponym in classical Arabic poetry.

Let go of Zayd and Mayya
(*Dīwān* 86–87, Escorial 16v–17r, Yale 45v)

Line 4: My essence (*dhātī*). Shushtarī defines *al-dhāt* as "unchanging reality" (*al-ḥaqīqa al-thābita*), (*'Ilmiyya* 164).

14: Zayd and Mayya are prototypical Arab lovers, the protagonists of many amorous verses, just as are Qays and Layla. To abandon him and her, Zayd and Mayya, is to give up the notion of duality and separateness that is inherent in any pair and to give up concern for worldly affairs.

17: The line might also be read as a series of adjectives, "wanton, a Shushtarī, unrepentant." The poetic "I" would be calling himself a follower of Shushtarī or an imitator of his ways. Corriente has expressed skepticism about the attribution of another poem with a similar reference. See *Poesía estrófica*, 19 n.1.

20: Draw near (*nuqbil*): the verb choice here echoes Qur'ān 28:31, when Moses recoils in fear after the staff he threw down at God's command turns into a snake and God calls out again: "Moses! **Draw near**! Do not be afraid, for you are one of those who are safe."

Many a cup (*Dīwān* 170–71, Escorial 34r–34v, Yale 34r–34v)

Line 5: Literally, "My throne encompasses my depths." This is an allusion to Qur'ān 2:255, a famously powerful description of the power and majesty of God: "God, there is no god but Him, the Ever Living, the Ever Watchful. Neither slumber nor sleep overtakes Him. All that is in the heavens and in the earth belongs to Him. Who is there that can intercede with Him except by His leave? He knows what is before them and what is behind them, but they do not comprehend any of His knowledge but what He wills. *His throne extends over the heavens and the earth*; it does not weary Him to preserve them both. He is the Most High, the Tremendous." This line and the one preceding it, attempt to communicate an unfathomable vastness.

9: I have chosen Escorial for my reading here—further supported by Yale Landberg (33r), Sprenger 1134 (18r), Wetzstein 195 (28r). Yale omits this stanza (lines 9–14) entirely. British Library 41r: reads "when I cast off sleep."

12: *Baʿd milk al-nās*, literally, "beyond what people possess." In common usage, applying the word *nās* to others often carries with it a certain elitism, verging on disdain for those who lack the wisdom or perspective of the speaker.

18: Strictly speaking, the word *dayr* refers to a Christian monastery. Monasteries were a common aspect of life in the medieval Islamic world, commonly serving as inns or taverns frequented by Muslims and Christians alike. When *dayr* refers to a place where drinkers gather, I have translated it "tavern," to demarcate it from instances in which the word *dayr* is used to refer to monasteries as places devoted to Christian worship; in those cases, I have translated it as monastery.

Wine from no wine press (*Dīwān* 139–40, Escorial 8v, continued on 9r after an interpolation, Yale 8v–9r)

Line 15: The Moroccan recensions of Shushtarī's *dīwān* here present a curious feature: two instances of Eastern dialectal usage: *bālak* in the sense of "beware," or "careful not to"; and *buwayḥ* meaning "loose-lipped," "overly talkative." The manuscripts written in an Eastern hand use instead the standard Arabic *iyāka* and *bawwāḥ*. The question, thus, is whether one or more early Eastern copyists "corrected" what had been an intentional interpolation of Eastern colloquial (perhaps to delight an Egyptian or Levantine audience with an Andalusian's appropriation of their local dialect). Or were the Moroccan manuscripts copied from Eastern manuscripts that had made a careless substitution?

At your service (*Dīwān* 101, Escorial 3v, Yale 3v)

Line 1: *Nuql,* literally candied almonds or nuts, sweets, dried fruits. The idea is a scene of leisurely indulgence.

8: *Iḥtisābī,* in the sense of something credited toward one's salvation. This usage is attested in the *ḥadīth*; see Wensinck, *Concordance,* 1:463–64.

11: *Ya huwa,* literally, "O Him," Him being a frequent way of referring to God, here translated "O Lord."

O perplexed heart! (*Dīwān* 174–76, Escorial 50r–51r, Yale 19r–20r)

Line 1: This intensely lyrical and intimate *muwashshaḥ* is marked by its many internal rhymes, spirited word play, and use of structured repetition. Although it utilizes a mostly classical diction, there are colloquialisms sprinkled throughout the poem.

5: The Eastern manuscripts read *kābid* (persist) rather than *kāna* (it was). I have chosen this reading over that given by Nashshār.

23: The idea that this wine has intoxicated others before echoes line 10 of "Ethereal wine."

39–40: As Ibn al-ʿArabī did in the *Tarjumān al-Ashwāq*, the poet here refers to passionate love, the love of Lubnā or Saʿada, as immortalized by the poets, or of whomever, as a pale reflection of divine love.

53–54: *Tafuz biha,* literally, "you will stumble across it" [the remains or traces of the lover] in the desert, marked with the sign "Here lies…" Thus the poet gestures allusively to the sorts of desert scenes common in the pre-Islamic odes that spoke precisely of the suffering lovers of Lubnā and others like her.

2. Love-crazed

Layla (*Dīwān* 81–82, Escorial 79r–79v, Yale 92v–93r)

Monorhyme *qaṣīda*, meter: *ramal*.

Line 1: *Shushtarī* plays here between *ḥayy*, "life," and *ḥayy*, "quarter" or "neighborhood." The line reads literally; "But for Layla, no life is seen in the neighborhood." The syntax of the second hemistich makes its meaning equivocal; "when in doubt, ask her about everything" is another plausible reading.

7: The suffering here is, of course, the suffering of the lover, an omnipresent motif in the poems of this section.

14: *Anthanā* could mean to incline, bow, turn away, or renounce. Each of these choices would result in vastly different readings. In my translation, the image is one of a Qays overcome with—perhaps stunned by—Layla's brilliance.

The torments of love (*Dīwān* 34–35, Escorial 63r, Yale 73v)

Monorhyme *qaṣīda*, meter: *ṭawīl*.

Line 2: The image here recalls schoolchildren reciting lessons written on a slate.

6: Cf. the saying attributed to Dhu 'l-Nūn that common men repent of sin (*al-dhunūb*) but the elect repent of forgetfulness (*al-ghafla*) (*Kitāb al-Lumaʿ*, 68).

Only love remains (*Dīwān* 35, Escorial 62r, Yale 72v)

Monorhyme *qaṣīda*, meter: *mujtathth*.

Line 2: That is, the heart can see what the eyes cannot.

4: The *ʿadhūl*, the naysayer or stern censurer, and the *raqīb*, the spy or guardian who breaks the lovers' secret, are the two quintessential obstacles faced by lovers in classical Arabic poetry.

My heart resides in the east (*Dīwān* 55–56, Yale 6r-6v)

Monorhyme *qaṣīda*, meter: *ramal.*

Line 5: The Arabic word for "east," *mashriq*, is derived from the verb *sharaqa*, "to rise" (sun) or "to shine," "radiate." The word for the west, *maghrib*, is derived from the verb *gharaba*, "to depart, withdraw," or in the case of the sun, "to set." Thus, the opposition here between east and west is one between illumination and darkness.

Before the morn (*Dīwān* 38)

Monorhyme *qaṣīda*, meter: *khafīf.*

Line 8: "My time (*waqtī*) is sweet": Sufi manuals contrast *waqt,* "instant" or "time" to "fixity" or "stability." Thus what is celebrated here is that fleeting ecstatic state that the mystic tries to make endure. Yet, Knysh reminds us that "*waqt* must not be understood as a temporal measure; it transcends measured and measurable time and can thus be seen as 'a unit of psychic measure' of this encounter, or of its absence. One can therefore describe *waqt* as a spiritual or psychological aspect of time" (Alexander D. Knysh, *Islamic Mysticism: A Short History* [Leiden: Brill, 2000], 305–6).

The Lover's Visit (*Dīwān* 89–91, Escorial 36v–37r, Yale 36v–37r)

Muwashshaḥ with Andalusian vernacular elements.

Line 4: *Raqīb,* "spy or censurer." A stock character in Arabic poetry whose aim is to prevent the lovers from meeting.

10: The printed *Dīwān* should read "*masarratī,*" joy or happiness, as per the manuscripts.

13: *Mishkātī*, my lamp, is an allusion to the celebrated verse of the Sūra of Light (Qur'ān 24:35): "God is the Light of the heavens and earth. His Light is like this: there is a niche, and in it is a lamp, the lamp inside a glass, a glass like a glittering star, fueled from a blessed olive tree from neither east nor west, whose oil almost gives light even when no fire touches it—light upon light—God guides whoever He will to his Light."

19–20: The speech of the birds takes on a religious dimension, for they not only are perched on "pulpits," but rather than sing, they preach or lecture (*takhtatib*).

47: Intimacy or joy (*uns*) is one of the mystical states. Abū Naṣr al-Sarrāj defines *uns* as relying on God, resting in God and turning to God for help. Ibrāhīm al-Mārastānī defines it as the heart's joy in the Beloved (*Kitāb al-Lumaʿ*, 96, 97).

Robbed of my senses (*Dīwān* 282–84, Escorial 3r–3v, Yale 3r–3v)

Zajal, in classical Arabic with numerous dialectalicisms.

While the previous poem spoke of losing oneself in mystical wine, here the beloved is portrayed as a thief who steals the lover's heart and even his ability to perceive himself. But the bulk of the poem is didactic, explaining the importance of humility and poverty and the need to shut out the voices of those who don't understand.

Line 41: This very catchy line (*ʿishqu-l-malīḥ yā ṣāḥ fannī* wa *shurbī min dannī*) closely echoes the refrain of "My art," found in Chapter 1.

My lover is beyond compare (*Dīwān* 94–96, Escorial 70v–71r, Yale 81r–82r)

Muwashshaḥ with numerous dialectal features.

This poem is discussed at some length in my article "Reading the Mystical Signs."

Line 1: Literally, "my lover (or beloved) has no second." This is at once a boast of the incomparability of the lover and an affirmation of monotheism.

5: "I am content in the Creator" (or pleased with the Creator) echoes the injunction in Qur'ānic verse 89:27: "Return to your Lord well pleased and well pleasing."

16: The edited text here reads *wa naqrā sirra maktūbī fī ṣūrati-l-ʿuqūd* that is, "I read the secret written for me in the image of the covenant(s)." Many manuscripts—including Escorial and Yale—read instead *sūrati-l-ʿuqūd,* that is, the Qur'anic *sūra al-ʿUqūd*. While there is no sūra by that name (hence the corruption in multiple copies of the text), the word *ʿuqūd* appears only once in the Qur'ān, in the first line of *Sūrat al-Mā'ida*, a sūra that focuses on obligations incumbent on the believer, yet also stresses, in language echoed by line 17 here, "Today the good things are permitted you"(5:5).

3. Denudatio/Stripping Bare

Burning all discernment (*Dīwān* 63–64, Escorial 66v–67r, Yale 77v–78r)

Monorhyme *qaṣīda,* meter: *basīṭ*.

Line 1b: *Mahabbatikum*, "your love." This poem is unusual for Shushtarī in that it employs the second person plural throughout, rather than the singular.

5c: The secret of the letters: It is unclear whether or not Shushtarī actively sought to uncover divine mysteries using esoteric techniques to decipher the occult meaning of letters. In the poem "The letters of His name," his meditation on the forms of the letters that spell Allah becomes the basis for devotion.

5d: *Look towards the mountain.* When Moses asked to see God, He replied: "You will never see Me, but *look at that mountain*: if it remains standing firm, you will see Me"(Qur'ān 7:143).

8a: *ʿAraftumūkum,* "You know Yourself." This is a prime example of how the poet at times destroys standard syntax, making a transitive verb reflexive in a way that is linguistically unnatural yet, at the same time, remains intelligible.

8b: *Al-khabīr* is the expert or experienced one, but it is also one of the names of God, the Knowing.

9c–d: An allusion to Qur'ān 21:37: "Man was created hasty: I will show you my signs soon, so do not ask Me to hasten them."

10c–d: The image of the moth burned in the flame harkens back to a *ḥadīth, al-farāsh al-mutahāfit* (see Wensinck, *Concordance*, 5:110.) As al-Ḥallāj explains the image, "the light of the flame is the knowledge of reality (*ʿilm al-ḥaqīqa*), the heat of flame is the reality of the reality (*ḥāqīqat-al-ḥaqīqa*) and union with [the flame] is the truth of reality (*ḥaqq al-ḥaqīqa*). [The moth] is satisfied neither with the light nor the heat, he flings himself into the flame completely" (al-Ḥallāj, *Dīwān*, 95). For a French translation, see Louis Massignon, *La passion de Hallaj*, 3:307. The English translation here is mine.)

Leaving my land (*Dīwān* 332–34, Escorial 38v–39v, Yale 38v–39v)

Muwashshaḥ in classical Arabic.

Nashshār notes that in one manuscript (British Library 9255) this poem is ascribed to Ibn al-Khatīb, the fourteenth-century Andalusian polymath known, among other things, for moving evocations of his homeland from which he was exiled.

The rank of the poor (*Dīwān* 64–65, Escorial 76r, Yale 86v–87r)

Monorhyme *qaṣīda*, meter: *munsariḥ*.

That the poor will enter heaven before the rich or more easily than the rich is an idea shared by both Muslims and Christians. One can cite numerous passages in the New Testament to this effect: "Blessed are the poor in spirit: for theirs is the kingdom of heaven" (Matt 5:3). "Hearken, my beloved brethren, Hath not God chosen the poor of this world rich in faith, and heirs of the kingdom which he hath promised to them that love him?" (Jas 2:5). Or, perhaps most famously, "Go to now, ye rich men, weep and howl for your miseries that shall come upon you" (Jas 5:1). And "It is harder for the rich man…" (Matt 19:16ff.; Mark 10:17ff.; and Luke 18:18ff.).

In Muslim tradition the idea of the precedence of the poor is made explicit in numerous *ḥadīth,* including one sacred tradition (*ḥadīth qudsī*). According to this *ḥadīth*, held to record a saying of the Prophet that had been revealed to him by God, "the Messenger of Allah (peace be upon him) said: Paradise and Hell-fire disputed together, and Hell-fire said: In me are the mighty and the haughty. Paradise said: In me are the weak and the poor. So Allah judged between them, [saying]:

You are Paradise, My mercy; through you I show mercy to those I wish. And you are Hell-fire, My punishment; through you I punish those I wish, and it is incumbent upon Me that each of you shall have its fill."In the "Baghdad Treatise," Shushtarī claims that the poor will enter heaven half a day before the rich, clarifying that he speaks of "the days of next world,"which are beyond calculation.

Line 1: The poem begins with the declaration of the existence of a nation or people of poverty. By the mid-thirteenth century, Sufism was becoming a thriving movement, no longer the province of small groups of visionaries, ascetics, and dissidents.

3: For the *ḥadīth* concerning the ordering of the ranks entering heaven, see Wensinck 5:187.

8: *Qisma*: A part or allotment. It can also refer to one's destiny or fate as foreordained by God. The lines here play on both senses of the word.

Purify the houses of God (*Dīwān* 57, Escorial 67r, Yale 78r)

Monorhyme *qaṣīda*, meter: *ṭawīl.*

Line 2: This is an allusion to the Qur'ān 20:10 and 28:29, which speak of how Moses saw fire on the mountain and told his people to remain while he went to seek guidance from it. The same motif appears in Shushtarī's poem "Is that a lamp?"

3: Literally, "there is no house but the heart."

Borrowed goods (*Dīwān* 192–94, Yale 61r–61v)

Zajal.

Line 1: I have translated "doesn't understand the signs"very colloquially here to match the extremely informal diction of the poem.

Poverty and riches (*Dīwān* 68–69, Escorial 63r–64v, Yale 73v–74r)

Monorhyme *qaṣīda*, meter: *mutaqārib.*

The seventeenth-century Syrian Sufi poet and scholar ʿAbd al-Ghānī al-Nābulusī glossed this poem in a *mukhammas*, a strophic poetic form that added lines matching the meter and rhyme of the base poem to form strophes of five lines (Nābulusī, *Dīwān al-Ḥaqā'iq* [Damascus: ʿAbd al-Wakīl al-Durūbī, 1968], 141–42). It is unclear whether the mistaken attribution of the base poem to Abū al-Ḥasan al-Shādhilī comes from al-Nābulusī himself, the compiler of his *dīwān,* or the modern editor of the volume.

Let go of delusions (*Dīwān* 112–14, Escorial 49r–49v, Yale 17v–18r)

Zajal with many colloquial Andalusian features.

Line 4: Faqrī, "poverty," here echoes the insistent theme of "Poor like me" that poverty, understood as the shedding of all attachments to the material world, is the natural condition of man.

20–22: The critique of the circularity of reason seen here is greatly elaborated in the *Nūniyya*, presented in the final chapter of this book.

Riding away (*Dīwān* 98–100, Escorial 2r–3r, Yale 2r–3r)

Zajal with abundant colloquial features including some Egyptian expressions.

Line 44: *Jawz al-ʿajā'ibī*. Nashshār suggests that this could simply mean "peanuts"; however, he cites a line of classical verse that suggests the word may already have a metaphorical association with empty words.

4. Among the Sufis

Little *shaykh* of Meknes (*Dīwān* 272–75, Escorial 76v–77v, Yale 90r–91v)

Zajal with a mix of dialectal features.

This is perhaps one of Shushtarī's most widely known poems; bits of it are found scattered in many later songbooks. Moroccan Sufis today are likely to mention (or even sing) this song when the poet's name is mentioned. Yet this popularity has rendered the poem one of the most problematic of those included in this collection. Most of the manuscript *dīwāns*—even the earliest ones—have several very dubious strophes that appear to have been appended by another author. I have chosen to omit those lines from the main body of the poem and reproduce them here because in both spirit and subject matter they seem at odds with the rest of the poet's work.

This is how he went about
praising Muḥammad.
and asking for blessings on his vizir,
Abu Bakr the illustrious,
and ʿUmar, who spoke the truth,
and the martyr of all martyrs.

And ʿAlī annihilator of the filthy ones,
the awesome striker.
What care have I for others?
What care have they for me?

O my God, I beg you
grant me repentance
By the Prophet, I ask of you
and by the Blessed Ones.
The devil did his work on me
and I was embroiled with him.

The devil filled my heart
with what he wished for me.

What care have I for others?
  What care have they for me?

So ends the description of the little *shaykh*
  in poetic symbols
And verily I am one of the elite and I recite
  my greetings to the fans of my art.
If you'll allow me,
  I'll repeat my opening words:

Little *shaykh* from Meknes
  wanders the souks and sings:
What care have I for others?
  What care have they for me?

The doubts about these final strophes arise from both structural and thematic issues. First, self-conscious or metapoetical references to the singer or the artistry of the poem are frequently used as a device to signal the end of the poem. Thus the lines that introduce the presumably final refrain, "those whose spirit is sweet/can forgive the singer" (lines 51–52 of the poem on page 76) mark the end of this poem. This alone calls attention to the subsequent verses, especially in a *zajal* that greatly exceeds the length of most of Shushtarī's *zajals*. Furthermore, the invocation of the Prophet and the early caliphs (lines 55–64) is atypical of Shushtarī, but it is a common feature of later Sufi poetry and song. Further doubt is cast upon these lines by the description of ʿAlī as "the annihilator of the filthy ones," a reference to ʿAlī's valor in the battle against the Jews of Khaybar. Such a hateful line is incongruous with Shushtarī's philosophy, which he repeats in nearly every one of his compositions, that is, that God is manifest in all of creation. Furthermore, the references to the devil (*al-rajīm*, *al-waswās*) and his power over the speaker (69–72) are completely anomalous. The poem, as recorded in several early *dīwāns*, employs a mixture of colloquial dialects, suggesting scribal additions or changes. The Escorial manuscript uses *shuwaykh*, the diminutive of *shaykh*, and *Ash* as an interrogative. By contrast, the Yale manuscript refers to *shaykh*, and uses *īsh* as an interrogative.

Line 1: In Arabic, *shaykh* literally means "old man." While the term is often used to refer to revered personages, from the master of a Sufi order to an elder or tribal chief, here the term appears to refer to an elderly ascetic, possibly viewed as an eccentric by many of those people (*nās*) whose judgment he disdains.

3–4: A more colloquial English translation might read: What do I care what people think of me? What do they care what I think of them?

25–30: These verses echo in the third person what the old man said in the previous verse. This sort of repetition from a slightly different perspective is a typical feature of popular storytelling and oral literatures.

In my heart so near (*Dīwān* 87–89, Escorial 74r–74v, Yale 84r–85r)

Zajal with a mix of Andalusian dialectal and classical Arabic features.

This relatively short *zajal* is marked by the insistent repetition that characterizes the opening of each of the refrains (*markaz*), echoing the repetition in the opening verse, "Allah, Allah" (God, O God), a verse that is then repeated in the second line of each refrain. Thus the poem alternates between a series of commands: "Let me speak," "Listen," "Witness" and "Enter," and an exposition of the power of God's love and the rewards for the truly faithful.

Remembrance of God (*Dīwān* 351)

Monorhyme song or chant with no clear meter.

This song is marked by its insistent repetition, closing each line with "Allah/God." Whether or not this piece was actually composed by Shushtarī—and the fact that it is missing from the most reliable sources for his poetry points to a false attribution—it is emblematic of much of the apocryphal material attributed to him. Those poems tend to be simpler and more repetitious, often with repeated chants of "Allah, Allah, Allah," and far more likely to include pious—and quite formulaic—references to the Prophet, his family, and his Companions.

Line 27: The "best of the messengers" is a reference to Muḥammad and Aḥmad (derived from the same root ḥ-m-d, with the meaning "most worthy of praise") is one of the names of the Prophet.

Shirts and caps (*Dīwān* 245–46)

Zajal in Andalusian vernacular Arabic.

The distinctive clothing worn by many Sufis is a frequent theme in Shushtarī's poetry and the subject of the Baghdad Treatise (included herein) in which he defended it against accusations that it was an innovation (*bidaʿ*) or even worse, a flagrant ostentation of one's piety. Here the subject is treated in the form of a dialogue between a suffering Sufi disciple, impatient to find contentment, and his teacher, who stresses poverty, emblematized in the characteristic dress of the Sufis.

Line 1: *Khirqa* is a Sufi robe of investiture, often made of patchwork, traditionally presented by a master to a disciple. In many cases this would mean that this disciple could in turn present a *khirqa* to future disciples and thus preserve a body of knowledge or devotional practice and extend a chain of spiritual authority. The word derives from the root *kh-r-q*, associated with the notion of tearing or rending (fabric).

2: The *shāshiyya* is a kind of cap worn by North Africans in the Middle Ages. That this particular item of clothing is not mentioned in the *Baghdad Treatise*, which examines and defends Sufi dress rather systematically, raises some questions about the certainty of attribution of this poem, found only in a handful of Moroccan manuscripts.

4: *Khalwa*, here rendered "seclusion," can mean a place for religious retreat. In North Africa, *zāwiyas* became walled-off centers for mystical communities, including a mosque, Qur'ān school, and the tomb of the order's founder. The full development of the institution of the *zāwiya* comes in the fourteenth century, casting additional doubt on Shushtarī's authorship of this poem.

7: The four schools: the four juridical schools in Sunni Islam—Ḥanafī, Mālikī, Shāfiʿī, and Hanbalī—which, insofar as they are concerned with exoteric religious practice, are here placed in contrast to the esoterism of the mystics.

8: The most distinguished station (*al-maqām al-akramā*) here clearly intends to signal a worldly station of prestige and honor among men, a station that entails wearing haughty robes. This is precisely what the *shaykh* then warns against.

Poor like me / By God, natural (*Dīwān* 184–90, Escorial 25v–27r, Yale 55v–57v)

Zajal in Andalusian vernacular.

As this poem repeats its insistent refrain, *maṭbūʿ maṭbūʿ* (rendered here as "natural"), it explores the myriad meanings and associations of its root, *ṭabaʿa*, which literally means "to stamp"or "to seal," but in the passive voice has the meaning of having a natural aptitude or propensity, or a natural disposition.

Line 4: *Sharshuh*: According to Nashshār, this is a knapsack hung from a stick. The line actually says it is *fī ʿunquh* ("on his neck"), which gives an image of the stick resting on the neck/shoulder area.

28: *Muwallah*: One of the attributes of the lovers of God in Shushtarī's verse, meaning giddy, distracted, madly in love.

48: *Ṭarjahāra*, a word of Persian origin, which R. P. A. Dozy lists as an "espèce de plateau ou d'assiette" (Supplement Aux Dictionairies Arabes, 2 vols. [1881; Beirut: Libraire deu Liban, 1981], 2:30). Nashshār notes that in Eastern usage the word denotes a musical instrument similar to the oud.

5. Deciphering the Signs of God

Just understand me (*Dīwān* 176–80, Yale 62r–64r)

Zajal with Andalusian dialectal features.

Line 44: Presence, *ḥaḍra*, is used by mystics to refer to being in the presence of God. It is paired with absence, *ghayba*, in the sense of being absent from everything but God.

53–57: These lines move from an abstract treatment of the mystical imperative to the concrete invitation to join with the community of mystics. *Al-rijāl*, literally "the men," here refers to the members of the Sufi order. In this context *Al-ḥadra* is a Sufi gathering for *dhikhr* and *samā'*. The clothing of perfection is the garb of the Sufi. *Busuṭ*, "carpets," is derived from *basuṭa*, "to spread," "to unfurl," or "to unroll." In its intransitive form, *basuṭa*, the verb means "to be simple, open-hearted, or frank," qualities which Shushtarī, in other poems, more explicitly links to the perfection of the Sufi.

59: *Dhawq* in common usage means "taste," such as for food. By extension, just as in English, it can refer to aesthetic or literary sensibilities, and Sufis use it to refer to the mystical senses, to insight, or to intuitive perception.

66: Several of Shushtarī's poems move toward their conclusion with a similar line, *khudh 'annī*, "take or accept from me," an expression that echoes the "believe what I am saying" meaning of the colloquial English expression "take it from me." The Arabic has other layers, however: "follow my example," "adopt my method." The line here reads *takhudhū* (the colloquial form of the plural imperative) *mimman sharṭ* that is, "follow the example of the one who placed the condition," referring to the condition set forth in the previous line.

69: *Aḥwāl al-rijāl*, literally, "the states of men," here the ecstatic states of the mystics that he warns—as do many other Sufis—are not ends in themselves. For those states themselves will ultimately be annihilated in the divine.

I translated an illegible letter (*Dīwān* 277–80, Escorial 44v–45v, Yale 13v–14v)

Zajal with some Andalusian dialectal features.

Line 1: The verb *tarjama* can mean to translate from one language to another, but it also can mean to comment upon something. Here, the poet seems to speak of the aporia of the mystic, the inability to render in human language truths that lie beyond it.

3: "The dot of *ba*": *Ba* is the second letter of the Arabic alphabet but also the consonant for the preposition *bi*, which defines a variety of relationships, from instrumentality, innerness, and the direction of motion. It is a preposition that Shushtarī repeats in some poems to emphasize the complete dependence of creation on the Creator. See especially, "My lover is beyond compare."

4: The rank of *alif* would then define an upward motion, to the first letter of the alphabet, which is also the first letter in Allah.

14: This difficult and ambiguous expression echoes an oath found in the Qur'ān, "by the even and the odd" (89:3). As Abdel Haleem explains in a footnote to his translation of the Qur'ān, "this has been interpreted in many ways: as a reference to numbers (as translated here); or e.g. as the multiple (God's creation) and the One (God himself)" (*The Qur'an*, trans. M. A. Abdel Haleem [Oxford: Oxford University Press, 2004], 420). Shushtarī uses similar expressions in a number of his poems, often suggesting some sort of paradox.

46: "In the midst of gloom and blindness" (*mā bayn ʿabas wa ʿammā*): The line makes sense read at its surface level—that confusion about the Names of God and the deep hermeneutical questions raised in attempting to reconcile strict monotheism with the idea of God's multiple names and attributes—however, the fact that *ʿabas* is the first word of Sūra 78 ("The Announcement") and *ʿammā* is the first word of Sūra 80 ("He frowned") suggests the possibility of additional readings. Both Sūra 78 and Sūra 79 (the two Sūras between those two words) speak of judgment day, and while the fulfillments of Paradise are mentioned here, the severity of God's judgment against the transgressors is described in much more vivid detail.

The letters of His name (*Dīwān* 243–44, Escorial 20r–20v, Yale 48v–49v)

Zajal with a few Andalusian dialectal features.

The idea of seeking meaning in the letters of the name Allah is not a new one (see *Kitāb al-Lumaʿ*, 125). Nashshār claims that this poem is often recited in Syria during Ramadan. The poem was commented on by Ibn ʿAjība.

Line 4: When *Lām* comes at the end of a word, it takes on a distinctive form ل, this is a form that many medieval copyists took special delight in highlighting and elongating. Here, Shushtarī calls the two *Lāms* in the middle of the word Allah incorporeal, partly because the word initial or medial form of *Lam* is rather unassuming: لـ, but also, of course, to highlight that God himself is incorporeal, beyond place.

11: Shrouded: This might seem like an odd choice here, but remember that the soul is on its way to oblivion. According to Nashshār's commentary, the heart will be placed between two coffins that represent mortality and spirituality or concrete and abstract or the divine Omnipotence and wisdom. When the person loses hope and lusts, he is wrapped in two garments; one of them is a garment of light, and the other is a garment of darkness.

14–17: Nashshār asserts that here Shushtarī maintains that he is the radiant guide of his era, claiming the great sainthood, or the Great Axis of his time. I find it hard to agree with such a conclusion. Shushtarī's radical monism is incompatible with claims to *personal* sanctity and superiority over other mystics. While he certainly vigorously defended the superiority of his views over those of other mystics, philosophers and jurists (see, for example the *Nūniyya*, in which he undertakes a systematic critique of many of his predecessors), I find nothing in any of his writings that would support Nashshār's interpretation.

Master of illusion (*Dīwān* 141–45, Escorial 58v–59v, Yale 28v–29v)

Muwashshaḥ in classical Arabic.

Line 9: "The universe was there to Him even before He made it": Given the heated controversy in Islam surrounding the question of the eternity or createdness of the universe, a debate that often pitted philosophers (arguing for the eternity of the world) against theologians (arguing the contrary), this seems to be a way of bridging the difference.

31–32: This is a variation on the metaphor of the stars seeming bright until the vastly brighter sun comes into view (see "Riding away," lines 37–38). The beauty and appeal of icy water seems insignificant when compared to the source.

51: The line is ambiguous, the pronoun (*hā*) seems to refer to remembering "the string"(*khuyūṭ*), that is, man's complete dependence on God. *Dhikr*, of course, signifies both memory or recollection and invocation, as in the specialized Sufi use of the term.

57–58: I understand this to mean that divine revelation gives man the tools to "read" the veils.

Don't say He forgot you (*Dīwān* 203–04, Escorial 55v–56r, Yale 24v–25v)

Muwashshaḥ, mostly in classical Arabic.

Lines 1–4: These lines echo the opening line of "The night's journey."

31–34: These lines highlight the question of predestination, which is a frequent theme in Shushtarī's poetry. The poetic treatment of the subject affords quite a lot of interpretative latitude.

39: Literally, "Don't hope except in God," a construction that parallels the profession of faith, "there is no god but God."

I'm a sight to see (*Dīwān* 266–68, Escorial 46r–46v, Yale 14v–15r)

Muwashshaḥ, in classical Arabic with some dialectal features.

Line 1: The Arabic here, *laqad anā shayun ʿajīb liman rānī*, is quite playfully polysemic. *ʿAjīb* ranges in meaning from "wonderful, marvelous, or astonishing" to "strange or odd."

34: "The seven *mathānī*" are traditionally understood to refer to the *fātiḥa*, the opening Sūra of the Qur'ān, thus, the seven oft-recited verses. (I borrow the translation from Abdel Haleem.) See Qur'ān 15:87: "We have given you the seven oft-recited verses and the whole glorious Qur'ān."

I sang to the moon (*Dīwān* 147–49, Escorial 17r–18r, Yale 45v–46v)

This *zajal*-like *muwashshaḥ* employs a highly colloquial and informal diction throughout. The effect is especially pronounced in the very informal asides to himself.

Line 1: The opening line announces the highly informal register and constant verbal play that characterize this poem. The use of the vocative *ya* with the first person is contrary to the logic of the language; the destabilizing effect is intensified with the following second person *aysh khabarak*, which could be translated, "what's happening?" "what's up?" If in the first hemistich Shushtarī breaks conventions regarding prepositions, rendering directional prepositions almost maddeningly circular, in the second hemistich it is conventions of person. Thus from the very first line, I and you, human and divine are confused and the poem jumps back and forth between declarations made by God to those more appropriate to God's creatures. For this reason, in this poem I have opted to make no attempt to reduce the ambiguity through the use of capitalization.

43–44: Another example of Shushtarī's proclamation of the apparently counterintuitive idea that focusing on the search for God will not lead to God.

47: "The names": The Names of God.

51–54: The *kharja* of this poem is borrowed from Ibn Zaydūn (1003–71) and is repeated in "In my heart's eye."

Breaking the talisman (*Dīwān* 46–47, Escorial 76r–76v, Yale 87r)

Monorhyme *qaṣīda*, meter: *sarīʿ*.

Line 1: Here it would seem that Shushtarī is using talisman in the same sense that Ibn al-ʿArabī does when he says: "hence everything given power to rule is a talisman, as long as it keep its ruling power. One kind of talisman has power to rule over the rational faculties. It is the strongest of talismans, since it does not let the rational faculties accept from the divine reports and the prophetic sciences of unveiling anything except that which can come under their interpretation (*ta'wīl*) and the weighing of their scale" (Chittick, *Sufi Path of Knowledge*, 184). The word appears in several other poems by Shushtarī and in its verbal form in a letter cited by Ibn al-Khaṭīb, "*Kanz al-wujūd al-ladhī ṭallasamahu al-insān*" (*Iḥāṭa*, 4:214).

4: An allusion to Qur'ān 74:50–51, which describes how the unbelievers turn away from the Prophet's warnings "like frightened asses fleeing from a lion."

5: *al-ḥusnā'*: I have translated this as the Beautiful Ones, that is, the ninety-nine names of God; however the word could also mean the planet Venus. The word play continues in the remainder of the line. The luminous seven here could refer to the seven verses of the *fātiḥa* (the opening sūra of the Qur'ān) or the seven planets.

7: Literally, he loosened, untied the lock of the names. The biggest problem posed by this poem is understanding whom or what Shushtarī is calling *khalīfa al-ḥaqq*, that is, the caliph of God.

In my heart's eye (*Dīwān* 150–51, Escorial 40v–41r, Yale 41r–41v)

Muwashshaḥ in classical Arabic.

This short poem is also included in Zarrūq's *Sharḥ al-Naṣīḥa al-Kāfiya* (MS 3024 Alexandria). It repeats the same *kharja* taken from Ibn Zaydūn that is found at the end of "I sang to the moon."

Line 24: "He wants to test you": This idea is frequently expressed in the Qur'ān, for example, Qur'ān 5:49 "If God had so willed, He would have made you one community, but He wanted to test you through that which He has given you."

Hidden in plain sight (*Dīwān* 134–36, Escorial 51r–52r, Yale 20r–20v)

Muwashshaḥ with occasional dialectal features.

Line 9: Literally: "One with no second," echoing the phrasing in "My lover is beyond compare."

23: *Al-'ayn:* "the where" or place.

25: *Iqtaṣar*, from the root *q-ṣ-r*, "to be short or limited," here could mean something on the order of "suit yourself," "restrict or limit yourself." Given that Shushtarī's poems frequently feature injunctions to stop making excuses or protesting his advice, I understand it in that vein.

27–34: This series of rhetorical questions, which I believe the poet means to dismiss, are contrasted with the understanding and discernment of the sensible one, who follows the road of truth.

Stop tiring yourself (*Dīwān* 105–08, Escorial 34v–35v, Yale 34v–35v)

Muwashshaḥ in classical Arabic with occasional Andalusian dialectal features.

While the opening line of each refrain features a repetition much like that seen in "In my heart so near," this is a deeply enigmatic poem, with rapid shifts in voice and perspective that constantly destabilize the reader.

6. Desert Wanderings

The night's journey (*Dīwān* 50, Escorial 63v, Yale 74r)

Monorhyme *qaṣīda*, meter: *ramal.*

Line 4: This verse is a paraphrase of the Arabic proverb *ʿinda al-ṣabāh yaḥmadu al-qawm al-surā* (at daybreak, the party commend night-journeying), often directed to someone enduring difficulties, urging patience. Of course, for the mystics the night journey (*surā* or *isrā*) refers both to Muḥammad's night journey from Mecca to Jerusalem and from there to heaven and back again (Qur'ān 17:1, 60, 53:1–18) and, by extension to the spiritual journey of every seeker.

When lightning flashes (*Dīwān* 45–46, Escorial 75v–76r, Yale 86r)

Monorhyme *qaṣīda*, meter: *munsariḥ.*

Line 1: *Ḥimā* is a frequent topos in the desert ode. As a common noun, it means a sanctuary. In pre-Islamic Arabia the *ḥimā* was an inviolable space protected by tribal deities.

1–2: The word play between *shāma*, (to watch for, to be on the lookout, to hope or expect) and *sha'ma* (to take something as an evil sign or bad omen) evokes both the anxious scanning of the skies and possible misreading of the brilliant flash of light.

4–5: That blinding light is quickly linked through the disorientation and perplexity that it provokes to the mystical wine carried by the cupbearer.

8: The equivocal *al-kibār* (great ones), frequently refers to great or eminent men, but in this context of drunkenness should likely be read as "great sins."

9: This wine, once tasted, leaves the drinker with no choice but to persist in his "wantonness."

10: The builder of the wall appears to be a reference to al-Khiḍr (also known as al-Khaḍir). This is the name commonly associated with the unnamed figure in Qur'ān 18:60–82 who meets Moses and then tests his patience by performing a series of odd and initially inexplicable actions, including repairing the wall of a town that had refused them both hospitality. At the end of their meeting, the stranger tells Moses the meaning of the things he had not been able to bear patiently. Among Sufi mystics, al-Khiḍhr is seen as a prototypical *shaykh* or teacher who leads the student from bewilderment to understanding.

11–13: The mystical understanding brings about a paradigm shift, a radically new perception, here exemplified in the reassessment of the story of Qays and Layla. The story of the love-mad Qays, who wandered through the desert anguished at his separation from Layla, is a frequent theme in Arabic and Persian poetry and *adab*. Shushtarī closes a number of poems with references to this tale, always showing how the popular understanding of the tale distorts or misreads its deeper meaning. Here he claims that Qays' madness was not brought on by Layla's departure, for she never left him. He fails to perceive her through her veil, but even more surprising, and the true sign of his madness, is that when she reveals herself to him, he, perhaps worried about maintaining appearances or too wrapped up in the petty morality of others, calls it a disgrace.

Pay no attention (*Dīwān* 48-49, Escorial 75v–76r, Yale 86v)

Monorhyme *qaṣīda*, meter: *sarīʿ*.

According to al-Ghubrīnī (240), Shushtarī composed this poem shortly after arriving in Gabes (Qābis), a Tunisian coastal city, and stopping at a Sufi lodge (*ribāṭ*) known as the Ṣahrīj Mosque. A lofty delegation headed by Abū Isḥāq al-Warqānī and Abū ʿAbd Allah al-Ṣanhājī came to visit him and found that he had gone on an errand that had taken him out of town. They hadn't waited long before he arrived, greeted everyone, kissed the Sufis, and with a tear running down his cheek, asked for writing implements, and with moans that by themselves moved the audience, he wrote these lines.

Line 2: These are all common tropes of the Arabian *qaṣīda*, illusions the poet warns against. The insistent repetition of the interrogative or exclamatory particle *mā* (which translated literally would read "what [is] a flock, what [is] a ban tree") gives the line a dramatic quality. The ban tree, which grows tall and slender, is often used as a simile for an attractive beloved. Laʿlaʿ is a place name, but it can also mean glimmer or mirage. In his commentary on the poems of *Tarjumān al-Ashwāq*, Ibn al-ʿArabī calls this a mystic station of bewilderment or perplexity and infatuation (*tawalluʿ*). Khayf, another toponym, refers to the slope or the peak of a mountain and has come to be associated with Mina. The gazelle of Bani Amr can be read as a reference to Layla, the beloved of Qays.

6: "The first and the last"are two of the beautiful Names of God, widely used in a Sufi context to refer to all of the ninety-nine Names of God because as opposite attributes they synthesize all of the (apparent) contradictions in the essence of God. These two attributes are also coupled with *ẓāhir* and *bāṭin*, that is, the manifest and the hidden.

But you *are* in the Najd (*Dīwān* 65)

Monorhyme *qaṣīda*, meter: *basīṭ*.

Ibn al-Khaṭīb attributes this poem to Ibn Sabʿīn (*Iḥāṭa*, 2:37). It is not found in the Eastern recensions of Shushtarī's *dīwān*.

Line 3: This line suggests a reply (or a partial reply) to the fifth poem in Ibn al-ʿArabī's *Tarjumān al-Ashwāq*, "*Anjada al-shawq wa athama al-ghurām*." In Michael Sells's translation, the first line reads:

Yearning sought the highlands.
Heartbreak sought the plain.
I was trapped somewhere in between
Najd and Tihām. (*Stations of Desire*, 60)

The Najd, or the uplands, are the plateau region lying to the east of al-Tihāma, the Red Sea lowlands. Shushtarī can't seem to resist the verbal play between the topographical designation, al-Tihāma and *muttaham*, (suspected, suspicious), derived from the root *w-h-m*, which is related to ideas of delusion, conjecture, and self-deception.

4: This verse echoes the opening line of "Layla."

Desire drives the camels (*Dīwān* 49, Escorial 64r, Yale 74v)

Monorhyme *qaṣīda*, meter: *kāmil.*

Line 3: Salʿ is a hill in the marketplace of, or a spot near, Medina; Yāqūt, 5:107.

5: Al-ʿAqīq (literally, "the ravine") here refers to a location near Medina (Yāqūt, 4:199). The lines recall verses of Ibn al-Fāriḍ, here translated by Arberry:

By God, if you pass by al-ʿAqīq in the forenoon, recite a
greeting to them, and that unaffectedly,
And say, "I left behind me, struck down among your
dwellings, one living, and yet as if dead, that lends
sickness even to sickness' self."

(*Mystical poems of Ibn al-Fāriḍ* [Dublin: Emery Walker, 1956], 95; I have modified Arberry's translation)

6: "Earth stands in for water" refers to the dispensation granted for ablutions, which can be performed with sand or soil when water is unavailable. (Qur'ān 5:6).

Drop all pretense of shame (*Dīwān* 38–39, Escorial 63v–64r, Yale 74r–74v)

Monorhyme *qaṣīda*, meter: *khafīf.*

Line 1: Here the poet alludes to the rich poetic tradition that describes the weariness and emaciation of the camels after an arduous journey. He sees no need to repeat those tropes, compare with these lines of Ibn al-Fāriḍ:

> Ease the pace of your journey, O camel driver,
> truly it is upon my heart that you are driving.
> Don't you see how the red-roan camels hunger and thirst,
> urged on and yearning for the Spring of the grassy encampments?
> The deserts have not left any body to them at all,
> save skin stretched over protruding bones;
> and their pads have become attenuated,
> and they march chafed like glowing coals on ashes.
> Weariness has emaciated them. (Arberry, *Mystical Poems of Ibn al-Fāriḍ*, 39; I have modified Arberry's translation)

7: *Asfār* (sing. *safar*), which I have translated as "wandering," also plays on *asfār* (sing. *sifr*), which means "books," especially the scriptures.

8: *Mizmār* is a musical reed or pipe, here translated "flute."

12: Sabʿīnī, that is, a follower of Ibn Sabʿīn. *Ṣaḥwa* is associated with the notion of wakefulness, clarity, serenity, and recovering from drunkenness. *Miḍmār* is a richly suggestive word here; while the noun commonly denotes a fixed space for an athletic activity, a race course, or an arena, the word is etymologically linked to notions as diverse as weight loss, hiding something away, stripping someone in the sight of others (such as while washing a cadaver), thinking to oneself, or undertaking some course of action with great assiduousness and zeal. The final phrase is thus remarkably polysemic. Does it refer to a clarity that follows the mystic's erasure of self? Or perhaps to that state of heightened consciousness that leads to a more zealous observance? Or a greater awareness of what is innermost?

If the scold could see (*Dīwān* 41)

Monorhyme *qaṣīda*, meter: *kāmil.*

When Moses performed miracles and brought God's clear signs to his people, they mocked him and called the signs conjuring tricks. In the Qur'an, the disbelief and mockery that Moses encountered prefigures the resistance that Muḥammad encounters to his message. Shushtarī draws here on the same story, alluding to Qur'an 28:36.

7. At the Monastery

Is that a lamp? (*Dīwān* 41–44, Yale 93r–94v, Escorial 79b)

Monorhyme *qaṣīda*, meter: *ṭawīl*

Line 3: The first enigma is that the bright glow is not constant; it is visible at night, brilliant even, but then it disappears. The travelers are confused as to its nature. This back and forth, the idea that the spiritual quest is not linear, is repeated in several different ways: In the sobriety after the obliteration (line 15), and in the ebb and flow in the waves of the great ocean of knowledge (line 32).

5: The polyvalence of the word *zujāj* is fully at play here. At root is the meaning of glass and its clarity. The word can refer to a glass bottle or a glass candle holder as well as to a drinking glass.

6: Literally, "by what is due the Messiah."

7: Seth: The third son of Adam and Eve, the ancestor of all humankind, for his older brothers, Cain and Abel, left no progeny. Although he is not mentioned in the Qur'an, there is quite a lot about him in the *Qiṣāṣ anbiyā* literature. One story about Seth that ties him to a journey is that his father had fallen ill and sent Seth to Mount Sinai to ask God for some olives and oil from Paradise.

10: The travelers accept the hospitality of the monastery, aware that this may lead to criticism or insults from those who find this improper. This can be read on several different levels, for example, that it is improper for Muslims to drink at all, or that partaking of wine with sacramental value—as is clearly implied—is an improper action between Christians and Muslims.

11: This difficult and ambiguous expression echoes an oath found in the Qur'ān, "by the even and the odd" (89:3). As Abdel Haleem explains, "This has been interpreted in many ways: as a reference to numbers (as translated here); or, for example, as the multiple (God's creation) and the One (God himself)" (420). Shushtarī uses similar expressions in a number of his poems, often suggesting some sort of paradox.

12: *Tajawharnā* can be translated "to become substance," but given *jawhar's* meaning as "essence, substance."

15: Literally, Shushtarī's chest tightened or contracted.

16: This is likely a reference to Abū Bakr ibn al-ʿArabī (d.543/1148), a leading *faqīh* of his era and—at least for a time—an admirer and imitator of al-Ghazālī's writings. See Maribel Fierro, "Opposition to Sufism in al-Andalus," in *Islamic Mysticism Contested: Thirteen Centuries of Controversies and Polemics*, eds. Frederick de Jong and Bernd Radtke (Leiden: Brill, 1999), 185.

17: That is, *faqīh* and *faqīr* become united, undistinguishable. The division between the exoteric knowledge of the law and esoteric practice is erased. *Fakka min al-qahr*, release from subjugation, compulsion, coercion, sorrow or grief. Some manuscripts read instead *fakka min al-qabr,* or release from the grave.

22: *Al-kalīm* here clearly refers to Moses, known in Islamic tradition as kalīm Allah or the one who spoke with God (or to whom spoke God). This is an allusion to Qur'ān 20:10 and 28:29, which speak of how Moses saw fire on the mountain and told his people to remain while he went to seek guidance from it. The same motif appears in Shushtarī's poem "Purify the houses of God,"24.

24: Reference to Qur'ān 20:12: a frequent Sufi trope, see *Khalʿ al-Naʿlayn* Ibn Qasī (twelfth-century). Ibn Qasī is remembered principally as the leader of a Sufi revolt against the Almoravids (see Goodrich, "A Sufi Revolt in Portugal"). Ibn Qasī's writings continued to exert some influence in al-Andalus in the following century: Ibn al-ʿArabi wrote a commentary on *Khalʿ al-Nalayn*, and Shushtarī makes numerous references to him as well.

25: It is not entirely clear to what the pronoun *huwa* here is referring.

26: Although Shushtarī's exact meaning is unclear, he appears to use the term *talisman* in a similar sense to that employed by Ibn al-ʿArabī, as practices or objects that hold power or control over human beings and prevent them from perceiving the fullness of reality.

Ṣabgha has several meanings here. In the context of a discussion of Christian sacramental theology, "baptism" is a key meaning, here described as the breaking of or breaking with lowness, shame, ignominy, and disgrace. Of course, for Christians, baptism represents the washing away of original sin, a breaking of the punishment imposed on man because of Adam. But the word also has meanings related to alchemy, and here it seems that this language of talismans and magic is being used to explore man's access to knowledge.

30: *Tajrīd* comes from a root that means "to peel, remove a shell, to peel away, to strip or denude."

31: The root *ḥ b r* and its many meanings: pope, a learned man among the Christians or the Jews, or learned men.

34: Grammatical imagery.

37: *Iftiqāruhu*, his impoverishment, that is, his abandonment of the material for a spiritual path.

The monastery door (*Dīwān* 58, Yale 76b, Escorial 65B)

Line 1: *Ta'addab bi-bāb al-dayr: ta'addab* (imperative form), can mean "to educate oneself" or "to be guided." Here, the crossing of the threshold into the monastery symbolizes also a submission to the discipline (*ta'dīb*) and an openness to the customs of the monks.

8: Religious icons being such a point of contention between Muslims and Christians—especially the orthodox Christians that Shushtarī would have encountered in the Levant—the reminder that the church the pilgrim will enter contains images of Jesus fashioned by the monks highlights the unusual nature of this poem.

8. The Nūniyya

Although this poem is not collected in the Eastern recensions of the *Dīwān*, it is widely known in the West, reproduced by Ibn al-Khaṭīb (713/1313–776/1375) in two of his works: *Rawdat al-taʿrīf* (ed. Aḥmad Ata, 606–10, ed. Kettanī 609–13) and the Iḥāta, 4:208–11. The Moroccan Sufi leaders Aḥmad Zarrūq and Ibn ʿAjība both wrote extensive commentaries on the poem.

Line 1: This line alludes to Qur'ān 10:26: "Those who did well will have the best reward and more besides." Ibn ʿAjiba writes: "The best reward is not heaven, which is understood (*fassirat*) as the best reward." "The something more" mentioned in the Qur'ānic verse is gazing with an everlasting vision (or knowledge) on the countenance of God (al-Karīm). An ever-rising ascent. So their desire was to grasp their high aspirations and lift them completely out of the cosmos, for heaven belongs to the cosmos. For he who in his heart departs from this world (*al-dunya*), seeking paradise and its embellishments, has simply left one world for another. He is like a donkey pulling a millstone; he cannot get away from it. Ibn ʿAjība cites a similar verse of Ibn al-Fāriḍ.

3: In his commentary, Ibn ʿAjība lists three levels of "pleasures of the low places," pleasures that bring no contentment to those with higher aspirations. These are bodily pleasures, such as food, drink, and women; pleasures of the heart, such as the love of money, power, rank, and praise; and spiritual pleasures, such as the desire for miracles and grace for pious deeds.

"Distant purpose," *Al-maqṣid al-aqṣā*, means Paradise, and "the most brilliant quest," the presence of God.

11: "The most perfect of men": Muḥammad.

18: "The banners on the right": Sūra 56: "That which is coming, vividly depicts how people will be divided on judgment day. The people on the right will enjoy God's reward, while those on the left will be subject to torment."

19: *ʿiqāl min al-ʿaql*: literally, the binding-cord of reason. Shushtarī seems to suggest that even at a linguistic level there is an association between reason and binding.

40: Hermes (*Hirmis*) is held to be the author of a large body of philosophical, theological, and magical texts. A large number of Arabic texts have also been attributed to Hermes (for details and bibliography, see "Hirmis" in *Encyclopedia of Islam*, 2nd ed. (Leiden: E.J. Brill, 1954–).

On Islamic ideas about Socrates, including the idea that he lived in a barrel in the desert, see Ilai Alon, *Socrates in Medieval Arabic Literature* (Leiden: Brill, 1991).

43: Dhū al-Qarnayn, literally, "the two-horned one," is discussed in the Qur'ān 18:82–98. Most scholars hold that this refers to Alexander the Great, who in many versions of his tales is said to have gone on a quest for the spring of eternal youth. There is an extensive bibliography on this figure, his portrayal in the Qur'ān and other sources and his interpretation by commentators (see Brannon Wheeler, "Moses or Alexander? Early Islamic Exegesis of Qur'ān 18:60–65," *Journal of Near Eastern Studies* 57 [1998]).

45: Ḥusayn ibn Manṣur al-Ḥallāj (244/857–309/922), an influential and polarizing figure in the history of Islamic mysticism, without a doubt one of Shushtarī's most important influences. Yet, Shushtarī criticizes him on several occasions for his failure to conceal his mystical rapture (and the ecstatic utterances that are popularly held to have led to his execution as a heretic). Although recent scholarship has superceded some of the details of Massignon's work, *The Passion of al-Hallaj* (Princeton, NJ: Princeton University Press, 1982) is still an indispensable reference.

47: Abū Bakr al-Shiblī (247/861–334/945): a student of al-Junayd, also associated with al-Ḥallāj (although he is said to have denied him before the vizier and accused him at the foot of the scaffold). Known for eccentric behavior, ecstatic utterances, and extravagant claims about his powers. Many poems are attributed to him. See *Dīwān Abī Bakr al-Shiblī*, ed. Muwaffiq Fawzī al-Jabr (Damascus: Dār Batrā, 1999).

48: Al-Niffarī, Muḥammad ibn ʿAbd al-Jabbār, d. 366/976–7: Sufi mystic of Iraq. His works, *The Book of Spiritual Stayings [or Standings] (Kitāb al mawāqif)* and *The Book of Spiritual Addresses* (*Kitāb al-mukhtabāt*) are marked by the influence of al-Ḥallāj. See the translation by A. J. Arberry. His work was later commented by Ibn al-ʿArabī. According to Chittick, seventy-eight chapters of the *Futuḥāt al-Makkiyya*—5 percent of this massive text—are devoted to this commentary (William Chittick, *Sufism: A Short Introduction* [Oxford:

One World, 2000], 144). His work was also commented by ʿAfīf al-Dīn al-Tilimsānī (see *Sharḥ al-Mawāqif,* ed. Jamāl Aḥmad Marzūqī [Cairo: Markaz al-Maḥrūsa, 1997]).

50: Ibn Jinnī (d. 392–1002): noted grammarian credited with inventing the science of etymology. Ibn ʿAjība quotes Zarrūq as saying that he wrote a book called *Tajrīd Khalq al-Insān* on grammar and logic. His explanation of this line is that the vastness of the subject matter led to Ibn Jinnī's silence.

51: Qaḍīb al-Bān: Mystic of Mosul, known for changing his appearance (from Kurd, to Bedouin, to doctor of theology). See R. A. Nicholson, *The Mystics of Islam* (New York: Schocken, 1975), 144–45.

52: Abū ʿAbd Allah al-Shūdhī, also known as al-Ḥalwī: said to be a Sufi from Seville, a teacher of Ibn Sabʿīn. Although his name surfaces occasionally, little is known about him. See Muḥammad ibn Muḥammad Ibn Maryam, *Al-Bustān fī dhikr al-awliyā' wa-al-ʿulamā' bi-Tilimsān* (Algiers: Dīwān al-Maṭbūʿāt al-Jāmʿiyya, 1986), 68–70; and Abū al-Wafā al-Ghunaymī al-Taftāzānī, "Al-Madrasa al-Shūdhiyya fī al-taṣawwuf al-andalusī," *Revista del Instituto Egipcio de Estudios Islámicos* 23 (1985). Ibn ʿAjība's identification of him with ʿAfīf al-Tilimsānī (d.1291) is highly improbable.

54: Ibn Qasī (d. 546/1151): leader of the anti-Almoravid revolt and a member of the Almeria school of Sufism, author of *Khalaʿ al-Naʿlayn.* This work was later commented by Ibn al-ʿArabī (see Goodrich, *A Sufi Revolt in Portugal).*

55: Ibn Masarra (269/883–319/931): Andalusian philosopher and mystic born in Córdoba. A pivotal figure in the development of Andalusian Sufism. He lived during a period of time in which the Mālikī *fuqahā'* of Spain actively persecuted those deemed heterodox. He is credited with writing two books, *Kitāb al-tabṣira* and *Kitāb al-ḥurūf,* neither of which is extant (see Miguel Asín Palacios, *The Mystical Philosophy of Ibn Masarra and His Followers,* trans. Elmer H. Douglas and Howard W. Yoder [Leiden: Brill, 1978]).

56: Ibn Sīnā (d.1111): towering Islamic philosopher, held by many also to have some mystical inclinations, known in Europe as Avicenna.

57: Abū Ḥamid al-Ghazālī Al-Tūsī (1058–1111): noted theologian, mystic and religious reformer, called the Proof of Islam (*Ḥujjat al-Islām*). An especially controversial figure in al-Andalus, where alliances were made and sundered based on one's support or opposition to his famous mystical work, *The Revival of the Religious Sciences* (*Iḥyā ʿUlūm al-Dīn*). Before his turn to Sufism, he had eagerly pursued philosophy, an approach he later rejected in his book *The Incoherence of the Philosophers* (*Tahāfut al-falāsifa*).

58: Ibn Ṭufayl (d.1185 or 1186): prominent Andalusian physician and philosopher—like Shushtarī, a native of Guadix—author of celebrated philosophical allegory *Ḥayy ibn Yaqẓān.*

59: Abū Madyan Al-Shuʿayb (1126–98): Andalusian mystic, born near Seville. After studying with several masters in North Africa and in the East, he eventually settled in Bougie (Bijāya, a seaport in modern Algeria). Although few of his writings survive, he continues to be held in high esteem as one of the great figures of Andalusian and North African Sufism. Shushtarī may have been a disciple of his for a time (see Cornell, *The Way of Abū Madyan).*

60–61: Muḥyi al-Dīn Ibn al-ʿArabī (al-Tayy): The appellation "spirit of the Spirit"comes from several lines of verse in his "Kitāb al-Isrā illā maqām al-asrā" in *Rasā'il Ibn ʿArabī* (Beirut: Dār Ṣādir, 1997), 171–235; this poem, 173). Shushtarī wrote a type of poetic gloss, called a *mukhammis*, on those lines. The bibliography on this figure is immense. A good starting point is Claude Addas, *Quest for the Red Sulphur: The Life of Ibn Arabi* (Cambridge: Islamic Texts Society, 1993).

62: Ibn al-Fāriḍ (1181–1235): one of the most renowned Sufi poets writing in Arabic. For a translation of much of his work, see E. Homerin, trans., *ʿUmar Ibn al-Fāriḍ* (New York: Paulist Press, 2001).

63: Abū al-Ḥasan al-Harrālī (d.1240): A Moroccan Sufi, the author of *Kitāb miftāḥ al-bāb al-muqfal* [Book of the key to the locked door] (BN Paris, MS 1398). Paul Nwyia calls him a writer with a difficult style, who creates a new language. See *Ibn 'Aṭā' Allāh et la naissance de la confrérie shādhilite* (Beirut: Dar el-Machreq, 1972), 56–62.

64: Al-Umawī: This obscure figure was unknown to both Zarrūq and Ibn ʿAjība. Zarrūq claims to have heard of him but cannot add any details. Massignon identifies him—giving no indication as to how he came to his conclusion—as Shaykh ʿAdī ibn Musāfir (d.~1162), who established a *zāwiya* for his followers, the ʿAdawiyya, in Qarafa in Cairo (see Massignon, "Ibn Sabʿīn et la "conspiration ḥallāgienne," 667).

65: Al-Ghāfiqī, that is: Ibn Sabʿīn, Shushtarī's most influential spiritual master.

NOTES

PART ONE: Praising God in the Language of Everyday Life

1. Ganjavi Niẓāmī, *The Story of Layla and Majnun,* trans. Rudolf Gelpke (Boulder, CO: Shambhala, 1978), 13.

2. Peter J. Chelkowski, "Niẓāmī." *Encyclopedia of Islam. CD-ROM edition* (Leiden: Brill, 1999).

3. The most complete account of Shushtarī's life and reception is in Nashshār's introduction to his edition of the poet's *dīwān*, ʿAlī Sāmī al-Nashshār, ed., *Dīwān Abī al-Ḥasan al-Shushtarī* (Alexandria: Dār al-Maʿārif, 1960). The Spanish linguist Federico Corriente, who by his own admission is primarily concerned with Shushtarī as a rich primary source for a philological study of medieval Andalusian Arabic, published an edition of the poet's *dīwān* in Latin transliteration with a literal Spanish translation, *Poesia estrófica: céjeles y/o muwaššaḥāt* (Madrid: CSIC, 1988). Bibliography on Shushtarī in European languages is limited; see also Ali Sami El-Nashar, "Abul Hasan al-Sustari místico andaluz y autor de zejeles y su influencia en el mundo musulmán," *Revista del Instituto Egipcio de Estudios Islámicos* 1.1 (1953); Louis Massignon, "Investigaciones sobre Šuštarī, poeta andaluz enterrado en Damieta," *al-Andalus* 14 (1949); René Perez, "Le dépoillement (tajrîd) dans le cheminement spirituel d'Abû l'Hassan al-Shushtari," *al-Tawāṣul al-Ṣūfī bayna misr wa al-maghrib*, ed. ʿAbd al-Jawād al-Saqqāt (Rabat: Jāmiʿat al-Ḥasan al-Thānī, 2000); Omaima Abou-Bakr, "The Symbolic Function of Metaphor in Medieval Sufi Poetry: The Case of Shushtari," *Alif* 12 (1992); Maribel Fierro, "al-Shushtarī," *Encyclopedia of Islam*, ed. C.E. Bosworth (1996); and Lourdes Alvarez, "The Mystical Language of Daily Life: The Arabic Vernacular Songs of Abū al-Ḥasan al-Shushtarī." *Exemplaria* 17:1(2005), and "Reading the Mystical Signs in the Songs of Abū al-Ḥasan al-Shushtarī" in *Muwashshaḥāt: Proceedings of the International Conference on Arabic and Hebrew Strophic Poetry and Its Romance Parallels, School of Oriental and African Studies, London, 8-10 October 2004* (London: RNR Books and School of Oriental and

African Studies, Music Department, forthcoming). Arthur Wormhoudt's "translations" of Shushtarī (*Selections from the Diwan of Abu al-Hasan ʿAli Ibn Abd Allah al-Shushtari,* (Oskaloosa, IA: William Penn College, 1992) are best described as idiosyncratic.

4. Ibn al-ʿArabī's *muwashshaḥāt* are scattered throughout the published versions of his *Dīwān* (Dār al-Kutub al-ʿIlmiyya, 1996). Federico Corriente and Ed Emery are currently preparing a monograph on these strophic poems.

5. Massignon, "Investigaciones sobre Šuštarī," 35.

6. Shushtarī's *Nūniyya* was commented by Aḥmad Zarrūq (Escorial MS 40186) and Ibn ʿAjība, "Sharḥ Nūniyya al-Imām al-Shushtarī," *Silsilāt Nūrāniyya farīda.* ed. al-ʿImrānī al-Khālidī ʿAbd al-Salām. (Maktabat al-Rashād, 1997). The qaṣīda *Ta'addab bi-bāb al-dayr* (presented here as "At the Monastery Door") was commented by ʿAbd al-Ghanī al-Nābulusī, "Radd al-Muftarī ʿan al-ṭaʿan fī al-Shushtarī," *al-Mashriq* 54 (1960): 629–39.

7. Aḥmad ibn ʿAbd al-Ḥalīm Ibn Taymīyah, *Majmūʿat al-rasā'il wa-al-masā'il*, ed. Muḥammad Rashīd Riḍā. 4 vols. ([Cairo]: Lajnat al-Turāth al-ʿArabī, 1976), I: 67.

8. See Lisān al-Dīn Ibn al-Khaṭīb, *Dīwān Lisān al-Dīn ibn al-Khaṭīb*, ed. Muḥammad Miftāḥ (Casablanca: Dār al-Thaqāfah lil-Nashr wa-al-Tawẓī, 1989). This volume has only nine of his *muwashshaḥāt*, pp. 783–96. Additional examples can be found scattered in other writings and in his own anthology of *muwashshaḥāt*, *Jaysh al-Tawshīh*, ed. Alan Jones (Cambridge, England: Trustees of the E.J.W. Gibb Memorial, 1997).

9. Muḥammad ibn Ibrahīm Ibn ʿAbbād, *al-Rasā'il al-kubrā.* ([Fez]: Matbaʿat al-ʿArabī al-Arzaq, 1902), 197.

10. Ibn Khaldun, *The Muqaddimah: An Introduction to History*, ed. and trans. Franz Rosenthal, 2d ed., 3 vols. (Princeton, NJ: Princeton University Press, 1967).

11. Although the last couple of decades have seen several new Arabic language monographs on Ibn Sabʿīn, he has still not received much attention from Western scholars. See V. J. Cornell, "The Way of the Axial Intellect: The Islamic Hermeticism of Ibn Sabʿīn." *Journal of the Muhyiddin Ibn Arabi Society* (1997): 41-79. Louis Massignon's "Ibn Sab`īn et la conspiration antihallegienne en Andalousie et en Orient du XIIIe siècle," *Études d'orientalisme dédiées à la mémoire de Lévi-Provençal*, vol. 2 (Paris: G.-P. Maisonneuve et Larose, 1962) remains useful, although it is marked by Massignon's tendency to exaggerate the importance of al-Ḥallāj. For useful excerpts from various

biographical accounts, as well as a translation of one of the philosopher's concise expositions of his thought, see M. A. F. Mehren, "Correspondance du philosophe Soufi Ibn Sab'în ʿAbd Oul-Haqq avec l'empereur Frédéric II de Hohenstaufen," *Journal Asiatique* 14 (7th series) (1879).

12. Aḥmad ibn Muḥammad al-Maqqarī, *Nafḥ al-Ṭīb min ghuṣn al-Andalus al-raṭīb*, ed. Iḥsān ʿAbbās, 8 vols. (Beirut: Dār Ṣādir, 1968), 2:185.

13. Al-Ghubrīnī, *ʿUnwān al-dirāya* (Beirut: Lajnat al-taʿlīf wa-l-tarjama wa-l-nashr, 1969), 239. [This translation and all other unattributed translations of Arabic sources are my own.]

14. This borrowing was first pointed out by Massignon. See his "Investigaciones," 30–31. See Ramon Llull, *Llibre de Evariste e Blanquerna* (Barcelona: Barcino, 1935), 2:238. English translation here is that of Allison Peers, *Blanquerna: A Thirteenth Century Romance* (London: Jarrolds, 1926), 392.

15. Abū ʿAbd Allah Muḥammad ibn al-Ḥusayn al-Ḥā'ik, *Kunnāsh al-Hā'ik*, ed. ʿAbbās al-Jarrārī (Rabat: Matbūʿāt Akādīmiyya al-Mamlaka al-Maghribiyya, 1999), 45.

16. Some noteworthy recordings include Ihsan Rmiki and Ensemble al-Jūd, *Al-Samâa: audition spirituelle extatique* (Institut du Monde Arabe, 2004); Amina Alaoui and Ahmad Piro et son orchestre, *Gharnati* (Auvidis France, 1995); Cofradía al-Shushtari and Omar Metioui, *Dhikr Y Samáʿ: Canto religioso de la Cofradía Sufi-Andalusí al-Shushtari* (Pneuma, 1999); Omar Metioui and Cofradía al-Harraqiyya, *Misticismo: Música sufí andalusí, cantos místicos de la Cofradía Al-Harraqiyya* (Pneuma, 2000); and Omar Metioui and Mohamed Mehdi Temsamani, *Ritual sufi-andalusi* (Sony Spain, 1998).

17. The show *al-Mūsīqā wa-l-Samāʿ al-Ṣūfī ʿabra al-ʿālam* [Sufi music and *samāʿ* around the world] is broadcast on Medi 1, which can be heard throughout Morocco, Algeria, Tunisia, Mauritania, parts of Libya, and southern Europe. Complete audio archives of the program are available on the Internet at http://www.medi1.com/musique/soufi.php. This particular quotation comes from the show entitled "Poete Soufi: Abou H. Chouchtari."

18. It should be noted that the errors in the 1960 *Dīwān* came about during the typesetting process and do not reflect Nashshār's actual reading of the manuscripts. Comparing the printed *Dīwān* with Nashshār's dissertation (Cambridge, 1951)—which cannot be reproduced because there is no signed permission to do so on file at Cambridge—one can find dozens of instances in which the dissertation correctly reflects the manuscript sources, while the published edition does not.

19. Corriente's book is clearly aimed at non-Arab specialists in Arabic linguistics rather than at a general Arab readership. Aside from the problems inherent in fixing the stress pattern and vowelling of the poems, it should also be noted that reading Arabic transliterated into another writing system presents a cognitive challenge that detracts from the pleasure of the text.

20. There is a break in the Escorial manuscript corresponding to over fourteen poems. Comparing the order of poems in that manuscript with Yale, Sprenger 1134, Yale Landberg, it is clear that all these copies come from a common source, but the Escorial manuscript shuffled sections (each run of poems follows an identical order, however) and omitted one. Nothing about the omitted section would lead one to believe that the omission was intentional.

21. The manuscripts used are listed in the bibliography.

22. Nashshār divides the collection into five sections, each of which he numbers separately: (1) Monorhyme poetry (*qaṣīdas* and *muqaṭṭaʿāt*), designated in the notes by Q followed by Nashshār's numbering; (2) strophic poetry (*muwashshaḥāt and zajals*) of reasonably certain attribution, designated in the notes by an M and Nashshār's number; (3) strophic poetry about which some doubt has been raised by a scribe or copyist, designated by *M; (4) strophic poems found in a series of Moroccan manuscripts that Nashshār calls the *Dīwān Saghīr* or Minor Dīwān, designated by DS; and (5) poetic fragments from the *Minor Dīwān*. None of these is included in the current volume.

23. However, modern American popular musical culture provides many examples of songs in which a voice speaking an exaggerated standard diction is juxtaposed with—and clearly mocked by—another voice speaking in the slang of inner-city youth or rappers.

24. The standard work on the rise of the Sufi brotherhoods remains J. Spencer Trimingham, *The Sufi Orders in Islam*, 2d ed. (Oxford: Oxford University Press, 1998).

25. Abū al-Ḥasan al-Shushtarī, *Al-Risāla al-Shushtariyya aw Al-Risāla al-ʿIlmiyya*, abridged by Ibn Luyūn (Casablanca: Dār al-Thaqāfa, 2004), 139. Curiously, at another point in the treatise, in what may well be an editorial note by Ibn Luyūn—for the use of the term *fuqarāʾ* is otherwise absolutely invariable—he says the *fuqarāʾ al-mutajarradūn* are "now called *qalandariyya*"(138).

26. Asín Palacios's efforts to tie the later development of Andalusian Sufism with the "school of Ibn Masarra" (*The Mystical Philosophy of Ibn Masarra and His Followers*, trans. by Elmer H. Douglas and Howard W. Yoder. [Leiden: Brill, 1978]) have been discredited by later scholars. The dis-

covery of authentic works by Ibn Masarra further calls into question many of Asín's conclusions. See S. M. Stern, "Ibn Masarra, Follower of Pseudo-Empedocles, an Illusion,"in *Medieval Arabic and Hebrew Thought*, ed. F. W. Zimmermann (London: Variorum Reprints, 1983).

27. For a helpful approach to some of the questions surrounding the early development of Sufism in al-Andalus, see Maria Isabel Fierro, "The Polemic about the Karāmāt al-awliyā' and the Development of Sufism in al-Andalus (4th–10th/5th–11th centuries)," *Bulletin of the School for Oriental and African Studies* 55 (1992).

28. See Ibn al-ʿArīf, *Maḥāsin al-Majālis*, ed. and trans. Miguel Asín Palacios (Paris: Librairie Orientaliste Paul Geuthner, 1933), 4. Only one work of Ibn Barrajān survives: see *Sarḥ asmā' allah Al-ḥusnā = Comentario sobre los nombres más bellos de Dios*, ed. Purificación de la Torre (Madrid: Consejo Superior de Investigaciones Científicas; Agencia Española de Cooperación Internacional, 2000).

29. See J. Dreher, "L'imamat d'Ibn Qasi à Mértola (automne 1144-été 1145): Légitimité d'une domination soufie?" *Mélanges* (Institut Dominicain d'Études Orientales du Caire) 18 (1988); D. R. Goodrich, "A Sufi Revolt in Portugal: Ibn Qasi and His Kitab *Khal' al-na'layn*"(PhD diss., Columbia University, 1978).

30. Ambrosio Huici Miranda, *Historia política del imperio almohade* (Tetuan: Editora Marroquí, 1956).

31. For example, in his preface to his edition of *al-Risāla al-ʿIlmiyya*, Muḥammad al-ʿAdlūnī al-Idrīsī writes that Shushtarī's first trip to the Maghreb was "definitely" to Meknes, as evidenced by the poem (p. 13). Massignon, in "Investigaciones sobre Shushtarī,"voices reservations about the ascribing any historical significance to the rhyme in "Maknās." (p. 33). Massignon does infer biographical details from certain other poems, but his inferences are usually supported by other historical sources.

32. Rachel Arié, *España musulmana (siglos VIII-XV)* (Barcelona: Labor, 1984), 35.

33. Aḥmad ibn Aḥmad al-Ghubrīnī, *ʿUnwān al-dirāyah* (Beirut: Lajnat al-taʿlīf wa-l-tarjama wa-l-nashr, 1969), 239–42.

34. Al-Maqqarī, *Nafḥ al-Ṭīb*, 2:185.

35. As Gerhard Endress explains, the word *ṭīna* is rich in religious and philosophical associations. The word appears in the Qur'ān as the matter that God infuses with life, for example, "He [God] is the one who created you from clay (ṭīn) (6: 2). The term also appears in Ibn Tufayl's *Ḥayy ibn Yaqẓān* as the

primordial stuff from which the protagonist Ḥayy was spontaneously generated. "Ṭīna,"*Encyclopedia of Islam, CD-ROM edition* (Leiden: Brill, 1999).

36. Abū ʿUthmān Ibn Luyūn al-Tujībī, *al-Risāla al-Shushtariyya, aw al-Risāla al-ʿIlmiyya fī al-taṣawwuf*, ed. Muḥammad al-ʿAdlūnī al-Idrīsī (Casablanca: Dār al-Thaqāfa, 2004). The biography supplied by Ibn Luyūn in introducing his abridgement of Shushtarī's treatise forms the basis for Lisān al-Dīn Ibn al-Khaṭīb's account in *al-Iḥāṭa fī akhbār Gharnāṭa*, ed. Muḥammad ʿAbd Allah ʿInān (Cairo: Maktabat al-Khanjī, 1973), 4: 205–16, and that of al-Maqqarī, *Nafḥ al-Ṭīb*, 2:185–87.

37. On the importance of Almería as a Sufi center dating back to the time of Ibn Masarra, see Asín Palacios, ed. and trans., *Mahāsin al-Majālis* by Ibn al-ʿArīf (Paris: Librairie Orientaliste Paul Geuthner, 1933), 3.

38. Ibn Luyūn mentions that one of these followers of Suhrawardī was the *qāḍī* Muḥyī al-dīn Abī al-Qāsim Muḥammad Ibn Ibrahīm Ibn Ḥusayn Ibn Sarāqa al-Ansārī al-Shātibī (that is, from Jativa), *Al-Risāla al-ʿIlmiyya*, 43.

39. Ibn Luyūn, *Al-Risāla al-ʿIlmiyya*, 53.

40. Al-Ghubrīnī, *ʿUnwān al-dirāya*, 239.

41. According to ʿAsqalanī, after his break with Ibn Sabʿīn the poet followed a now-forgotten figure by the name of Abū Isḥāq Ibrahīm ibn ʿAbīdīs.

42. Ibn ʿAjība, "Sharḥ li-Nūniyyya al-imām al-Shushtarī." In *Silsilāt Nūrāniyya farīda* (n.p.: Maktabat al-Rashād, 1997), 9.

43. Further doubt on the question of a rift is cast by a manuscript containing the writings of Shushtarī's student, Abū Yaqub Ibn Abī al-Ḥasan Ibn Mubashshir. Yale Arabic Mss Supplement 104 contains Shushtarī's *al-Risāla al-Miʿrājiyya*, as well as three treatises of Ibn al-Mubashshir that make frequent reference to both Shushtarī and his teacher. In a number of writings, that refer to both Ibn Sabʿīn and Shushtarī using the honorifics reserved for the dead, Ibn Mubashshir speaks of them with extreme reverence, quoting extensively from both. The manuscript also contains two works by Ibn al-ʿArabī, *Risāla al-talāwa* and *Kitāb al-isrā'*.

44. Alexander D. Knysh, *Ibn ʿArabī in the Later Islamic Tradition* (Albany: State University of New York Press, 1999), 2.

45. Shuʿayb ibn al-Ḥusayn al-Anṣārī Abū Madyan, *The Way of Abū Madyan: Doctrinal and Poetic Works of Abū Madyan Shuʿayb*, ed. and trans. Vincent Cornell (Cambridge, UK: Islamic Texts Society, 1996), 4-5.

46. Passages found throughout seem to be paraphrases or direct quotations from Sarrāj's tenth-century manual of Sufism. For example, Shushtarī's glossary of mystical expressions ("fī al-alfāẓ al-dā'ira baynahum,"chapter 10

of the *Risāla al-ʿIlmiyya*, 159–71) is an abridged version of Sarrāj's glossary ("bāb bayān hadhihi-l-alfāẓ," 411–56)

47. The *Kitāb al-Isrā'* can be found in *Rasā'il Ibn ʿArabī,* intro. Maḥmūd Maḥmūd al-Ghurāb (Beirut: Dār Ṣādir, 1997), 173. Shushtarī's *takhmīs*, not included in this volume, can be found in the *Dīwān*, 244–46.

48. See Gerald T. Elmore, "Ibn al-'Arabi's 'cinquain' (takhmis) on a poem by Abu Madyan,"*Arabica* 46 (1998).

49. See Th. Emil Homerin, *From Arab Poet to Muslim Saint: Ibn al-Fāriḍ, His Verse, and His Shrine* (Columbia: University of South Carolina, 1994); and ʿUmar ibn ʿAlī Ibn al-Fāriḍ, *ʿUmar ibn al-Fāriḍ: Sufi Verse, Saintly Life*, trans. Th. Emil Homerin (New York: Paulist Press, 2000).

50. Like Ibn al-ʿArabī, who wrote a commentary on Ibn Qāsī's *Khalaʿ Naʿlayn [The Shedding of the Sandals*], Shushtarī makes frequent allusions to Ibn Qāsī's work, mentioning him by name in the *Nūniyya.*

51. On Niffarī, see *The Mawáqif and Mukháṭabāt of Muḥammad Ibn ʿAbdi l-Jabbár al-Niffarí*, trans. A. J. Arberry (London: J. W. Gibb Memorial, 1935); and Michael Anthony Sells, *Early Islamic Mysticism: Sufi, Qur'an, Miraj, Poetic and Theological Writings* (New York: Paulist Press, 1996), 281–301.

52. Ibn al-Khaṭīb lists the following titles: *al-ʿUrwa al-wathqī fī bayān al-sunan wa iḥṣā' al-ʿulūm* [*The Firm Bond in the Clarification of the Sunna and the Calculation of the [Religious] Sciences*], *al-Maqālīd al-wujūdiyya fī asrār ishārāt al-Ṣūfiyya* [*The Keys of the Universe in the Secrets of Sufi Symbolism*], *al-Risāla al-Qudsiyya fī tawḥīd al-ʿamma wa-l-khāṣṣa* [*The Jerusalem Letter on Unity between the Masses and the Elites*] and *al-Marātib al-īmāniyya wa-l-islāmiyya wa-l-iḥsāniyya* [*Stages of Faith, Surrender, and Praise*] and *al-Risāla al-ʿIlmiyya* [*The Treatise on Knowledge*].

53. According to Sarrāj's *Kitāb al-Lumaʿ*, the use of the term fuqarā' for Sufis originated in Syria (al-Sham), 46. Abū ʿUthmān Ibn Luyūn al-Tujībī, *al-Risāla al-Shushtariyya, aw al-Risāla al-ʿIlmiyya fī al-taṣawwuf*, ed. Muḥammad al-ʿAdlūnī al-Idrīsī, al-Tab`ah (Casablanca: Dār al-Thaqāfa, 2004), 45.

54. See note 43.

55. Shushtarī details eight levels or steps (*marātib*) in that ascent: contemplation (*al-tadbīr*), command (*al-amr*), heavens (*al-samā'*), earth (*al-ard*), ascent (*al-ʿurūj*), day (*al-yawm*), measure (*al-miqdār*), and millenium (*al-alf sana*).

56. Muḥammad ibn al-Ḥasan Zubaydī, *Laḥn al-ʿawāmm* ([Cairo: Maktabat Dār al-ʿUrūbah], 1964), 6-7, cited in and translated by Ch. Pellat, "Laḥn al-ʿāmma," *Encyclopedia of Islam*. CD-ROM ed. (Leiden: Brill, 1999). See also George Krotkoff, "The 'Laḥn al-ʿAwwām' of Abū Bakr al-Zubaydī," *Bulletin of the College of Arts and Sciences* [Baghdad] 2 (1957).

57. The recent bibliography on the *muwashshaḥāt* is imposing. The following works are particularly important: Samuel Miklos Stern, *Hispano-Arabic Strophic Poetry: Studies*, ed. L. P. Harvey (Oxford: Clarendon Press, 1974). Although García Gómez has been criticized for taking excessive liberties in vocalizing and emending the texts in accordance with the stress-syllabic scansion that he championed, his *Las jarchas romances de la serie árabe en su marco* (Madrid: Alianza Editorial, 1990) is still the standard work in the field and the most complete Spanish translation of *muwashshaḥāt*. Other noteworthy works include Alan Jones, *Romance Kharjas in Andalusian Arabic Muwaššah Poetry: A Palaeographical Analysis* (London: Ithaca Press, 1988) and his painstaking diplomatic editions of the two most important texts for the study of Hispano-Arabic poetry, *The 'Uddat al-jalīs of ʿAlī ibn Bishrī: An Anthology of Andalusian Arabic Muwashshaḥāt* (Cambridge: E.J.W. Gibb Memorial, 1992) and *The Jaysh al-tawshīh of Lisān al-Dīn Ibn al-Khaṭīb: An Anthology of Andalusian Arabic Muwashshaḥāt*, (Cambridge: E.J.W. Gibb Memorial, 1997). See also Alvaro Galmés de Fuentes, *Las jarchas mozárabes* (Madrid: Crítica, 1994), Otto Zwartjes, *Love Songs from al-Andalus: History, Structure and Meaning of the Kharja* (Leiden: Brill, 1997), J. A. Abu-Haidar, *Hispano-Arabic Literature and the Early Provençal Lyrics* (Richmond, Surrey: Curzon, 2001).

58. MS. Berlin, no. 7681. An edition of his *Dīwān* was published by ʿAfīfah Maḥmūd Dīrānī. (Beirut: Dār al-Thaqāfa, 1964).

59. MS. British Library no. 605. The edition of the *Dīwān* published in 1963 by Iḥsān ʿAbbās is based on Cairo MS. Dār al-kutub no. 593 and British Library Add. 6673.

60. Julián Ribera y Tarragó, *Manuscritos árabes y aljamiados de la Biblioteca de la Junta* (Madrid: Centro de Estudios Históricos, 1912). For the *muwashshaḥāt* written by or preserved by Moriscos, see LXIV, 5; C, 4. The coplas in honor of Muhammad written in *aljamía* with the refrain in Arabic are found on pages IX, 2; XIII, 25, 40, 41.

61. The section, entitled "May the word *ʿishq* be applied to love for God and from God?"immediately follows the preface and enumeration of the chapters in the book. See Abū 'l-Hasan ʿAlī ibn Muḥammad Daylamī, *A Treatise*

on Mystical Love, trans. Joseph Norment Bell and Hassan Mahmood Abdul Latif Al Shafie (Edinburgh: Edinburgh University Press, 2005), 8–9. The larger question of classifying and defining terminology for different kinds of love is discussed at length in Joseph Norment Bell, *Love Theory in Later Hanbalite Islam* (Albany: State University of New York Press, 1979), 148–81.

62. Ibn al-ʿArabī, *Dīwān* (Beirut: Dār al-Kutub al-ʿIlmiyya, 1996), 283, translation mine.

PART TWO: Poems and Songs

Chapter 1: Intoxicated by the Divine

1. See Massignon, *Essay on the Origins of the Technical Language of Islamic Mysticism,* trans. Benjamin Clark (Notre Dame, IN: University of Notre Dame Press, 1997), 19.

2. Th. Emil Homerin, "Tangled Words," in *Reorientations/Arabic and Persian Poetry*, ed. Suzanne Pinckney Stetkevych (Bloomington: Indiana University Press, 1994), 191.

3. For recent English translations of both of these poems, see Homerin, *ʿUmar Ibn al-Fāriḍ*, 73–291, and 45–51.

4. Kalābādhī, *Doctrine of the Sufis*, trans. A. J. Arberry (Cambridge: Cambridge University Press, 1935), 95.

Chapter 2: Love-crazed

1. In the introduction to his edition and translation of *Tarjumán al-Ashwáq* (especially pp. 2–8), Nicholson examines the textual history of the multiple recensions of this poetic collection, the addition of the poet's commentary, and the controversy surrounding the date these poems were composed.

2. Ibn al-ʿArabī, *Tarjumán al-Ashwáq,* 123–24. Similar examples can be found in almost every poem in the collection.

3. Jaroslav Stetkevych, *The Zephrys of Najd* (Chicago: University of Chicago Press, 1993), 92.

4. Kalābādhī, *Doctrine of the Sufis*, 102.

5. Kalābādhī, *Doctrine of the Sufis*, 141.

Chapter 3: Denudatio/Stripping Bare

1. John Cassian, *The Institutes*, trans. Boniface Ramsey, *Ancient Christian Writers; no. 58* (New York: Newman Press, 2000), book VII, chap. 24.

2. Shushtarī, *al-Risāla al-ʿIlmiyya*, 135.

3. Shushtarī, *al-Risāla al-ʿIlmiyya,* 55.

4. Shushtarī, *al-Risāla al-ʿIlmiyya*, 48; and Baghdad Treatise, pg. 147, in the present volume.

Chapter 4: Among the Sufis

1. One songbook, Wetzstein 222, lists it as being sung to two different *nawbas* or melodies. As is often the case with songbooks, only the most popular verses are recorded as a complete performance of the poem as recorded in the *Dīwān* would be quite lengthy.

Chapter 5: Deciphering the Signs of God

1. T. Fahd, "ʿIlm al-Ḥurūf," *Encyclopedia of Islam*, CD-ROM edition.

Chapter 6: Desert Wanderings

1. Muhyi'ddīn Ibn al-ʿArabī, *Tarjumān al-Ashwāq*, trans. Reynold A. Nicholson (London: Theosophical Publishing House, 1978), 59, 122, 43.

2. Stetkevych, *The Zephyrs of Najd*, 81.

Chapter 7: At the Monastery

1. Ghāzī, Sayyid. *Dīwān al-muwashshaḥāt al-andalusiyya.* (Alexandria: Munsha'at al-maʿārif, 1979) 1: 303–4.

2. See John Walbridge, *The Wisdom of the Mystic East: Suhrawardī and Platonic Orientalism* (Albany: SUNY Press, 2001); and Cornell, "The Way of the Axial Intellect."

3. An example of this can be seen in chapter 352 of *Futuḥāt al-Makkiyya*, where he speaks of reflection, imagination, and habits as talismans that must be overcome. He says, "This [talisman] is the most intractable ruling power in the cosmos, for the person put under its charge loses abundant

knowledge of God. This talisman is reflection." See Chittick, *Sufi Path of Knowledge* (Albany: SUNY Press, 1989) 184–85; cf. Chittick's *The Self-Disclosure of God* (Albany: SUNY Press, 1998), 342.

4. ʿAbd al-Ghanī al-Nābulusī, "Radd al-Muftarī ʿan al-ṭaʿan fī al-Shushtarī,"*al-Mashriq* 54 (1960). Portions of this essay are translated and discussed in Dominique and Marie Thérèse Urvoy, "Les thèmes chrétiens chez Ibn Sab'în et la question de la spécificité de sa pensée,"*Studia Islamica* 44 (1976). The essay is also discussed in Omaima Abou-Bakr, "The Symbolic Function of Metaphor in Medieval Sufi Poetry: The Case of Shushtari,"*Alif* 12 (1992).

5. Stetkevych, *Zephyrs of Najd*, 97.

6. Stetkevych, *Zephyrs of Najd*, 96–97. Although Stetkevych's comments are directed to Nābulusī's commentary on Ibn al-Fāriḍ, the same holds true for his commentary on Shushtarī.

7. Nābulusī, "Radd al-Muftarī,"631.

8. Nābulusī, "Radd al-Muftarī,"632.

Chapter 8: Ode Rhyming in Nūn

1. Ibn al-Khaṭīb, *Iḥāṭa*, 4:211.

2. Quoted in Ibn ʿAjība, *Sharḥ Nūniyya al-Imām al-Shushtarī*, 11.

3. Michael Sells, *Early Islamic Mysticism: Sufi, Qur'an Miraj, Poetic and Theological Writings* (New York: Paulist Press, 1996), 151.

4. Ibn ʿAjība, *Sharḥ Nūniyya al-Imām al-Shushtarī*, 11.

PART THREE: Prose

Baghdad Treatise [on Sufī customs]

1. Escorial Ms. Arab 763, ff. 75r–79v. The Arabic text was edited with a brief French introduction by Marie-Thérèse Urvoy, "La Risāla Bagdādīya de Šuštarī,"*Bulletin d'études Orientales* 28 (1976). The manuscript is generally clear, although the hand is rushed. I was able to resolve many of the difficulties she had in transcribing the manuscript by referring to the *ḥadīth* cited by Shushtarī. The translation given here reflects my corrections to her transcription of the manuscript.

2. Ibn al-Jawzī, *Devil's Delusion*, trans. Margoliuth, *Islamic Culture* 11 (1937), 239.

3. This *ḥadīth* is cited in Al-Sarrāj, Abū Naṣr, *Kitāb al-Lumaʿ fi al-*

taṣawwuf. Edited by ʿAbd al-Ḥalīm Maḥmūd. Port Said (Egypt): Maktabat al-Thaqawfa al-Dīniyya, 2002). 166.

4. This *ḥadīth* has been taken by Shiites to define the members of the Ahl al-bayt.

5. Arent J. Wensinck, *Concordance et indices de la tradition musulmane* (Leiden: Brill, 1992), 2:290.

6. The reference is to Ibn al-Jawzī, author of *Ṣifat al- Ṣafwā*.

7. A long outer garment.

8. My reading of the manuscript is *al-ḥarīr* (silk), while Urvoy reads *al-ḥadīr* which she ammends to read *al-jadīd* (new). Although Shushtarī is defending the use of patches and worn clothing (among other things), I see no basis on which he would claim that new clothing is not permissible. Furthermore, well-defined traditions forbid the wearing of silk by men.

9. Cf. *Kitāb al-Lumaʿ*, 185.

10. The Qur'ān frequently mentions the countenance of God (*wajh Allah*) as the goal of the believer. A similar linkage between the signs of God on earth and coming before God is found in 30:37-38, "There truly are signs in this for those who believe. So give their due to the near relative, the needy, the wayfarer—that is best for those whose goal is God's countenance."

11. A saying commonly attributed to the Prophet by the Sufis.

12. For a discussion of God's two hands, see Michael Sells, *The Mystical Languages of Unsaying* (Chicago: Chicago University Press, 1994), 84–87.

13. Besides meaning simply listening or hearing, *samāʿ* is also the term used by Sufis to describe the act of listening to religious poetry or music as part of a mystical gathering.

14. A group of Muḥammad's Companions who typify the idea of poverty and piety.

15. That is, that he slept on a rough mat without pillows or cushions.

16. See Wensinck, *Concordance*, 2:105.

17. Here, Shushtarī limits the potential meanings of *zafna*, which can also be understood as "to play"or "sport."

18. The conclusion of the sūra would, of course, be known to the reader: "...seeking His approval, and do not let your eyes turn away from them out of desire for the attractions of this worldly life."

19. This is one of the places where my reading of the manuscript differs from that of Urvoy.

Bibliography

Manuscripts of Shushtarī's Work

Dīwān (in chronological order)

Escorial 278 [956 AH=1549 CE]. This manuscript is missing fourteen poems found in most copies of the Eastern recension of Shushtarī's *dīwān*.

Beinecke Library, Yale University. Arabic MS 21 [1000 AH-1591 CE]. An excellent early manuscript; vowelling is somewhat less dialectal than in Escorial 278.

British Library 9255 [late tenth century AH? =sixteenth century CE].

British Library 26127 [eleventh century AH=sixteenth-seventeenth centuries CE]. Poor hand, many mistakes, missing many poems.

Staatsbibliothek zu Berlin. Sprenger 1134 [1012 AH=1603 CE].

Staatsbibliothek zu Berlin. Wetzstein 195 [twelfth century AH?]. Beautifully presented.

Staatsbibliothek zu Berlin. Wetzstein 222 [1111 AH=1699 CE].

Beinecke Library, Yale University. Landberg 484 [1129 AH=1717 CE].

Staatsbibliothek zu Berlin. Wetzstein 209 [1256 AH-1840 CE]. Organized for singing.

Staatsbibliothek zu Berlin. Sprenger 1126. Many errors; hand is poor.

Prose Works

al-Risāla al-Baghdādiyya. Escorial 763.
al-Risāla al-Mi'rājiyya. Beinecke Library, Yale University. Arabic MS Supp. 104.
al-Maqālīd al-wujudiyya fī asrār a-ṣūfiyya (Cairo Taymūr MS 149 ff., 413–43). This manuscript, written in a Maghrebī script by a number of different copyists, is largely devoted to the writings of Ibn Sab'īn.
al-Risāla al-qudsiyya fī tawḥīd al-'amma wa-l-khaṣṣa (Cairo Taymūr MS 149 ff.; Istanbul, Şehit Ali 1389/6).

Other Manuscripts

Zarrūq, Aḥmad ibn Aḥmad. *Sharḥ Zarrūq al-Fāsī li-Nūniyya al-Shushtarī*. Escorial 40186.
———. *Tarjama al-Shaykh Abī al-Ḥasan al-Shushtarī naqlan 'an mukhtaṣar al-naṣīḥa al-kāfiyya*. Alexandria, MS 3024.

Published Works

Primary Sources

Abū Madyan, Shu'ayb ibn al-Ḥusayn al-Anṣārī. *The Way of Abū Madyan: Doctrinal and Poetic Works of Abū Madyan Shu'ayb*. Edited and translated by Vincent Cornell. Cambridge [England]: Islamic Texts Society, 1996.
Abū Nūwās. *Dīwān*. Beirut: Dār Ṣādir, 1996.
Avempace [Ibn Bājja, Abū Bakr Muḥammad], *Kitāb tadbīr al-mutawaḥḥid*. [Beirut]: Dār al-Fikr al-Islāmī, 1978. Translated by Joaquín Lomba Fuentes as *El régimen del solitario*. Madrid: Editorial Trotta, 1997.
Balyānī, Awḥad al-Dīn. *Kitāb al-Waḥda al-Muṭlaqa [Epîstre sur l'Unicité Absolue]*. Translated by Michel Chodkiewicz. Paris: Les Deux Oceans, 1982.
Daylamī, Abū 'l-Ḥasan 'Alī ibn Muḥammad. *A Treatise on Mystical Love*.

Translated by Joseph Norment Bell and Hassan Mahmood Abdul Latif Al Shafie. Edinburgh: Edinburgh University Press, 2005.

al-Ghubrīnī, Aḥmad ibn Aḥmad. *ʿUnwān al-dirāyah*. Beirut: Lajnat al-taʿlīf wa-l-tarjama wa-l-nashr, 1969.

al-Hā'ik, Abū ʿAbd Allah Muḥammad ibn al-Ḥusayn. *Kunnāsh al-Hā'ik*. Edited by ʿAbbās al-Jarrārī. Rabat: Matbūʿāt Akādīmiyya al-Mamlaka al-Maghribiyya, 1999.

al-Ḥallāj, al-Ḥusayn ibn Manṣūr. *Dīwān*. Beirut: Dār al-Kutub al-ʿilmiyya, 1998. Translated into French by Sami-Ali as *Poèmes Mystiques*. Paris: Albin Michel, 1998.

Ibn ʿAbbā, Muḥammad ibn Ibrahim. *al-Rasā'il al-kubrā*. [Fez]: Matbaʿat al-ʿArabī al-Arzaq.

Ibn ʿAjība, Aḥmad ibn Muḥammad. *The Autobiography of the Moroccan Sufi Ibn Ajiba*. Translated by Jean-Louis Michon and David Streight. Louisville, KY: Fons Vitae, 1999.

———. "Sharḥ li-baʿd muqtaʿāt al-Shushtarī." In *Silsilāt Nūrāniyya farīda*, 3:35–61. Edited by al-ʿImrānī al-Khālidī ʿAbd al-Salām. N.p.: Maktabat al-Rashād, 1997.

———. "Sharḥ li-nūniyya al-imām al-Shushtarī."In *Silsilāt Nūrāniyya farīda*, 5:1–74. Edited by al-ʿImrānī al-Khālidī ʿAbd al-Salām. N.p.: Maktabat al-Rashād, 1997.

Ibn al-ʿArabī. *Dīwān*. Beirut: Dār al-Kutub al-ʿIlmiyya, 1996.

———. *Rasā'il Ibn ʿArabī*. Introduction by Maḥmūd Maḥmūd al-Ghurāb. Beirut: Dār Ṣādir, 1997.

———. *Tarjumān al-Ashwāq*. Beirut: Dār al-Ṣādir, n.d. Translated by Reynold A. Nicholson. London: Theosophical Publishing House, 1978. Selection translated by Michael Sells as *Stations of Desire: Love Elegies from Ibn 'Arabi and New Poems*. Jerusalem: Ibis Editions, 2000.

Ibn al-ʿArīf, [Abū al-ʿAbbās Aḥmad]. *Maḥāsin al-Majālis*. Edited and translated by Miguel Asín Palacios. Paris: Librairie Orientaliste Paul Geuthner, 1933.

Ibn Barrajān, ʿAbd al-Salām ibn ʿAbd al-Raḥmān ibn Muḥammad. *Sarḥ asma' allah Al-husnà = Comentario sobre los nombres más bellos de Dios*. Edited by Purificación de la Torre. Madrid: Consejo Superior de Investigaciones Científicas, 2000.

Ibn al-Fāriḍ, ʿUmar ibn ʿAlī. *Dīwān*. Edited by ʿAbd al-Khāliq Maḥmūd. Al-Haram: ʿAyn lil-dirāsāt wa al-buḥūth al-insāniyya wa-l-ijtimāʿiyya, 1995. Translated by A. J. Arberry as *The Poem of the Way* (London: E. Walker, 1952), and *The Mystical Poems of Ibn al-Fāriḍ* (Dublin: Emery Walker, 1956). Selections translated by Th. Emil Homerin as *ʿUmar ibn al-Fāriḍ: Sufi Verse, Saintly Life*. Mahwah, NJ: Paulist Press, 2000.

Ibn Ḥajar al-ʿAsqalānī, Aḥmad ibn ʿAlī. *Lisān al-mīzān*, 1971.

Ibn al-Jawzī, Abū al-Farāj ʿAbd al-Raḥmān ibn ʿAlī. *Kitāb Ṣifat al-Ṣafwā*. Hyderabad: Maṭbaʿat Dā'irat al-Maʿārif al-ʿUthmāniyyah, 1968.

———. *Talbīs Iblīs*. Translated by D. S. Margoliuth as "The Devil's Delusion." *Islamic Culture* 9 (1935): 1–21, 186–208, 377–99; 533–57; 10 (1936): 169–92, 339–68, 633–47; 11 (1937): 266–73, 391–403, 529–33; 12 (1938): 108–18, 235–40, 447–58.

Ibn Khaldun. *The Muqaddimah: An Introduction to History*. Edited and translated by Franz Rosenthal. 2d ed. 3 vols. Princeton, NJ: Princeton University Press, 1967.

———. *Shifā al-sā'il li-tahdhīb al-masā'il*. Edited by Abū Yaʿrub Marzūqī. [Tunis]: al-Dār al-ʿArabiyyah lil-Kitāb, 1991.

Ibn al-Khaṭīb, Lisān al-Dīn. *Dīwān Lisān al-Dīn ibn al-Khaṭīb*. Edited by Muḥammad Miftāh. Casablanca: Dār al-Thaqāfah lil-Nashr wa-al-Tawẓī, 1989.

———. *al-Iḥāṭah fī akhbār Gharnāṭa*. Edited by Muḥammad ʿAbd Allah ʿInān. Cairo: Maktabat al-Khanjī, 1973.

———. *The Jaysh al-tawshīḥ of Lisān al-Dīn Ibn al-Khaṭīb: An Anthology of Andalusian Arabic Muwashshaḥāt*. Edited by Alan Jones. Cambridge, England: Trustees of the E. J. W. Gibb Memorial, 1997.

———. *Libro de la magia y de la poesía [Kitāb al-siḥr wa l-shiʿr]*. Translated by J. M. Continente Ferrer. Madrid: Instituto Hispano-árabe de Cultura, 1981.

———. *Rawdat al-taʿrīf bil-ḥubb al-Sharīf*. Cairo: Dār al-fikr al-ʿArabī, 1968.

Ibn Luyūn al-Tujībī, Abū ʿUthmān. *Al-Risāla al-Shushtariyya, aw al-Risāla al-ʿIlmiyya fī al-taṣawwuf*. Edited by Muḥammad al-ʿAdlūnī al-Idrīsī. Casablanca: Dār al-Thaqāfa, 2004.

Ibn Qasī, Aḥmad ibn Ḥusayn. *Kitāb Khalaʿ al-Naʿlayn*. Edited by Muḥammad al-Amrānī. Safi, Morocco: M. al-Amrānī, 1997.

Ibn Quzmān. *Dīwān*. Edited by Federico Corriente. Madrid: al-Maʿhad al-Isbānī al-ʿArabī lil-Thaqāfah, 1980. Translated by Corriente as *Cancionero andalusí*. Madrid: Hiperión, 1996. Translated by Julián Ribera y Tarragó as *El cancionero de Abencuzmán. Disertaciones y opúsculos*. Madrid: Maestre, 1912.

Ibn Sabʿīn, ʿAbd al-Ḥaqq. *Budd al-ʿārif*. Edited by Jūrj Kattūrah. Beirut: Dār al-Andalus: Dār al-Kindī, 1978.

———. *Rasā'il*. Edited by ʿAbd al-Raḥmān Badawī. Cairo: al-Mu'assasa al-miṣriyya al-ʿamma lil-taʿlīf wal-anbā'a wal-nashr, 1965.

Ibn al-Ṣiddiq, ʿAbd al-ʿAzīz ibn Muḥammad. *Sharḥ Bada'tu bi-dhikr maqtaʿāt al-ḥabib*. Cairo: Dār al-Shabāb lil-Ṭibaʿah, 1984.

Ibn Taymīyah, Aḥmad ibn ʿAbd al-Ḥalīm. *Majmūʿat al-rasā'il wa-al-masā'il*. Edited by Muḥammad Rashīd Riḍā. 5 vols. Beirut: Dār al-Kutub al-ʿIlmiyyah, 1983.

Ibn Zaydūn. *Dīwān Ibn Zaydūn wa rasā'iluh*. Edited by ʿAlī ʿAbd al-ʿAẓīm. Cairo, 1957.

———. *Poesías*. Edited and translated by Mahmud Sobh. Introduction by E. Terés. Madrid: Instituto Hispano-árabe de Cultura, 1979.

Imru'al-Qays. *Imrulkais of Kinda, Poet: circa A.D. 500–535*. Translated by Charles Greville Tuetey. London: Diploma Press, 1977.

Kalābādhī, Muḥammad ibn Ibrāhīm. *The Doctrine of the Ṣūfīs [Kitāb al-taʿarruf li-madhhab ahl al-taṣawwuf]*. Translated by A. J. Arberry. Cambridge; New York: Cambridge University Press, 1977.

al-Maqqarī, Aḥmad ibn Muḥammad. *Nafḥ al-Ṭīb min ghuṣn al-Andalus al-raṭīb*. Edited by Iḥsān ʿAbbās. 8 vols. Beirut: Dār Ṣādir, 1968.

al-Nābulusī, ʿAbd al-Ghanī. *Dīwān al-ḥaqā'iq wa-majmʿū al-raqā'iq*. [Damascus: ʿAbd al-Wakīl al-Durūbī, 1968].

———. "Radd al-Muftarī ʿan al-ṭaʿan fī al-Shushtarī." *al-Mashriq* 54 (1960): 629-39.

al-Niffarī, Muḥammad ibn ʿAbd al-Jabbār. *The Mawáqif and Mukháṭabāt of Muḥammad Ibn ʿAbdi l-Jabbár Al-Niffarí*. Translated by A. J. Arberry. London: J. W. Gibb Memorial, 1935.

Niẓāmī, Ganjavi. *Mirror of the Invisible World: Tales from the Khamseh of Nizami*. Edited and translated by Peter J. Chelkowski. New York: Metropolitan Museum of Art, 1975.

———. *The Story of Layla and Majnun*. Translated by Rudolf Gelpke. Boulder, CO: Shambhala, 1978.

The Qur'an. Translated by M. A. Abdel Haleem. Oxford: Oxford University Press, 2004.

al-Sarrāj, Abū Naṣr. *Kitāb al-luma' fī al-Taṣawwuf*. Edited by 'Abd al-Ḥalīm Maḥmūd. Port Said (Egypt): Maktabat al-Thaqawfa al-Dīniyya, 2002.

Shābb al-Ẓarīf, Muḥamad ibn Sulayman. *Dīwān Al-Shābb Al-Ẓarīf*. Beirut: Maktabat al-Nahdah al-'Arabiyyah: 'Alam al-Kutub, 1985.

al-Shiblī, Abū Bakr. *Dīwān Abī Bakr al-Shiblī*. Edited by Muwaffiq Fawzī al-Jabr. Damascus: Dār Batrā, 1999.

al-Shushtarī, Abū al-Ḥasan. *Dīwān*. Edited by 'Alī Sāmī al-Nashshār. Alexandria: Dār al-Ma'ārif, 1960.

———. "Al-Risāla al-Baghdadiyya." Edited by Marie-Thérèse Urvoy. *Bulletin d'études orientales* 28 (1976), 259–66.

———. [al-Shushtarī, 'Alī ibn 'Abd Allah]. *Poesía estrófica: céjeles y/o muwaššaḥāt*. Edited and translated by F. Corriente. Madrid: Consejo Superior de Investigaciones Científicas, Instituto de Filología, Departamento de Estudios Árabes, 1988.

Tilimsānī, 'Afīf al-Dīn Sulaymān ibn 'Alī. *Sharḥ Mawāqif Al-Niffarī*. Edited by Jamāl Aḥmad Marzūqī. Cairo: Markaz al-Maḥrūsa, 1997.

Zarrūq, Aḥmad ibn Aḥmad. Zarrūq, Aḥmad ibn Aḥmad. *al-Naṣīḥah al-kāfiyah*. Riyad: Maktabat al-Imām al-Shāfi'ī, 1993.

Secondary Sources

Abou-Bakr, Omaima. "The Religious Other: Christian Images in Sufi Poetry." In *Images of the Other: Europe and the Muslim World before 1700*, ed. by David R. Blanks. Cairo: American University in Cairo Press, 1997.

———. "A Study of the Poetry of al-Shushtari." PhD diss., University of California, 1987.

———. "The Symbolic Function of Metaphor in Medieval Sufi Poetry: The Case of Shushtari." *Alif* 12 (1992): 40–57.

Addas, Claude. "Andalusi Mysticism and the Rise of Ibn Arabi." In *The Legacy of Muslim Spain*, ed. S. Kh. Jayyusi. Leiden: Brill, 1992.

———. "L'oeuvre poétique d'Ibn Arabi et sa réception." *Studia Islamica* (2000): 23–36.

———. *Quest for the Red Sulphur: The Life of Ibn Arabi*. Golden Palm series. Cambridge: Islamic Texts Society, 1993.

Alon, Ilai. *Socrates in Mediaeval Arabic Literature*. Leiden: Brill, 1991.

Alvarez, Lourdes María. "The Mystical Language of Daily Life: The Arabic Vernacular Songs of Abū al-Ḥasan al-Shushtarī." *Exemplaria* 17, no. 1 (2005): 1–32.

———. "Reading the Mystical Signs in the Songs of Abū al-Ḥasan al-Shushtarī." In *Muwashshaḥāt: Proceedings of the International Conference on Arabic and Hebrew Strophic Poetry and Its Romance Parallels, School of Oriental and African Studies, London, 8–10 October 2004, 23–35*. London: RNR Books and School of Oriental and African Studies, Music Department, 2006.

Arié, Rachel. *España musulmana (siglos VIII–XV), Historia de España*. Barcelona: Labor, 1984.

Asín Palacios, Miguel, *The Mystical Philosophy of Ibn Masarra and His Followers*. Translated by Elmer H. Douglas and Howard W. Yoder. Leiden: Brill, 1978.

Attar, Sulayman. *al-Khayāl wa-al-shiʿr fī taṣawwuf al-Andalus: Ibn ʿArabi, Abū al-Ḥasan al-Shushtarī, wa-Ibn Khumayyis al-Tilimsani*. Cairo: Dār al-Maʿārif, 1981.

Badawi, A. "Ahd Ibn Sabʿīn li-talāmīdhih." *Revista del Instituto Egipcio de Estudios Islámicos* (1957): 1–103, 249–53.

———. "Ibn Sabʿîn y la oración mental." *Revista del Instituto Egipcio de Estudios Islámicos* (1956): 131–35.

Baldick, Julian. "Medieval Ṣūfī Poetry up to the 15th Century." In *History of Persian Literature: from the Beginning of the Islamic Period to the Present Day*, ed. George Morrison, 111–32. Leiden: Brill, 1981.

———. *Mystical Islam: An Introduction to Sufism*. New York: New York University Press, 1989.

Bell, Joseph Norment. *Love Theory in Later Hanbalite Islam*. Albany: State University of New York Press, 1979.

Bruijn, J. T. P. de. *Persian Sufi poetry: An Introduction to the Mystical Use of Classical Persian Poems*. Richmond, Surrey: Curzon, 1997.

Brustad, Kristen. *The Syntax of Spoken Arabic: A Comparative Study of Moroccan, Egyptian, Syrian, and Kuwaiti Dialects*. Washington, DC: Georgetown University Press, 2000.

Burrows, Mark S. "Raiding the Inarticulate: Mysticism, Poetics, and the Unlanguageable."*Spiritus* 4 (2004): 173–94.

Cantarino, Vicente. *Casidas de amor profano y místico, Ibn Zaydun, Ibn Arabi. Estudio y traducción*. Mexico: Porrúa, 1977.

Cassian, John. *John Cassian, The Institutes*. Edited and translated by Boniface Ramsey. New York: Newman Press, 2000.

Chelkowski, Peter J. "Nizāmī." *Encyclopedia of Islam. CD-ROM Edition*. Leiden: Brill, 1999.

Chittick, William. *Faith and Practice of Islam: Three Thirteenth Century Sufi Texts*. Albany: State University of New York Press, 1992.

———. *Imaginal Worlds: Ibn al-ʿArabī and the Problem of Religious Diversity*. Albany: State University of New York Press, 1994.

———. "Rumi and waḥdat al-wujūd." In *Poetry and Mysticism in Islam: The Heritage of Rumi*, ed. Amin Banani. New York: Cambridge University Press, 1994.

———. *The Self-Disclosure of God: Principles of Ibn al-ʿArabī's Cosmology*. Albany: State University of New York Press, 1998.

———. *The Sufi Path of Knowledge: Ibn al-ʿArabī's Metaphysics of Imagination*. Albany: State University of New York Press, 1989.

———. *Sufism: A Short Introduction*. Oxford: Oneworld, 2000.

Corriente, Federico. *A Dictionary of Andalusi Arabic*. Leiden: Brill, 1997.

———. "Observaciones sobre la métrica de as-Šuštari: Materiales para un estudio diacrónico del zejel y el muwaššaḥ."*Awraq* 5–6 (1982–83): 39–87.

———. "La poesía estrófica de Ibn Arabi de Murcia." *Sharq al-Andalus* 3 (1986): 19–24.

Cornell, Vincent J. "Faqīh versus Faqīr in Marinid Morocco: Epistemological Dimensions of a Polemic." In *Islamic Mysticism Contested: Thirteen Centuries of Controversies and Polemics*, ed. Frederick de Jong and Bernd Radtke, 207–24. Leiden: Brill, 1999.

———. *Realm of the Saint: Power and Authority in Moroccan Sufism*. Austin: University of Texas Press, 1998.

———. "The Way of the Axial Intellect: The Islamic Hermeticism of Ibn Sabʿīn."*Journal of the Muhyiddin Ibn Arabi Society* (1997): 41–79.

Cortes García, Manuela. "Nuevos datos para el estudio de la música en al-Andalus de dos autores granadinos: Aš-Šustari e Ibn al-Jatib." *Música Oral del Sur* 1 (1995): 177–94.

Dozy, R. P. A. *Supplément Aux Dictionaires Arabes*. 2 vols. 1881. Beirut: Librairie deu Liban, 1981.

Dreher, J. "L'imamat d'Ibn Qasi à Mértola (automne 1144-été 1145): Légitimité d'une domination soufie?" *Mélanges de l'Institut Dominicain d'Études Orientales du Caire* 18 (1988).

Elmore, Gerald T. "Ibn al-'Arabi's "cinquain" (*takhmīs*) on a Poem by Abū Madyan." *Arabica* 46 (1998): 62–96.

Endress, G[erhard]. "Ṭīna," *Encyclopedia of Islam. CD-ROM edition*. Leiden: Brill, 1999.

Fenton, Paul B. "Judeo-Arabic Mystical Writings." In *Judeo Arabic Studies*, ed, Norman Golb, 87–101. Amsterdam: Harwood Academic Publishers, 1997.

Fenton, Paul, Roland Goetschel, and Centre d'études juives de Paris-Sorbonne. *Expérience et écriture mystiques dans les religions du livre: actes d'un colloque international tenu par le Centre d'études juives Université de Paris IV-Sorbonne 1994*. Leiden: Brill, 2000.

Fierro, Maribel. Fierro, Maria Isabel. "Mahdisme et eschatologie dans al-Andalus." In *Mahdisme. Crise et changement dans l'histoire du Maroc*, ed. A. Kaddouri. Rabat, 1994.

———. "Opposition to Sufism in al-Andalus." In *Islamic Mysticism Contested: Thirteen Centuries of Controversies and Polemics*, ed. Frederick de Jong and Bernd Radtke, 174–206. Leiden: Brill, 1999.

———. "The Polemic about the Karāmāt al-Awliyā' and the Development of Sufism in al-Andalus (4th–10th/5th–11th centuries)." *Bulletin of the School for Oriental and African Studies* 55 (1992).

———. "al-Shushtarī." In *Encyclopedia of Islam, CD-ROM edition*. Leiden: Brill, 1999.

———. "The Treatises against Innovations (Kutub al-Bidaʿ)." *Islam* 69, no. 2 (1992): 204–46.

Galindo-Aguilar, Emilio. *Šuštarī: Peregrino y juglar del amor*. Madrid: Darek-Nyumba, 2000.

Galmés de Fuentes, Álvaro. *Las jarchas mozárabes: forma y significado*. Madrid: Crítica, 1994.

García Gómez, Emilio. *Las jarchas romances de la serie árabe en su marco: edición en caracteres latinos, versión española en calco rítmico y estudio de 43 moaxajas andaluzas*. 3d. ed. Madrid: Alianza Editorial, 1990.

Goodrich, D. R. "A Sufi Revolt in Portugal: Ibn Qasi and his Kitab Khalʿ al-naʿlayn." PhD diss., Columbia University, 1978.

Gribetz, A. "The Samaʿ Controversy: Sufi vs. Legalist." *Studia Islamica* 74 (1991): 43–62.

Hallaq, Wael B., ed. *Ibn Taymiyya against the Greek Logicians.* Oxford: Clarendon Press, 1993.

Homerin, Th. Emil. *From Arab Poet to Muslim Saint: Ibn al-Fāriḍ, His Verse, and His Shrine*. Columbia: University of South Carolina, 1994.

———. "'Tangled Words': Toward a Stylistics of Arabic Mystical Verse."In *Reorientations/Arabic and Persian Poetry*. ed. Suzanne Pinckney Stetkevych, 190–98. Bloomington: Indiana University Press, 1994.

Jones, Alan. *Romance Kharjas in Andalusian Arabic Muwaššaḥ Poetry: A Palaeographical Analysis*. London: Ithaca Press for the Board of the Faculty of Oriental Studies, Oxford University, 1988.

Karamustafa, Ahmet T. *God's Unruly Friends: Dervish Groups in the Islamic Later Middle Period, 1200–1550*. Salt Lake City: University of Utah Press, 1994.

Kazimirski, Albert de Biberstein. *Qāmūs al-lughatayn al-ʿArabiyyah wa-al-Farānsāwiyyah. Dictionnaire arabe-français*. Beirut: Librairie du Liban, 1970.

Kennedy, Hugh. *Muslim Spain and Portugal: A Political History of al-Andalus*. London: Longman, 1996.

Kennedy, Phillip F. *The Wine Song in Classical Arabic Poetry: Abū Nūwās and the Literary Tradition*. Oxford: Clarendon Press, 1997.

Knysh, Alexander D. *Ibn ʿArabi in the Later Islamic Tradition*. Albany: State University of New York Press, 1999.

———. *Islamic Mysticism: A Short History*. Leiden: Brill, 2000.

Krotkoff, G. "The 'Laḥn al-ʿAwwām' of Abū Bakr al-Zubaydī." *Bulletin of the College of Arts and Sciences* [Baghdad] 2 (1957): 183–95.

Llull, Ramon. *Libre de Evast e Blanquerna*. Edited by Salvador Galmés. Barcelona: Editorial Barcino, 1935. Translated by E. Allison Peers as *Blanquerna: A Thirteenth Century Romance*. London: Jarrolds, 1926.

Massignon, Louis. *Essay on the Origins of the Technical Language of Islamic Mysticism*. Translated by Benjamin Clark. Notre Dame, IN: University of Notre Dame Press, 1997.

———. "'Ibn Sabʿ īn et la conspiration anti-hallegienne' en Andalousie et en Orient du XIIIe siècle." In *Études d'orientalisme dédiées à la mémoire de Lévi-Provençal*, 661–83. Paris: G.-P. Maisonneuve et Larose, 1962.

———. "Investigaciones sobre Šuštarī, poeta andaluz enterrado en Damieta." *al-Andalus* 14 (1949): 29–57.

———. *La Passion de Husayn Ibn Mansûr Hallâj: martyr mystique de l'Islam, exécuté à Bagdad le 26 mars 922: étude d'histoire religieuse*. New ed. 4 vols. [Paris]: Gallimard, 1975. Translated by Herbert Mason as *The Passion of al-Hallāj: Mystic and Martyr of Islam*. 4 vols. Princeton, NJ: Princeton University Press, 1982.

McGinn, Bernard. *The Flowering of Mysticism: Men and Women in the New Mysticism (1200–1350)*. New York: Crossroad, 1998.

Mehren, M. A. F. "Correspondance du philosophe Soufi Ibn Sabʿîn ʿAbd Oul-Ḥaqq avec l'empereur Frédéric II de Hohenstaufen." *Journal Asiatique* 14 (7th series) (1879): 377ff.

Michon, Jean-Louis. *Le Soufi marocain Aḥmad ibn ʿAjība et son miʿrāj: Glossaire de la mystique musulmane*. Paris: Librarie Philosophique J. Vrin, 1990.

Morris, James Winston. "Ibn 'Arabi and his Interpreters. Part I: Recent French Translations." *Journal of the American Oriental Society* 106, no. 3 (1986): 539–51.

———. "Ibn 'Arabi and his Interpreters. Part II: Influences and Interpretations." *Journal of the American Oriental Society* 106, no. 4 (1986): 733–56.

Nashshar, Sami El-. "The Poetry and Mystical Philosophy of Abu al-Hasan al-Shushtari."PhD diss,. Cambridge University, 1951.

———. "Abul Hasan al-Šuštari místico andaluz y autor de zejeles y su influencia en el mundo musulmán."*Revista del Instituto Egipcio de Estudios Islámicos* 1 (1953): 122–55.

Nicholson, Reynold Alleyne. *The Mystics of Islam*. New York: Schocken, 1975.

Nurbakhsh, Javad. *Sufism*. New York: Khaniqahi-Nimatullahi Publications, 1982.

Nwyia, Paul. *Ibn 'Abbād de Ronda, 1332–1390; un mystique prédicateur à la Qarawīyīn de Fès*. Beirut: Impr. catholique, 1961.

———. *Ibn 'Aṭā' Allāh (m. 709/1309) et la naissance de la confrérie shādhilite*. Beirut: Dar el-Machreq, 1972.

Perez, René. "Le dépoillement (tajrîd) dans le cheminement spirituel d'Abû l'Hasan al-Shushtari." In *al-Tawāṣṣul al-Ṣūfī bayna miṣr wa al-maghrib*. ed. ʿAbd al-Jawād al-Saqqāṭ, 1–11. Rabat: Jāmiʿat al-Ḥasan al-Thānī, 2000.

Ribera y Tarragó, Julián, and M. Asín. *Manuscritos árabes y aljamiados de la Biblioteca de la Junta*. Madrid: Centro de Estudios Históricos, 1912.

Saleh, Walid A. *The Formation of the Classical Tafsīr Tradition: The Qur'an Commentary of al-Tha'labī (d.427/1035)*. Boston: Brill, 2004.

Santiago Simón, Emilio de. "Jatiibiana mística I: El Kitaab Rawdat al-Ta'riif. Su temática." *Andalucía Islámica, Textos y Estudios* 1 (1980): 105–22.

———. *El polígrafo granadino Ibn al-Jatīb y el sufismo: aportaciones para su estudio*. Granada: Instituto Provincial de Estudios y Promoción Cultural, Departamento de Historia del Islam de la Universidad, 1983.

Schimmel, Annemarie. "The Influence of Sufism on Indo-Muslim Poetry." In *Anagogic Qualities of Literature*, ed. J. P. Strelka, 181–210. University Park: Pennsylvania State University Press, 1971.

———. *Mystical Dimensions of Islam*. Chapel Hill: University of North Carolina Press, 1975.

———. *Rumi's World: The Life and Work of the Great Sufi Poet*. Boston: Shambhala, 2001.

Sells, Michael. "Bewildered Tongue: The Semantics of Mystical Union in Islam." In *Mystical Union in Judaism, Christianity, and Islam: An Ecumenical Dialogue*, ed. Moshe Idel and Bernard McGinn, 87–124. New York: Continuum, 1996.

———. *Desert Tracings: Six Classic Arabian Odes*. Middletown, CT: Wesleyan University Press, 1989.

———. *Early Islamic Mysticism: Sufi, Qur'an, Miraj, Poetic and Theological Writings*. New York: Paulist Press, 1996.

———. "Longing, Belonging, and Pilgrimage in Ibn 'Arabi's Interpreter of Desires (Tarjuman al-Ashwaq)." In *Languages of Power in Islamic Spain*, ed. Ross Brann and David I. Owen, 178–96. Bethesda, MD: CDL Press, 1997.

———. *Mystical Languages of Unsaying*. Chicago: University of Chicago Press, 1994.

Sharaf, Muḥammad Yāsir. *Falsafat al taṣawwuf al-Sabʿīnī*. Damascus: Wizārat al-Thaqāfa fī al-Jumhūriyya al-ʿArabiyya al-Sūriyya, 1990.

———. *Falsafat al-waḥda al-muṭlaqa ʿinda Ibn Sabʿīn*. Baghdad: Dār al-Rashīd lil-Nashr, 1981.

Stern, Samuel Miklos. *Hispano-Arabic Strophic Poetry: Studies*. Edited by L. P. Harvey. Oxford: Clarendon Press, 1974.

———. "Ibn Masarra, Follower of Pseudo-Empedocles, an Illusion." In *Medieval Arabic and Hebrew Thought,* ed. F. W. Zimmermann. London: Variorum Reprints, 1983.

Stetkevych, Jaroslav. *Muḥammad and the Golden Bough: Reconstructing Arabian Myth*. Bloomington: Indiana University Press, 1996.

———. The *Zephyrs of Najd: The Poetics of Nostalgia in the Classical Arabic Nasīb*. Chicago: University of Chicago Press, 1993.

al-Taftāzānī, Abū al-Wafā al-Ghunaymī. *Ibn Sabʿīn wa falsafatuhu al-Ṣūfī*. Beirut: Dār al-Kitāb al-Lubnānī, 1973.

———. "Al-Madrasa al-Shūdhiyya fī al-taṣawwuf al-andalusī." *Revista del Instituto Egipcio de Estudios Islámicos* 23 (1985): 173–81.

Trimingham, J. Spencer. *The Sufi Orders in Islam*, 2d ed. Oxford: Oxford University Press, 1998.

Urvoy, Dominique, and Marie Thérèse Urvoy. "Les thèmes chrétiens chez Ibn Sabʿîn et la question de la spécificité de sa pensée." *Studia Islamica* 44 (1976): 99–121.

Walbridge, John. *The Wisdom of the Mystic East: Suhrawardī and Platonic Orientalism*. Albany: State University of New York Press, 2001.

Wensinck, Arent Jan. *Concordance et indices de la tradition musulmane*. 2d ed. Leiden: Brill, 1992.

Wheeler, Brannon. "Moses or Alexander? Early Islamic Exegesis of Qur'an 18:60-65." *Journal of Near Eastern Studies* 57, no. 3 (1998): 191–215.

Wilson, Peter Lamborn. "In the Mirror of a Man: Eros and Literary Style in Ibn 'Arabi's Tarjuman al-Ashwaq." *Studies in Mystical Literature* 2 (1982): 1–25.

Wormhoudt, Arthur, ed. and trans. *Selections from Diwan of Abu al Hasan 'Ali ibn 'Abdallah Al-Shushtarī*. [Oskaloosa, IA]: William Penn College, 1992.

Yāqūt ibn ʿAbd Allāh, al-Hamawī. *Muʿjam al-buldān*. 5 vols. Beirut: Dār Ṣādir, 1955.

Zayn, Samīḥ. *Ibn Sabʿīn: al-ṭuruq al-Ṣūfīyah: dirāsa wa-taḥlīl*. Beirut: al-Sharikah al-ʿAlamiyyah lil-Kitāb, 1988.
Zwartjes, Otto. *Love Songs from al-Andalus: History, Structure, and Meaning of the Kharja*. Leiden: Brill, 1997.

INDEX

Other Volumes in This Series

Abraham Isaac Kook • THE LIGHTS OF PENITENCE, LIGHTS OF HOLINESS, THE MORAL PRINCIPLES, ESSAYS, LETTERS, AND POEMS
Abraham Miguel Cardozo • SELECTED WRITINGS
Albert and Thomas • SELECTED WRITINGS
Alphonsus de Liguori • SELECTED WRITINGS
Anchoritic Spirituality •ANCRENE WISSE AND ASSOCIATED WORKS
Angela of Foligno • COMPLETE WORKS
Angelic Spirituality • MEDIEVAL PERSPECTIVES ON THE WAYS OF ANGELS
Angelus Silesius • THE CHERUBINIC WANDERER
Anglo-Saxon Spirituality • SELECTED WRITINGS
Apocalyptic Spirituality • TREATISES AND LETTERS OF LACTANTIUS, ADSO OF MONTIER-EN-DER, JOACHIM OF FIORE, THE FRANCISCAN SPIRITUALS, SAVONAROLA
Athanasius • THE LIFE OF ANTONY, AND THE LETTER TO MARCELLINUS
Augustine of Hippo • SELECTED WRITINGS
Bernard of Clairvaux • SELECTED WORKS
Bérulle and the French School • SELECTED WRITINGS
Birgitta of Sweden • LIFE AND SELECTED REVELATIONS
Bonaventure • THE SOUL'S JOURNEY INTO GOD, THE TREE OF LIFE, THE LIFE OF ST. FRANCIS
Cambridge Platonist Spirituality •
Carthusian Spirituality • THE WRITINGS OF HUGH OF BALMA AND GUIGO DE PONTE
Catherine of Genoa • PURGATION AND PURGATORY, THE SPIRITUAL DIALOGUE
Catherine of Siena • THE DIALOGUE
Celtic Spirituality •
Classic Midrash, The • TANNAITIC COMMENTARIES ON THE BIBLE
Cloud of Unknowing, The •
Devotio Moderna • BASIC WRITINGS
Dominican Penitent Women •
Early Anabaptist Spirituality • SELECTED WRITINGS
Early Dominicans • SELECTED WRITINGS
Early Islamic Mysticism • SUFI, QUR'AN, MI'RAJ, POETIC AND THEOLOGICAL WRITINGS
Early Kabbalah, The •
Early Protestant Spirituality •
Elijah Benamozegh • ISRAEL AND HUMANITY
Elisabeth Leseur • SELECTED WRITINGS
Elisabeth of Schönau • THE COMPLETE WORKS

Other Volumes in This Series

Emanuel Swedenborg • THE UNIVERSAL HUMAN AND SOUL-BODY INTERACTION
Ephrem the Syrian • HYMNS
Fakhruddin 'Iraqi • DIVINE FLASHES
Farid ad-Din 'Attār's Memorial of God's Friends • LIVES AND SAYINGS OF SUFIS
Fénelon • SELECTED WRITINGS
Francis and Clare • THE COMPLETE WORKS
Francis de Sales, Jane de Chantal • LETTERS OF SPIRITUAL DIRECTION
Francisco de Osuna • THE THIRD SPIRITUAL ALPHABET
George Herbert • THE COUNTRY PARSON, THE TEMPLE
Gertrude of Helfta • THE HERALD OF DIVINE LOVE
Gregory of Nyssa • THE LIFE OF MOSES
Gregory Palamas • THE TRIADS
Hadewijch • THE COMPLETE WORKS
Henry Suso • THE EXEMPLAR, WITH TWO GERMAN SERMONS
Hildegard of Bingen • SCIVIAS
Ibn 'Abbād of Ronda • LETTERS ON THE ṢŪFĪ PATH
Ibn Al'-Arabī • THE BEZELS OF WISDOM
Ibn 'Ata' Illah • THE BOOK OF WISDOM AND KWAJA ABDULLAH ANSARI: INTIMATE CONVERSATIONS
Ignatius of Loyola • SPIRITUAL EXERCISES AND SELECTED WORKS
Isaiah Horowitz • THE GENERATIONS OF ADAM
Jacob Boehme • THE WAY TO CHRIST
Jacopone da Todi • THE LAUDS
Jean Gerson • EARLY WORKS
Jeremy Taylor • SELECTED WORKS
Jewish Mystical Autobiographies • BOOK OF VISIONS AND BOOK OF SECRETS
Johann Arndt • TRUE CHRISTIANITY
Johannes Tauler • SERMONS
John Baptist de La Salle • THE SPIRITUALITY OF CHRISTIAN EDUCATION
John Calvin • WRITINGS ON PASTORAL PIETY
John Cassian • CONFERENCES
John and Charles Wesley • SELECTED WRITINGS AND HYMNS
John Climacus • THE LADDER OF DIVINE ASCENT
John Comenius • THE LABYRINTH OF THE WORLD AND THE PARADISE OF THE HEART
John of Avila • AUDI, FILIA—LISTEN, O DAUGHTER
John of the Cross • SELECTED WRITINGS

Other Volumes in This Series

John Donne • SELECTIONS FROM DIVINE POEMS, SERMONS, DEVOTIONS AND PRAYERS
John Henry Newman • SELECTED SERMONS
John Ruusbroec • THE SPIRITUAL ESPOUSALS AND OTHER WORKS
Julian of Norwich • SHOWINGS
Knowledge of God in Classical Sufism • FOUNDATIONS OF ISLAMIC MYSTICAL THEOLOGY
Late Medieval Mysticism of the Low Countries •
Luis de León • THE NAMES OF CHRIST
Luther's Spirituality •
Margaret Ebner • MAJOR WORKS
Marguerite Porete • THE MIRROR OF SIMPLE SOULS
Maria Maddalena de' Pazzi • SELECTED REVELATIONS
Martin Luther • THEOLOGIA GERMANICA
Maximus Confessor • SELECTED WRITINGS
Mechthild of Magdeburg • THE FLOWING LIGHT OF THE GODHEAD
Meister Eckhart • THE ESSENTIAL SERMONS, COMMENTARIES, TREATISES AND DEFENSE
Meister Eckhart • TEACHER AND PREACHER
Menahem Nahum of Chernobyl • UPRIGHT PRACTICES, THE LIGHT OF THE EYES
Nahman of Bratslav • THE TALES
Native Mesoamerican Spirituality • ANCIENT MYTHS, DISCOURSES, STORIES, DOCTRINES, HYMNS, POEMS FROM THE AZTEC, YUCATEC, QUICHE-MAYA AND OTHER SACRED TRADITIONS
Native North American Spirituality of the Eastern Woodlands • SACRED MYTHS, DREAMS, VISIONS, SPEECHES, HEALING FORMULAS, RITUALS AND CEREMONIALS
Nicholas of Cusa • SELECTED SPIRITUAL WRITINGS
Nicodemos of the Holy Mountain • A HANDBOOK OF SPIRITUAL COUNSEL
Nil Sorsky • THE COMPLETE WRITINGS
Nizam ad-din Awliya • MORALS FOR THE HEART
Norbert and Early Norbertine Spirituality •
Origen • AN EXHORTATION TO MARTYRDOM, PRAYER AND SELECTED WORKS
Philo of Alexandria • THE CONTEMPLATIVE LIFE, THE GIANTS, AND SELECTIONS
Pietists • SELECTED WRITINGS
Pilgrim's Tale, The •
Pseudo-Dionysius • THE COMPLETE WORKS

Other Volumes in This Series

Pseudo-Macarius • THE FIFTY SPIRITUAL HOMILIES AND THE GREAT LETTER
Pursuit of Wisdom, The • AND OTHER WORKS BY THE AUTHOR OF THE CLOUD OF UNKNOWING
Quaker Spirituality • SELECTED WRITINGS
Rabbinic Stories •
Richard Rolle • THE ENGLISH WRITINGS
Richard of St. Victor • THE TWELVE PATRIARCHS, THE MYSTICAL ARK, BOOK THREE OF THE TRINITY
Robert Bellarmine • SPIRITUAL WRITINGS
Safed Spirituality • RULES OF MYSTICAL PIETY, THE BEGINNING OF WISDOM
Shakers, The • TWO CENTURIES OF SPIRITUAL REFLECTION
Sharafuddin Maneri • THE HUNDRED LETTERS
Sor Juana Inés de la Cruz • SELECTED WRITINGS
Spirituality of the German Awakening, The •
Symeon the New Theologian • THE DISCOURSES
Talmud, The • SELECTED WRITINGS
Teresa of Avila • THE INTERIOR CASTLE
Theatine Spirituality • SELECTED WRITINGS
'Umar Ibn al-Fāriḍ • SUFI VERSE, SAINTLY LIFE
Valentin Weigel • SELECTED SPIRITUAL WRITINGS
Vincent de Paul and Louise de Marillac • RULES, CONFERENCES, AND WRITINGS
Walter Hilton • THE SCALE OF PERFECTION
William Law • A SERIOUS CALL TO A DEVOUT AND HOLY LIFE, THE SPIRIT OF LOVE
Zohar • THE BOOK OF ENLIGHTENMENT

The Classics of Western Spirituality is a ground-breaking collection of the original writings of more than 100 universally acknowledged teachers within the Catholic, Protestant, Eastern Orthodox, Jewish, Islamic, and Native American Indian traditions.